Praise for Pigs at the Trough

"Huffington yanks back the curtains on the '90s 'go-go market' to reveal a portrait of Dorian Greed. . . . wicked gallows humor . . . Democrats and Republicans sizzle like bacon under her broiling spotlight. Scrupulous detail . . . real porcine heft."
— *Christian Science Monitor*

"A rousing call to action. As only she can, Arianna breathes energy and passion into the reform agenda. A withering, breathtaking, quintessentially controversial book that will inspire, inflame, and educate." —**Senator John McCain**

"Arianna Huffington makes an appealing and compelling argument for the repeal of human nature—that part of it that indulges savage, unconscionable, and despicable greed."
—**Walter Cronkite**

"Even the most worldly activist and most cynical political observers will be shocked by what they read here. A powerful book, brimming with wit and sulphurous satire."
—*Publishers Weekly*

"With a passion for the truth and an eye for detail, Arianna Huffington reports on the hijacking of democracy. Read it and weep—then head for the barricades. We have work to do."
—**Bill Moyers**

"Arianna Huffington has written the most entertaining tour guide to hell since Virgil led Dante through the Inferno. Crooked CEOs beware!" —**Bill Maher**

Also by Arianna Huffington

PIGS AT THE TROUGH

How Corporate Greed and
Political Corruption Are
Undermining America

ARIANNA HUFFINGTON

 THREE RIVERS PRESS • NEW YORK

Published by Three Rivers Press, New York, New York.
Member of the Crown Publishing Group, a division of Random House, Inc.
www.crownpublishing.com

THREE RIVERS PRESS and the Tugboat design are
registered trademarks of Random House, Inc.

Originally published in hardcover in slightly different form by
Crown Publishers, a division of Random House, Inc., New York, in 2003.

Printed in the United States of America

DESIGN BY BARBARA STURMAN

Library of Congress Cataloging-in-Publication Data
is available upon request.

ISBN 1-4000-5126-6

10 9 8 7 6 5 4 3 2 1

First Paperback Edition

For Isabella,
my youngest daughter,
with much love

Acknowledgments

Writing this book was a juggling act—keeping the big themes clear while tracking all the startling details unfolding every day on the front pages of our newspapers. Keeping ahead of this moving target could not have been done without a great team. Deep thanks go to Billy Kimball, who was shuttling back and forth between L.A. and Long Island, and to Peter Abbott, who landed here for a year from Cambridge, our shared alma mater in England, and went back the day after the book went to press. I hope that his decision to return to Cambridge to do a Ph.D. on the use of "terror" in Greek and Shakespearean tragedy was not entirely the result of researching the "pigs." Additional thanks to Chris Kyle, Moira Brennan, Jon Hotchkiss, Roy Sekoff, Stephen Sherrill, Victor Abalos, Leslie Borja, Mia Mazadiego, Prof. Christopher Gill, and to my good friends Mary Arno, David Booth, Bob Borosage, Marc Cooper, David Corn, Lynda Obst, and Lynn Sweet, who read the manuscript at different stages and greatly improved it.

Many thanks also to my anonymous sources, both at the top of the corporate world and among the recently downsized who provided fascinating leads and key details. Like Deep Throat, my inside sources reminded me to "follow the money." I can't name them but my thanks go to them all the same.

I can name, however, Steven Weiss of the Center for Responsive Politics (www.opensecrets.org), Scott Klinger of United for a Fair Economy (www.ufenet.org), Russell Mokhiber of the *Corporate Crime Reporter* (www.corporatecrimereporter.com), Robert Weissman of the *Multinational Monitor* (www.multinationalmonitor.org), and Micah Sifry of Public Campaign (www.publiccampaign.org). I've included their websites because I know that my readers will find them as useful as I did.

All my gratitude to my amazing editor Emily Loose, whose outrage at the pigs never flagged, even after her fourth masterly editorial pass on the same text; and to my incredible agent Richard Pine, whose involvement embraced every detail from the book's contract to the book's content. To Steve Ross, who welcomed me back into the Crown fold, Barbara Marks for the enthusiasm she brought to the book's promotion, and Caroline Sincerbeaux for all the many ways she helped the pigs come to life. Many thanks also to Barbara Sturman for her work in creating an attractive design for the book, to Amy Boorstein for her expert management of the copyediting, and to Derek McNally for his efforts to make this book come in on time.

The book is dedicated to my younger daughter Isabella who together with her older sister, Christina, provided constant joyous interruptions.

Contents

PIGS AT THE TROUGH

INTRODUCTION

Twilight of the Corporate Gods

"Old truths have been relearned; untruths have been un-learned. We have always known that heedless self-interest was bad morals; we know now that it is bad economics. Out of the collapse of a prosperity whose builders boasted their practicality has come the conviction that in the long run economic morality pays."

FRANKLIN D. ROOSEVELT
(Second Inaugural Address, January 20, 1937)

IN AUGUST OF 2002 I received a politely phrased notice from my cable company, Adelphia, addressed to "Dear Valued Customer" announcing that my monthly cable fee would be increasing. The letter explained that, "like other businesses, Adelphia constantly faces increases in operational expenses such as wages, specialized training for our employees, utilities, fuel, insurance, equipment. . . ." Missing from the missive? Any mention of another operational expense that no one at Adelphia seemed too happy to discuss. During the unfortunate latter days of his reign, former CEO John Rigas had borrowed $3.1 billion from the company and spread the money around like seed on a sun-scorched lawn. His own lawn, of course. He spent $13 million to build a golf course in his backyard, $150 million to buy the Buffalo Sabres hockey team, $65 million to fund a venture capital group run by his son-in-law, thousands to maintain his three private jets, and $700,000 for a country-club membership. It's a wonder my bill's not going up a million dollars a month. I just hope Adelphia's subscribers aren't also paying for his bail.

In the super-heated nineties we were told repeatedly that the "democratization of capital" and unparalleled increases in productivity would level the playing field and produce unprecedented gains in everyone's standard of living. Well, far from closing the vast gap between the haves and the have-nots, the lunatic excesses and the frenzy of fraud perpetrated by our high-flying corporate chieftains have left America's 401(k)s and pension plans in ruins and more than 8 million people out of work. Meanwhile, despite the much vaunted Corporate Responsibility Act and the highly publicized round up of a few of the most heinous offenders, the awful truth is that the corporate tricksters have pillaged the U.S. economy and gotten away with it. They're still living in their gargantuan houses, still feasting on their wildly inflated salaries, and engorging themselves on staggering sums of stock options, while the rest of America tries to figure out how to rebuild for retirement. Or send a kid to college on a worthless stock portfolio.

Ask yourself, Which America do you live in?

Do you live in a $90 million mansion in Bel-Air like Global Crossing founder and chairman Gary Winnick, financed by the cleverly timed sale of more than $730 million worth of stock in the now bankrupt telecom giant? Or do you have a house like Stephen Hilbert's in Carmel, Indiana, with a personal basketball court that's a full-sized replica of Indiana University's Assembly Hall? (Hilbert—an avid Hoosiers fan as you may have guessed—built the house during his disastrous tenure as CEO of Conseco, an insurance company whose stock dropped off the S&P 500 in the summer of 2002.)

Maybe you prefer to kick back, like former Tyco CEO Dennis Kozlowski, on beautiful Nantucket? Sea Rose Farm, Kozlowski's $5 million island spread, features magnificent ocean views, massive fireplaces, a resident chef, a four-bedroom guesthouse, and two seaside cottages—the cutely named "Sequin" and "Edward Cary"—each valued at an additional $2 to $3 million.

Or maybe you don't even bother with a house. Maybe you live on a yacht like *Sakura,* the 192-foot, five-deck, $10 million floating mansion owned by Oracle CEO Larry Ellison. Or the aptly named *Aquasition,* which you took off the hands of former WorldCom CEO Bernie Ebbers after the company he led hid more than $7 billion in losses and scuttled its stock. Or maybe these are just too small-time for you. If that's the case, try out Kozlowski's $25 million, 130-foot historic sloop *Endeavour,* which costs the Tyco tycoon $700,000 a year to maintain.

Or are you one of those corporate titans who has so many million-dollar residences scattered around the globe that you have trouble settling down? Perhaps you'd rather shuttle between homes on your corporate jet. Or is even that too restrictive? When General Electric's retired CEO Jack Welch got fed up with his fleet of cramped corporate jets, he did what any self-respecting capitalist idol would do. He went out and bought a couple of much larger Boeing 737-700s. His allergy to baggage claim is said to be so extreme that even in retirement GE kept a plane at the ready for his impulsive wanderings. Only after the arrangement was made public in his divorce filings did Welch agree to pay $2 million a year to reimburse GE for the jet and a few other perks.

How do you make the most of a long weekend? Instead of planning a backyard barbecue, do you take off for an afternoon at a beach halfway around the world, say in Fiji or Bora Bora, courtesy of your generous shareholders? Or do you line up a golf date with the president of the United States?

Why not jet off to a sunny spot closer to home like Bermuda or the Cayman Islands? CEOs like Joe Forehand of

Accenture and Herbert Henkel of Ingersoll-Rand can go there and still claim they're on the job because their companies are technically headquartered in these centers of high finance with warm tropical breezes and no taxes.

How about a little extra spending money? Are you crafty enough to line up the special kind of financing that netted Bernie Ebbers $408 million in loans? Hey, why bother with a nosy bank when you can just write yourself a check for a few hundred million from your very own corporate kitty, at no or extremely low interest? And if you can't pay it back, maybe your company will let you slide for a few months or years or even forgive the whole thing like E*Trade did with CEO Christos Cotsakos' $15 million loan? After all, you're the boss.

And what would happen if, God forbid, you caught a few bad breaks and were forced out of your job? Are you confident that even if you really messed up and not only lost all the company's money but also lost thousands of other people their jobs, you'd still walk away with millions of dollars in bonuses and options and an extremely generous annual pension payment?

If you answered yes to any of these questions, you live in a very special suburb of America: "CEO-ville." It's a cushy, exclusive enclave that has broken away from the rest of the Republic, where the motto is "Land of the free, home of the off-shore tax shelter." The currency is emblazoned with the inscription, "In God and crooked accountants we trust," and the Declaration of Independence includes the phrase: "all men are endowed by their creator with certain inalienable rights, that among these are stock options, golden parachutes, and the reckless pursuit of limitless wealth."

In all likelihood, though, you're living in the other America, the one 99.9999% of the country has to make do with. The one in which a record-breaking 1.5 million filed for bankruptcy between March 2001 and March 2002. The one in which investors have lost nearly $9 trillion since March 2000 and retirement assets lost 11% of their value—$630 billion—over roughly the same period.

How did this divisive and anti-democratic tale of two Americas come to pass? How did the impossibly rich upper crust get impossibly crustier? How did we allow the haves to have so insanely much while the rest of America got stuck with the bill? What did our fearless corporate leaders do to deserve such excessive pay and perks, and severance packages, as they laid off hundreds of thousands of hardworking Americans, and magically made trillions of dollars in pension plans and small investor shareholdings disappear?

It's not just that corporate America corrupted the watchdogs that were supposed to be guarding the public interest by feeding them under the table. While it is true that federal regulators, overseers, accountants, and the corporate boards were only too happy to lick the hands that fed them, corporate corruption will not just be chased away by a better-trained pack of Dobermans.

Most of us live our lives according to a set of generally accepted rules. Some are actual laws, which we may or may not be happy with—who likes paying taxes?—but which we follow anyway. Others are moral conventions governed by our sense of decency. We relinquish our seat to an elderly woman on a crowded bus. We hand back the extra money when a cashier gives us too much change. We don't gamble away our kids' allowance in the office football pool. And although we're ambitious, we don't cheat people just to speed up our own rise to the top.

A small group of Americans isn't happy with this arrangement. Not content to conduct themselves according to a code of fair play that allows more than ample opportunity for hardworking, talented, or just plain lucky people to prosper—even to become very rich—they've created their own set of rules that defy logic, violate basic decency, corrupt commerce, and laugh in the face of the laws and regulations established to protect the rest of us. These are the standards that comprise the Code of the Crooked CEO. It's a code of dishonor that rewards unprecedented avarice with gargantuan wealth and ensures a lifestyle of appalling excess—where "keeping up with the Gateses" means that having too much is never enough.

Whenever gang members mow each other down in inner-city shootouts, we are subjected to endless speculation about the root causes of their behavior. Was it a family breakdown, the absence of a father figure, the scourge of crack cocaine, the rising illegitimacy rate, or the collapse of religious values? Watching the latest installments of Must CEO TV—disgraced corporate execs carted off in handcuffs or robotically taking the Fifth in front of congressional committees—I find myself asking the same question: What led these men (and, Martha excepted, they are all men, though one suspects that behind more than a few avaricious men stand greedy women) to do the despicable things they did?

How could they show such wanton disregard for the well-being of so many? What makes them tick—and what made them into ticking financial time bombs? Perhaps instead of the usual talk-show pundits, it would be more useful to convene a roundtable discussion on the subject featuring Dr. Freud, Dr. Jung, and Dr. Phil. Call it "The Three Doctors."

I'd love to hear what these legendary explorers of the human psyche would make of the likes of John Rigas, Dennis Kozlowski, Bernie Ebbers, Sam Waksal, and those Three Horsemen of the Enron Apocalypse, Ken Lay, Jeff Skilling, and Andy Fastow. Were they, as some armchair analysts have theorized, kids who grew up with no love in their lives, now desperately trying to fill the inner void with money and material possessions? Were they suffering from reckless grandiosity? Grotesque delusions? Sheer madness?

In *Without Conscience,* renowned criminologist Dr. Robert Hare identified the key emotional traits of psychopaths.

Included in what he called "The Psychopathy Checklist" were: the inability to feel remorse, a grossly inflated view of oneself, a pronounced indifference to the suffering of others, and a pattern of deceitful behavior.

Could there be any better example of a person with a grandiose—and sociopathic—sense of entitlement, of feeling that the rules that mere mortals live by don't apply to him, than John Rigas? He thought nothing of "borrowing" $3.1 billion dollars from his shareholders so he and his sons could live like sultans—even though they were already fantastically rich, by anyone's definition, before raiding the company coffers.

If you're wondering what the inability to feel regret or shame looks like, take a good look at Dennis Kozlowski. He may have cost Tyco shareholders $92 billion in market value, and he may be facing criminal trials for tax fraud and for looting $600 million from the company, but "Deal-a-Day Dennis" refused to let a few unfortunate details like these stop him from shamelessly hosting a lavish and boisterous Fourth of July bash—only one month after his art fraud scheme was revealed—at his magnificent spread in Nantucket and aboard his antique racing sloop.

Whether it was a last hurrah or just excess as usual, Kozlowski spared no expense to guarantee that a good time was had by all. A legion of private security guards protected the cases of vintage wine and other goodies being delivered to the yacht, which sat on a mooring that costs Kozlowski $1.5 million a year. After a sail on the *Endeavour*, one eyewitness reported that "he cruised back into port at the helm—like he was a conquering hero." Unwilling to try his guests' sea legs further, Kozlowski next conquered a lavish repast at the elegant White Elephant restaurant, from which he watched the island's annual fireworks display. And just to show what a stand-up guy he is, Kozlowski stood a round of drinks for everyone at the restaurant's bar. And why not? It's not like it's his money.

You'd be hard pressed to find a man more willing to play fast and loose with the truth than that indefatigable social climber Dr. Sam Waksal. He didn't just lie about big things like the prospects of FDA approval for his company's cancer drug, Erbitux. No, Waksal lied even when there was nothing to gain from the deceit: he claimed he was 52 when he was actually 54, that he was raised in Toledo, Ohio, when he grew up in nearby Dayton. Either way, he's a middle-aged Middle American, so why the subterfuge?

As for Jeff Skilling, who abandoned Enron's sinking ship with his $100 million stock option lifejacket, he exhibits the psychopath's complete lack of remorse, unable to admit wrongdoing. Instead he continues to insist he "made the right decisions."

During the nineties, America fell under the spell of the corporate kingpins, putting a premium on charismatic CEOs who looked good on the cover of *Business Week* or being interviewed on *Squawk Box* (although many also mainstreamed themselves with appearances on *Larry King* or even *The Tonight Show*). It was the era of the rock star CEO. *Time* magazine even chose two businessmen—Amazon's Jeff Bezos and Intel's Andy Grove—as its Person of the Year in two of the past five years.

It turns out, of course, that far too many of these preening, pampered, overpaid, egocentric corporate American Idols were good on the tube or glad-handing Wall Street but tended to overlook mundane little things like where to list assets and where to list liabilities on a balance sheet.

The off-the-chart CEO extravagances would be a tad easier to stomach if they had been paid for with money earned as reward for superior performance. But they weren't. Many of these superstar executives were not even good at what they were overpaid to do. In fact, some were downright atrocious—to say nothing of felonious. But however much they ravaged their companies' bottom line, it never seemed to affect their own annual haul.

Consider the case of former Ford CEO Jacques Nasser,

who was rewarded with millions in stock and cash despite an awful 34-month reign that left the carmaker's revenue in a nosedive and 35,000 workers out of a job. It's hard to imagine that Ford could have done worse if they'd just made decisions by letting a monkey flip a coin.

In fact, the CEOs' lust for excess has been indulged at the direct expense of the pyramid of workers below them. The very system that the CEOs have taken advantage of depends upon the premise that the other America follows the other code—the one based on laws and morality. The scandals at Enron, Arthur Andersen, Global Crossing, Tyco, WorldCom, Xerox, Qwest, Merrill Lynch, and the rest have exposed a brutal disregard in the boardroom for the fate of those in the office cubicles or on the factory floor.

Against all odds, Kozlowski, Waksal, Rigas, and Fastow are actually being criminally prosecuted. But that doesn't happen very often, because most CEOs and their Praetorian Guard of lawyers, accountants, and advisors are smart enough not to break the law. They don't have to.

The mad stampede of greed that coincided with the waning of the bull market and the bursting of the loony tunes tech balloon would not have been possible without an unholy alliance between the CEO class and their buddies on Capitol Hill. For a small fee, payable at the beginning of each election cycle—some call such fees "political donations"; others, less concerned with semantics, political correctness, and charges of slander, call them "legal bribes"—corporate mandarins can purchase an all-access pass guaranteeing a sympathetic look the other way from our so-called public servants. Sure, for a few weeks last summer, when the WorldCom bomb made them fear for their political lives, our political leaders actually passed a set of reforms. But don't be fooled. Both political parties have a richly vested interest in corporate corruption.

The hustling salesmen known as stock "analysts," and their

unindicted co-conspirators, the handsomely attired and blow-dried anchors of the cable business news channels, hardly held CEOs' feet to the fire. Glaring disparities in compensation, along with an all-you-can-eat menu of ultra-cushy CEO perks—golden parachutes, interest-free loans, options with obscene returns—were not only tolerated but winked at. And why should the average American have begrudged the CEOs their fabulous pay packages? After all, we thought they were working hard for their money. When stock prices and corporate values were flying so high, why should small-stake stock punters not believe that high-priced executives were worth their inflated salaries, their personal jets, and their shareholder-funded mansions?

Now, of course, we know the appalling truth.

With the bull market a distant memory and nearly $9 trillion of market value lost, those who play by the rules are finally demanding justice. But the harsh and infuriating reality is that at the top of the economic heap, despite scandal after scandal, and the much-touted corporate reform bill, little has changed.

Confronted with the ever-growing litany of distasteful abuses, the defenders of the system of excess and fraud have protested, sometimes with some pro-forma show of regret, that the invisible hand of the market inevitably anoints both winners and losers.

They blithely sidestep the inconvenient fact that the democratic social contract depends upon the vast majority of citizens trusting that the economic game is not rigged like some shady ring-toss booth on a carnival midway. If the playing field isn't level, then the market isn't free—it's fixed. Despite the disingenuous protestations of the true believers, the fraud and deceit perpetrated in our corporate suites and boardrooms have nothing to do with the free market—and everything to do with the swindles and cons you traditionally associate with a rug bazaar.

"Businessmen," said Ayn Rand in 1961, "are the symbol of a free society—the symbol of America. If and when they perish, civilization will perish." Obviously the high priestess of free enterprise never met the men of Enron, Adelphia, and WorldCom.

In books such as *The Virtue of Selfishness* and *Atlas Shrugged*, the bibles of free marketeers like Alan Greenspan, Rand championed the idea that by doing what is best for yourself, you end up doing what is best for society. That equation has now been turned on its ear. The gross excesses of today's crony capitalists are no longer aligned with the interests of their shareholders or workers, or even with the long-term interests of the companies they run—not to mention society as a whole.

The orgy of money-grubbing by the corporate cabal has inflicted real, long-lasting pain on a host of deceived Americans: emptying their wallets, pillaging their 401(k) plans and dashing all their expectations for a comfortable retirement. The have-nots found themselves on the opposite side of an ever-widening economic Grand Canyon separating them from the have-way-too-muches.

UPSTAIRS/DOWNSTAIRS

"What we have in this country is socialism for the rich and free enterprise for the poor."
—Gore Vidal

"The only difference between the rich and other people is that the rich have more money," said literary critic Mary Colum during lunch with Ernest Hemingway in 1936. In truth, more money is hardly the only difference. No newsflash there. But what should be making headlines is the fact that the gap between what's going on upstairs in boardrooms, executive suites, and private planes and what's going on downstairs in office cubicles and on factory floors has become an abyss.

Upstairs: Former Kmart CEO Charles Conaway received nearly $23 million in compensation during his two-year tenure.
Downstairs: When Kmart filed for bankruptcy in 2002, 283 stores were closed and 22,000 employees lost their jobs. None of them received any severance pay whatsoever.

Upstairs: Former Tyco CEO Dennis Kozlowski made nearly $467 million in salary, bonuses and stock during his four-year tenure.
Downstairs: Shareholders lost a massive $92 billion when Tyco's market value plunged.

Upstairs: The CEOs of 23 large companies under investigation by the SEC and other agencies earned 70% more than the average CEO, banking a collective $1.4 billion between 1999 and 2001.
Downstairs: Since January 2001 the market value of these 23 companies nosedived by over $500 billion, or roughly 73%, and they have laid off over 160,000 employees.

Upstairs: In the year before Enron collapsed, about 100 executives and energy traders collected more than $300 million in cash payments from the company. More than $100 million went to former CEO Kenneth Lay.
Downstairs: After filing for bankruptcy, Enron lost $68 billion in market value, 5,000 employees lost their jobs, and Enron workers lost $800 million from their pension funds.

Upstairs: Wal-Mart CEO H. Lee Scott, Jr. received more than $17 million in total compensation in 2001.
Downstairs: Wal-Mart employees in 30 states are suing the company alleging that managers forced employees to punch

out after an eight-hour work day, and then continue working for no pay. This is a clear violation of the Fair Labor Standards Act, which says employees who work more than 40 hours a week must be paid time and a half for their overtime.

Upstairs "Penthouse A": Citigroup provided Enron with $8.5 billion in loans disguised as commodity trades. The deals allowed Enron to artificially inflate cash flow and hide debt, which deceptively boosted share price and ultimately led to the company's collapse.

Upstairs "Penthouse B": Citigroup offered hot initial public offering shares to WorldCom CEO Bernie Ebbers and other telecom titans in exchange for their investment banking business. Ebbers is alleged to have made nearly $11 million on IPO shares sold to him by Citigroup.

Downstairs: Citigroup agreed to pay $215 million in fines to the FTC to settle allegations of "predatory lending," loosely defined as mortgage lending that preys on customers, especially ones with bad credit, through abusive practices like deceptive marketing and inflated fees on unnecessary refinancings.

Upstairs: More than a million U.S. corporations and individuals have registered as citizens of Bermuda to avoid taxes, a practice okayed by the IRS. Although the exact number is unknown, the IRS estimates that "tax motivated expatriation" drains at least $70 billion a year from the U.S. Treasury.

Downstairs: If you were poor enough to apply for the Earned Income Tax Credit in 2001, your chance of being audited was one in 47. If you made more than $100,000 a year, your chance of being audited was one in 208.

Upstairs: The richest 20% of Americans earn almost 50% of the nation's income.

Downstairs: The poorest 20% of Americans earn 5.2%.

How can there be talk of a shared destiny in a nation where just over one percent of the population (170 billionaires, 25,000 deca-millionaires and 4.8 million millionaires) control approximately 50% of the entire country's personal wealth? Where the richest 20% earn 48.5% of the income and the poorest 20% merely 5.2%? Where, since 1980, real income for the bottom fifth of families fell by $800, while for the top fifth, it rose by $56,800?

The excesses of corporate America have become more than just a social crime; they are a direct threat to the well-being of our society. The bottom line is that the United States can no longer hold its head up as the world's standard-bearer of capitalist virtue.

Even as our country has taken steps to abolish welfare, forcing the poor to sink or swim, we've allowed the high-end corporate class to weave a giant safety net for its members. Is this corporate welfare really any different or less costly than the kind most of these people inveigh against? To use their own argument, how are we ever going to get them to act responsibly when we keep rewarding them for irresponsibility? To say nothing of criminality.

Those devoted to the principles of a free and fair market are the ones who should be working the hardest to put an end to the sorry state of affairs in which businessmen—those "symbols of America"—are richly rewarded for failing.

Indeed, a report from United for a Fair Economy and the Institute for Policy Studies revealed that CEOs of companies under investigation by the SEC, the Justice Department, and other agencies for accounting irregularities, received as much as 70% more than the average CEO. It's downright un-Randian. And, much more important for those of us who do not sleep with *Atlas Shrugged* under our pillow, it's downright un-American.

How did the free-market ideology of the Reagan revolution come to be the political consensus of our times? How did we get suckered by the fairy tale that as long as people kept shopping, the market could keep our prosperity expanding as far as the eye could see? And that by voting with our credit cards, we could spread the gospel of prosperous democracy to any corner of the earth where American products were made or consumed? Like all fairy tales, it's a nice story. But it's time to acknowledge that this one didn't have a happily-ever-after ending.

Over the last twenty years, Americans have been doused with regular sermons on the supposed correlation between un-regulated markets and higher standards of living. In the process, the American people were demoted from citizens to consumers, and sold a bill of goods (rather than a Bill of Rights) about how the almighty market was the essential foundation of democracy. Accepted notions of public protections—of the environment, of workers, of the poor—were scrapped, cast out as superannuated relics. Compassion became the 8-track player of public policy.

In the course of selling us on buying, the market worshippers shredded the modern social contract, the hard-fought consensus that had emerged since the New Deal, which ordered our political priorities, and expressed both our communal concern for the most vulnerable and our disapproval of huge inequalities. We were now supposed to believe that all that could be left up to the soulless, self-correcting calculus of supply and demand. The free market had become the People's Market and would, of course, take care of the people.

On June 26, 1995, President Clinton, speaking at the World Economic Forum in Davos, Switzerland, described the job of our generation: "to persuade people that democracy and free markets can give all people the opportunity to live out their dreams." Almost imperceptibly "free markets" had come to mean unregulated markets. As for democracy, well, it was a nice rhetorical flourish. But in reality, the fact that half of our citizens do not vote in presidential elections, while two-thirds don't bother to turn up for midterm elections did not seem to concern our political leaders.

Once the province of Republican supply-siders, this all-encompassing faith was warmly embraced in the nineties by New Democrats. And some old Democrats, too. Even Jesse Jackson rang the opening bell at the New York Stock Exchange and created a Wall Street Project.

The media dutifully did their part, hyping stories that made it seem like everyone was making money investing. Who can forget the Beardstown Ladies, those best-selling, stock-pickin' grannies from Illinois who were supposedly making a 23% return in the market? Or all those Millionaires Next Door—like Anne Scheiber, the lowly government auditor who, by patiently investing in stocks, turned $5,000 into a $22 million fortune?

Stressed out about retirement? Your kids' college tuition? A family health emergency? Not to worry! The market would take care of all that. Even being downsized could be made fun and profitable. After AT&T laid off 40,000 workers in January 1996, hedge-fund manager Jim Cramer wrote a cover story for the *New Republic* entitled "Let Them Eat Stocks." In it he proposed a simple solution. "Just give the laid-off employees stock options," he exulted, "let them participate in the stock appreciation that their firings caused." And why not toss in a year's worth of Turtle Wax while you're at it, Jim? So all social ills would be redressed by the market while the onward march of democracy would be guaranteed by the democratization of capital. "One dollar, one vote." The new evangelists had seen the future and it worked. Even when it was out of work.

The future that Wall Street had dreamt of for decades—free of snooping politicians, pesky regulators and profit-sapping social activists—had finally arrived in a golden, irrationally exuberant dawn. Just as communists had promised a utopia in which the state would wither away, the free-market ideologues in control in the nineties promised us that we would reach Nirvana when all government intervention would, well, just wither away.

We would then find ourselves in a glorious Brave New World. Marxists and MSNBC stock analysts together at last, holding hands and feverishly chanting: "From each according to his culpability, to each according to his greed."

I was lucky that I got my degree in economics at Cambridge, where I inhaled a healthy skepticism of the power of the free market to bring about the good society. After all, Cambridge was the home of John Maynard Keynes. I well remember a lecture in my freshman year in which free-market guru Milton Friedman was dismissed in one sentence as someone who did not understand Keynesian economics.

My first speech at the Cambridge Union was on the motion, "This House Believes That the Market Is a Snare and an Illusion." I was speaking on J. K. Galbraith's side against William F. Buckley. In 1978 I published a book, *The Other Revolution,* in which I marveled at the attempt of free-market ideologues to ascribe all public good to the invisible hand of the market. It took a while—and the fall of Ken Lay, Bernie Ebbers, Sam Waksal, et al.—before the invisible hand was exposed as a pickpocket. But even during my Republican interregnum in the early nineties I never believed that we could trust trickle-down economics to solve social problems. I've actually always agreed with Mark Russell, who defined trickle-down as, "something that benefits David Rockefeller now and Jay Rockefeller later." Or, to be a bit more current, George Herbert Walker Bush then, and George Walker Bush now.

But evidence can never, by itself, trump ideology. Forget the inconvenient fact that deregulation hasn't worked—that it's given us an airline industry on the verge of collapse, higher electric and cable bills, a savings and loan disaster, to say nothing of Enron, WorldCom, Adelphia, Xerox, and Merrill Lynch—the invisible hand is still the magical answer to all our woes. So even after the free-market parade had to be called off on account not of rain, but of fraud, we have begun to hear the trickle-down marching bands warming up in the distance, ready to play their familiar siren songs.

Like a lung-cancer patient reaching for a pack of smokes, the Bush administration has again and again greeted gloomy economic news with a nerve-settling puff of its favorite brand of economic relief: tax cuts for the rich. And considering the imprudence of that idea, maybe Team Bush is smoking something a little stronger than Marlboros.

What makes the free market ideology stronger than ever is that it is now powered by the nexus of money and politics that dominates our political process.

"No more easy money for corporate criminals, just hard time," President Bush said when he signed the corporate reform bill in July 2002. It was supposed to usher in the new era of corporate responsibility, but the new era message is nothing but a Madison Avenue gimmick—a "new and improved" label slapped on the same old package of deceit.

Watching the president smile for the cameras as he signed a reform bill he had never supported, I couldn't help but wonder if the glint in his eye was because he knew something the rest of us didn't. That for all his get-tough promises, the bill would actually do very little to reduce the level of corporate influence over our government.

It made me think of the time a friend took a family trip on a cruise ship. Her 10-year-old son kept pestering every crewmember he encountered, begging for a chance to drive the massive ocean liner. The captain finally invited the family up to the bridge, whereupon the boy grabbed hold of the wheel and began vigorously turning it. My friend panicked—until the captain leaned over and told her not to worry, that the ship was on autopilot, and that her son's antic maneuvers would have no effect.

It's the same with our leaders. They stand on the bridge making theatrical gestures they claim will steer us in a new direction while, down in the control room, the autopilot, programmed by politicians in the pocket of special interests, continues to guide the ship of state along its predetermined course. And you can bet that corporate America—with its Energizer Bunny lobbyists and wide-open checkbooks—will now be working overtime to further its own interests.

Although the corporate reform law was presented as a big win for the public interest, corporate lobbyists actually succeeded in fighting off a whole slew of potential reforms: stock options still don't have to be treated as a corporate expense, offshore tax havens continue to flourish, and there's been no pension fund reform.

What's more, industry lobbyists were able to water down many of the provisions that actually made it into the bill, including those affecting the ability of accounting firms to offer consulting services to the companies they audit—the fountainhead of so much dishonest bookkeeping. The new law doesn't ban such double-dipping—it only limits it. And even those limits can be overridden by the new accounting oversight board whose members will be appointed by an SEC still stocked with the industry's shills.

A few more "victories" like this and we're going to lose the war.

It's really pretty astounding when you think of it: with all the public outrage and media focus on corporate wrongdoing, moneyed interests are still able to undermine the public interest—as our political leaders shamelessly continue dancing to their tune.

How else to explain the brazen hypocrisy exhibited by the president after the ceremonial signing of the new bill? Less than eight hours after warning corporate crooks "you will be exposed," he furtively issued an interpretation of the law that undercuts a provision designed to make it easier for employees to—you got it—expose corporate crooks. According to the White House, whistleblowers would be protected only if their inside information is provided during the course of a formal congressional investigation.

When the president's action was harshly criticized by the provision's bipartisan co-sponsors, White House spokesman Ari Fleischer puffed out his chest and sniffed: "Welcome to the statutes. That's why statutes are often complicated, and that's why somebody created lawyers." In other words: "Forget it, Jake, it's Chinatown."

Over the last 10 years, corporations have doled out more than $1.08 billion in soft-money contributions. This down payment on preferential public policy has extended across party lines, with $636 million going to Republicans and $449 million to Democrats.

Indeed, what makes the corporate crime wave not just a

business scandal but a political one is precisely the fact that there is simply no consistent institutional opposition to the corporate takeover of our politics—certainly not from the Democratic Party. It was, after all, Tom Daschle who blocked the stock-option amendment proposed by John McCain. And all but two Democratic senators—Mark Dayton (Minn.) and Thomas Carper (Del.)—have accepted campaign contributions from WorldCom, Enron, or Arthur Andersen.

During his run for the White House, Bush fought long and hard to convince us that he was a new breed of conservative—a Compassionate Conservative. But recent events make clear that he is actually the standard bearer of a far more coldhearted breed. Call them the Enron Conservatives.

Enron Conservatives can be either Republicans or Democrats. They are people who use political money and connections as levers to free themselves of all accountability to laws, regulations, and responsibility—even to their own employees. Simply put, they are people who consistently, shamelessly, and aggressively put their self-interest above the public interest. And when the lives of others are destroyed in the process, they just look the other way and hope that the law does, too.

As emotionally satisfying as the Rigas-Sullivan-Fastow-Waksal-Kozlowski "Corporate Execs in Chains" filmfest was, in the end it was just political theater—a focus group–tested performance piece written by Karl Rove and directed by John Ashcroft. And with those guys calling the shots, it would be foolish to expect a long run for the production.

No public interest group is able to match the relentless lobbying and contributing by corporate heavy hitters. And until we have such a populist countervailing force, we are doomed to live in a less and less democratic society.

By the time you finish this book, it is my hope that you will be ready to join forces to storm the control room on the S.S. *America* and shut off the autopilot.

P.I.Q. TEST

Would you rather watch CNBC's *Business Center* than *Monday Night Football*? Do you sometimes fantasize that you're Mrs. Lou Dobbs? Well, whether you answered "yes" to these questions, or whether you don't know who Lou Dobbs is, take this test to determine your Porcine Intelligence Quotient (P.I.Q.). Some of the answers may surprise you. Don't worry, if you don't score well, you can always retake the test after you've read the book.

1. Bernie Ebbers is to WorldCom as Gary Winnick is to
   _____?
   a. Winnebago
   b. Slime mold
   c. Global Crossing
   d. Dennis Kozlowski

2. According to Martha Stewart, she had placed a "sell" order on her ImClone stock when the price hit what point?
   a. $50
   b. $60
   c. $65
   d. $70
   e. $1
   Bonus Question 1: Which is the proper spelling of Martha Stewart's broker's last name: "Bacanovic" or "Backanovic?"
   Bonus Question 2: What's the name of the broker's assistant?

3. *True or False?* Tyco has its world headquarters on the tiny picturesque island nation of Barbuda.

4. Retired General Electric CEO Jack Welch's girlfriend, Suzy Wetlaufer, is the former editor of which magazine?
   a. *Maxim*
   b. *Money*
   c. *Wall Street Weekly*
   d. *The Harvard Business Review*

5. Arthritis? Migraines? Cancer? Herpes? Which disease did ImClone hope to fight with a drug the FDA ultimately rejected in December of 2001?

6. In an effort to remain solvent, Kenneth Lay's wife, Linda, opened a secondhand store in Houston to unload some of her pricey baubles. The store was called _____?
   a. Jus' Stuff
   b. Things 'n' Such
   c. The Junk-O-Mat
   d. Stuff 'n' Things

7. *True or False?* One of the paintings Dennis Kozlowski had shipped to New Hampshire to avoid New York's sales tax was Renoir's *Brasseur D'Affaires Emprisonné*.
   Bonus Question: What is the English translation of *Brasseur D'Affaires Emprisonné?*

8. "Neutron" is to Jack Welch as _____ is to former Sunbeam CEO Al Dunlap.
   a. Blowtorch
   b. Chainsaw
   c. Dental drill
   d. Sunbeam juicer
   Bonus Question: Other than Sunbeam, name the two other companies Al Dunlap was fired from.

9. Name three Internet start-ups hyped by disgraced Merrill Lynch analyst Henry Blodget that have since gone belly up.

10. The mascot for Pets.com was:
    a. A snuggly teddy bear named "Peepers"
    b. An angry, cigar-smoking rat named "Mr. Krunk"
    c. An adorable wise-cracking sock puppet
    d. A lovable foul-mouthed dancing chicken

11. Of two years and two days, three years and three days, and one year and one day, how long was former Sotheby's boss Al Taubman sentenced to prison for?
    Bonus Question 1: What crime was Taubman convicted of?
    Bonus Question 2: Name the head of Christie's Auction House who was implicated in Taubman's scheme.

12. Of private plane, private yacht, or private island, where was Martha Stewart when she allegedly called her broker to sell her shares of ImClone?

13. What was the name of Bernie Ebbers' 60-foot yacht?
    a. *Sea-E-O*
    b. *Man Over Board-of-Directors*
    c. *Aquasition*
    d. *The In-Vest-Or*
    Bonus Question: What is the name of Oracle CEO Larry Ellison's $10 million, five-deck, 192-foot yacht?

14. *True or False?* Before becoming a powerful Washington lobbyist, Chet Lott, Senator Trent Lott's son, owned a Chuck E. Cheese pizza restaurant.

15. If everyone who works for Haley Barbour's lobbying firm is male and everyone is Republican, which then is also true?
    a. All the secretaries are female.
    b. All the men are gay.
    c. All the men are Republicans.
    d. No one makes a decent cup of coffee.

16. What happened to UBS PaineWebber broker Chung Wu
    when he warned clients that "Enron's financial condition
    is deteriorating?"
    a. Promoted by management
    b. Hailed as a "hero" by co-workers
    c. Fired by boss
    d. Shot at dawn

17. In the last five years, *Time* magazine has selected two
    CEOs as their "Person of the Year." Who are they?
    a. Bill Gates   e. Andrew Grove
    b. John Rigas   f. Larry Ellison
    c. Jeff Bezos   g. Steve Case
    d. Kenneth Lay   h. Jack Welch

18. *True or False?* In 2001 all 30 of the blue chip companies
    in the Dow Jones Industrial Average paid their account-
    ants more for consulting and tax service than for the
    company audit.

19. American Express. Daimler Chrysler. Dow Jones. Revlon.
    Sara Lee. Xerox. Callaway Golf. What do these companies
    have in common?
    a. Al Dunlap is a former CEO.
    b. Vernon Jordan sits on their boards.
    c. Martha Stewart sold their stock based on insider
       information.
    d. Each makes a simply delicious coffee cake.

20. Fill in the blank. In 1998, hot-shot Wall Street analyst
    Mary Meeker wrote a famous Internet stock report titled
    "Yahoo, Yippee, _____."
    Bonus Question: What firm does Mary Meeker work for?

21. Only one word can be made when you unscramble all the
    following letters. What is it? "YNTPCRKBUA."

22. Which of the following is NOT like the others: Bill Gates, Andrew Fastow, Larry Ellison, Rupert Murdoch, Warren Buffett.
    Bonus Question: Name the type of soda Warren Buffett drinks five cans of a day.

23. When asked about her dumping of ImClone stock during a cooking segment on *CBS This Morning,* Martha Stewart famously said:
    a. "My lawyer has urged me not to discuss this matter."
    b. "I want to focus on my salad."
    c. "It's only a matter of time before I'm declared innocent of all charges."
    d. "I want to talk about something that's really important: celery."

24. George W. Bush affectionately refers to his friend Kenneth Lay as . . .
    a. "Kenny My Man"
    b. "The Kenster!"
    c. "Kenny Boy"
    d. "The Lay-minator"

25. *True or False?* Salomon Smith Barney maintained "hold" ratings on eight companies up to the date the companies filed for bankruptcy.

26. In 100 words or less, what is the single most important lesson we can take from this recent corporate crisis, and what can we do to bring about fundamental reform?
    Send your responses to *pigs@ariannaonline.com.* Selected highlights from your responses will be posted on my website (www.pigsatthetrough.com).

Answers

1. c
2. b;
   Bonus #1: "Bacanovic";
   Bonus #2: Douglas Faneuil
3. False. It's Bermuda.
4. d
5. Cancer
6. a
7. False;
   Bonus: "Tycoon Imprisoned"
8. b;
   Bonus: Nitec and Max
   Phillips & Son
9. Aether Systems, Infospace
   and Excite@Home
10. c
11. One year and one day;
    Bonus #1: Price-fixing;
    Bonus #2: Sir Anthony
    Tennant
12. Private plane
13. c;
    Bonus: *Sakura*
14. False. He actually owned a
    Domino's Pizza franchise.
15. c
16. c
17. c & e
18. False. It was actually 26.
19. b
20. "Cowabunga";
    Bonus: Morgan Stanley
21. "Bankruptcy"
22. Andrew Fastow. The others
    are all CEOs.
    Bonus: Cherry Coke
23. b
24. c
25. True

Scoring

Zero correct answers: That banging you hear? It's the Emergency Medical Services. They want to make sure you're still alive.

1 to 7 correct answers: It's time to read something other than the *National Enquirer*.

8 to 13 correct answers: It's time to read something other than *People*.

14 to 22 correct answers: The good news is you buy the *Wall Street Journal*. The bad news is you left it on the subway.

23 to 30 correct answers: Congratulations! You'd be the Dow Jones Man of the Year, if such an award existed.

31 to 34 correct answers: That banging you hear? It's the police. You're under arrest for insider trading, or falsifying tax returns, or fraud, or stealing, or lying to Congress. If you know that much, you must be one of the Pigs.

PIGS ON PARADE

Power, Perks, and Impunity

◆

They hang the man and flog the woman that steal the
goose from off the common.
But let the greater villain loose that steals the common
from the goose.

ENGLISH FOLK POEM, c. 1764

SURVEYING THE STATE of corporate America from his
number two perch on *Forbes* magazine's list of the 400
Richest People in America, Warren Buffett, the avuncular sage
of American capitalism, opened fire with both barrels. At a
Berkshire Hathaway shareholder meeting in May 2002, Buffett
told his audience, among other things, that Wall Street loves a
crook, investment bankers have contempt for investors, stock-
option-engorged CEOs are shameless, and American business
is teeming with fraud.

Buffett's blast was a remarkably honest assessment—as
rare in the world of high finance as it was necessary. The litany
of sins committed by the high priests of profit is a study in
venality, deceit, theft, treachery, pride, and most of all, greed,
greed, and more greed.

And who do you think is paying the price for all of this
greed and corruption? The corporate criminals have made out
like bandits while the American public has been robbed. Buffett nailed it when he wrote in a recent letter to his sharehold-

ers that he is "disgusted by the situation, so common in the last few years, in which shareholders have suffered billions in losses while the CEOs, promoters, and other higher-ups who fathered these disasters have walked away with extraordinary wealth. To their shame, these business leaders view shareholders as patsies, not partners."

You know things have really gotten out of hand when the most scathing attacks on corporate greed and Wall Street malfeasance are being launched not by knee-jerk business haters and anti-globalization Jeremiahs but by the country's leading investment guru.

Family Pig: John Rigas

Rigas, Kozlowski, Waksal, Winnick, Lay, Skilling, Fastow, Ebbers, Sullivan. This rogues' gallery of corporate scoundrels has turned our country's state-of-the-art free enterprise system into a smorgasbord of corruption.

The stories of these pigs at the trough are as rich and varied as the personalities of their protagonists.

Take John Rigas, the small-town hero who turned into a big time crook. You couldn't make up a story as incredible as the all-too-true tale of Rigas' rise and fall—or a character as unforgettable.

Rigas is straight out of a Frank Capra movie: a self-made man who turned a $300 investment in a local cable franchise into a $7 billion communications empire; a Greek boy who remained true to his roots, refusing to move his company's headquarters out of the little Pennsylvania town where it got its start; a benevolent billionaire who treated his employees like family, put his home phone number on Adelphia cable bills, offered jobs and loans to those down on their luck, helped finance a medical center in his hometown, and every now and then collected tickets and made popcorn at the local movie theater he has owned for nearly half a century.

He clearly considers himself a very moral man. He steadfastly refused, for instance, to carry X-rated programming on Adelphia, even though it cost the company $10 to $20 million in annual revenue. That's what makes the revelations about Rigas's sleazy business practices all the more shocking. His morality is reminiscent of the 1980s televangelist Jim Bakker who, like Rigas, read from the "Good Book" on Sunday and cooked the books on Monday through Friday. Where Rigas is headed, Bakker has been, having served five years in prison for fleecing his flock out of $158 million. Of course, where both men are *ultimately* headed is up to a higher court than any here on Earth. But I have my suspicions that both are more likely to feel the poke of a pitchfork than try on angels' wings.

The problem is that Rigas, like so many CEOs in the headlines today, began to see himself and the multi-billion-dollar company he led as one and the same, adopting the outlook of France's Louis XIV, who notoriously proclaimed: *L'état c'est moi*—"I am the state."

Now he has been forced to resign from the company he founded and is facing charges that he and his sons engaged in conspiracy and securities, wire, and bank fraud. When Rigas and his two sons realized that they could no longer postpone the inevitable, they offered to present themselves discreetly to the authorities to be charged. However, the government declined. It needed pictures of CEOs in handcuffs to try to convince the public that there was just one set of laws for both the haves and the have-nots.

The Rigases chose to spend the day before their arrest in an all-American car-switching extravaganza. After renting a Chevy Lumina in New York City (surely a downgrade from what they were used to) and attempting to drive from Manhattan to their home in Coudersport, Pennsylvania, John and Michael Rigas noticed that they were being tailed. They pulled a quick U-ey and returned to the Big Apple. While this bizarre scene was being played out, Timothy Rigas was jumping on a train bound for Greenwich, Connecticut. At his destination he impulsively splurged on a 1997 Audi from a local dealer and drove back to New York. From overhead, they must have looked like rats in a maze.

The Rigas clan was reunited back in New York and rose early the next morning. When five armed postal policemen knocked on the door of their apartment, John and Michael Rigas were dressed in blue suits and white shirts, and ready to go. Tim Rigas, in blue blazer and khaki pants, was heard to joke: "We live on the farm. We get up early."

Anyway, the Rigases had enough spare change on hand to cover their $30 million bail and were back home in plenty of time for a nice family dinner. You know what they say: the family that eats together, cheats together.

Maybe at least one of them will end up in a cell next to Dennis Kozlowski, whose story could be subtitled "Still Life in Prison Stripes."

Boss Pig: Dennis Kozlowski

When Kozlowski was arrested in May 2002 on charges of evading $1 million in sales taxes on $13.2 million worth of paintings he bought—wryly described by the *New York Times* as "second-tier work by big-name artists"—the question on everyone's lips was: why?

Why would a man who earned $125 million in 2001, owned planes, yachts, and an assortment of multi-million-dollar homes, and who routinely donated millions to charity risk it all in an effort to save a million bucks—probably about what he spent each year to keep his fleet of Harley-Davidson motorcycles running?

But, after immersing myself in Kozlowski's business history, I came up with an altogether different question: Why was anyone surprised? The behavior that now has him facing the possibility of 30 years in prison is exactly the behavior that was the hallmark of his run as Tyco's swashbuckling, take-no-prisoners CEO.

Why is it so shocking to learn that Kozlowski cooked up a con job to avoid paying his personal taxes? After all, this is the same guy who, in 1997, moved his company's nominal headquarters offshore to Bermuda to avoid paying taxes on billions of dollars in overseas earnings. Apparently, life imitates business when it comes to the art of cutting corners.

According to the scabrous portrait painted by prosecutors, Kozlowski bought his extravagant artwork—which included a $3.95 million Monet and a $4.7 million Renoir—to accessorize his $18-million, 13-room apartment on Fifth Avenue. But he then cleverly had his pricey paintings routed through Tyco's offices in New Hampshire so he wouldn't have to spring for New York City's 8.25% sales tax.

In one case, cooperative art dealers didn't even bother to actually ship the paintings to New Hampshire. Instead, they sent them directly to Kozlowski's apartment, shipping empty crates to Tyco headquarters. Unfortunately for Kozlowski, along with creating a paper trail of phony invoices, his co-conspirators generated a number of other deeply incriminating documents. "Here are the five paintings to go to New Hampshire (wink, wink)," reads one smoking gun memo addressed to an art handler.

Adding to this murky moral landscape, it appears that Kozlowski funded some of his art purchases with no-interest loans drawn from a Tyco program designed to help employees buy company stock. Perhaps if he had made do with a few LeRoy Neiman sports scenes and that perennial classic, *Dogs Playing Poker,* he could have avoided downsizing employees and raiding their stock fund.

Like Rigas, somewhere along the way, Kozlowski, the son of a New Jersey cop, began to see himself and the multi-billion-dollar company he led as one and the same. So why not get Tyco to make charitable donations in his name and buy his Manhattan apartment and $11 million in furniture and knickknacks, including a $6,300 sewing basket, a $15,000 dog umbrella stand, and $2,900 worth of coat hangers? And why not get Tyco shareholders to fork out nearly $100,000 for flowers or a million bucks for his wife's fortieth birthday party on the island of Sardinia with Jimmy Buffett to serenade her? He viewed all of Tyco's assets as his because, well, without him Tyco was nothing.

Dennis the Public Menace's progress from tax aversion to alleged tax evasion began with his loophole-exploiting business practices and ended with his defrauding the public out of tax money New York desperately needs. With the city digging out from under a post-9/11 budget deficit, what are we to make of a clown like Dennis Kozlowski who steals $1 million from the public to decorate his apartment even after he's engorged himself with hundreds of millions from the company trough?

According to the financial press, we were supposed to admire him—until the scandal broke. Maneuvers like these had for years earned Kozlowski the admiration of Wall Street and a glowing reputation as America's "Most Aggressive CEO"—the title of a 2001 cover story in *Business Week.* The magazine even went so far as to laud Kozlowski—an accountant by trade—for his "willingness to test the limits of acceptable accounting and tax strategies." And yes, I believe that, in the same issue, street corner crack dealers were lauded for their "willingness to test the limits of acceptable commerce strategies."

These accounting strategies allowed the company to report billions of dollars in profits every year, while building up $26 billion in debt. Only after the Enron collapse did Wall Street stop applauding and start scrutinizing Tyco's business more closely. The result? The company's stock lost three-quarters of its value in 2002, costing investors $92 billion.

On September 12, 2002, three months after he was indicted for evading sales taxes, Kozlowski and former Tyco CFO Mark Swartz were charged with "enterprise corruption and grand larceny"—for treating Tyco as their "personal piggy bank," and raiding its coffers to the tune of more than $600 million. Former general counsel Mark Belnick was charged with falsifying business records and hiding more than $14 million in loans he took from the company.

The previous May, three weeks before he resigned, Kozlowski gave the commencement address at New Hampshire's St. Anselm's College. A psychoanalyst would have had a field day with the message he chose to impart to the school's Class of 2002. "You will be confronted," he warned them, "with questions every day that test your morals. Think carefully, and for your sake, do the right thing, not the easy thing." You could almost see his superego and his id duking it out underneath his mortarboard.

Doctor Pig: Sam Waksal

When it comes to Dr. Sam Waksal, the founder of ImClone who pleaded guilty to bank and securities fraud, conspiracy to obstruct justice, and perjury, it's clear that his id won out a long time ago.

A legendary charmer, Waksal helped turn ImClone, which he started in an old shoe factory with $4 million, into a

MATCH THE CEO TO THE MANSION

KEN LAY Enron	**Boca Raton, Florida** $13.5 million Mediterranean-style, waterfront estate. 15,000 square feet. Parquet and marble flooring. Complete with elevator, boat dock, pool, cabana, tennis courts, and fountain
JOE NACCHIO Qwest	**Nantucket, Massachusetts** "Sequin," a charming $2.5 million wharf-side cottage
DENNIS KOZLOWSKI Tyco	**Rye, New Hampshire** $2.3 million house in exclusive New Hampshire coastal community
JOHN RIGAS Adelphia	**Bachelor Gulch, Colorado** $8.5 million 7,800-square-foot, eight-bedroom, ten-bathroom house on almost 3 acres of land
GARY WINNICK Global Crossing	**Nantucket, Massachusetts** "Edward Cary," an intimate coastal cottage worth somewhere in the region of $2.5 million
BERNIE EBBERS WorldCom	**New York, New York** $18 million, 13-room apartment on Fifth Avenue, complete with $11 million worth of furnishings, including a $6,000 gold shower curtain and high-end art including works by Monet and Renoir
SAM WAKSAL ImClone	**Nantucket, Massachusetts** $5 million coastal mansion, in-house chef, three-bedroom guest house, and boat dock

(They all belong to former Tyco CEO Dennis Kozlowski.)

$5.5 billion juggernaut. Dr. Sam was credited with single-handedly making biotech sexy. Along the way, he developed a reputation as a relentless social climber who collected famous friends—among them Mariel Hemingway, Lorraine Bracco, Carl Icahn, Harvey Weinstein and Mick Jagger—as hungrily as he acquired the trappings of wealth, including a place in the Hamptons and a 7,000-square-foot SoHo loft festooned with $20 million worth of de Koonings, Rothkos, and Picassos. One acquisition he was less inclined to show off was a world-class—and rapidly appreciating—collection of lawsuits.

He even got an invitation to play golf with President Clinton. Waksal did not play golf, but he rushed out on a mad spending spree, buying every golfing accessory the well-turned-out golfer needs. Unfortunately, he could not buy the ability to play the game. Standing at the first tee, Bubba at his side, Waksal swung at the ball with all his strength, succeeding only in dislodging a massive divot from the ground. "Maybe you can just ride along in the cart for the rest of the game, Sam," the president suggested.

But even as he became a regular on both the society and the business pages of the New York papers, Waksal began to reveal himself as a pathological liar. At his birthday party at Nobu restaurant in New York a couple of years ago, billionaire financier Carl Icahn told the assembled guests, who included Martha Stewart, a story of walking with Waksal on the beach in East Hampton. Waksal pointed to a house and told Icahn that he had just bought it. A few days later, Icahn passed by the house and decided to say "hi" to his buddy. The person who answered the door had never heard of Waksal. All those at the birthday dinner laughed about their daredevil friend. But I hope there was at least some unease, if not outright consternation, beneath the laughter.

Waksal's shaky relationship with the truth has put the future of Erbitux, and the treatment of millions of cancer sufferers, in jeopardy, and placed his own father and daughter, to say nothing of pal Martha Stewart, in harm's way, facing potential prosecution and jail time.

In a matter of months, Waksal morphed from Jay Gatsby in a lab coat to a snake oil–peddling Ivan Boesky.

This is just a mere glimpse of the gluttonous CEOs who have fattened themselves at America's expense. They and their fellow swine have brought disgrace to themselves and uncertainty to the U.S. economy. What differentiates them from their Old West predecessors like Billy the Kid, Jesse James, and the Dalton Gang are just Armani suits in place of leather chaps, crooked accountants instead of guns, and private planes instead of horses.

Succeeding by Failure, the CEO Way

Since the beginning of the new century, over 570 public companies—including most famously Enron, Global Crossing, Adelphia, WorldCom and Kmart—have declared bankruptcy. 2.7 million Americans have lost their jobs. Nearly $9 trillion in market value has been lost on Wall Street. But while the average American has suffered staggering losses in 401(k) and pension value, and many have struggled to stay afloat, the average CEO has added millions to his personal wealth. In corporate America, apparently, nothing succeeds like utter failure.

At Enron, after tens of billions of dollars vanished—including over $1 billion in employees' pension funds—and over 4,000 employees had been laid off, Enron's "Kenny Boy" Lay strolled out the door with over $100 million. In his last three years at Tyco, Dennis Kozlowski received $466.7 million in salary, bonuses, and perks. He did such a bang-up job that, since the summer of 2001, Tyco has closed or consolidated 300 plants and laid off 11,000 workers.

Since 1999, Bernie Ebbers—who claims he didn't understand that WorldCom was defrauding investors of $7 billion—received over $44 million in pay.

When Ebbers resigned in April 2002, his severance package promised him $1.5 million a year for the rest of his life, and the use of the WorldCom jet for 30 hours a year. And medical benefits. And life insurance. And a desktop computer. Plus, 300,000 free night and weekend long-distance calling minutes a month. Okay, not that.

WorldCom's board of directors finally woke up in September 2002 and asked a bankruptcy court to rescind the package.

Since then, 18,550 WorldCom employees have lost their jobs, the NASDAQ has halted trading of WorldCom stock, and the SEC has brought fraud charges against the company. On the bright side, Ebbers received 18,550 calls during dinner the day the WorldCom scandal broke asking if he wanted to switch long-distance companies.

And this bad corporate habit of rewarding CEOs for failure has become the norm rather than the exception. For instance, in the last three years, the stock of SBC Communications (a company that provides the dialtone for one in three Americans) has dropped 27%. Meanwhile, SBC's CEO, Edward Whitacre, has seen his compensation rise. In 2001, the third year in a row that the value of SBC declined, Whitacre received his largest windfall ever: $82 million at present values. In April 2002, *The Wall Street Journal* reported that Oracle CEO Larry Ellison made $706.1 million in total compensation in 2001. Shareholder return for that year was a *negative* 57%. James McDonald, CEO of Scientific-Atlanta, Inc., made $86.6 million in the same year. His shareholders got a return of *negative* 45%. Tony White, of Applera, a company that provides equipment for scientific research, made $62 million in 2001 while shareholders lost 59% on their investments.

Some companies have gone even further out of their way to reward their CEOs for failure. I mean, if the corporate earnings game is proving too tough, why not simply widen the goalposts? That's exactly what Coca-Cola did for CEO Douglas Daft. In 2000 the company was in a nosedive. More than 5,000 employees—almost one-fifth of the company's workforce—lost their jobs. Assets held in the company's 401(k) plan went up in smoke as the stock dropped 31% between 1998 and 2001. In late 2000, the newly arrived Daft, brought in to turn the company around, was told that a million Coca-Cola shares—with a total value of almost $60 million—had been reserved for him on the condition that Coke's earnings per share grew at least 20% a year over the next five years. Daft would get nothing if annual growth fell below 15%, half the shares if it was exactly 15%; and between half and all if growth exceeded 15%.

Just four months later Daft realized he couldn't make the benchmarks. It was just too difficult and, to his credit, he told Coke's board so. Not to worry, the board told him, we don't want you upset, so we'll lower the target goals from 20% to 16% growth on the high end and from 15% to 11% on the low end. And we'll still keep the maximum reward at a million shares. How's that for daft behavior? Wouldn't it be great if all our bosses were so accommodating?

That year Coke's stock dropped 23%, but, thanks to his old options and his new deal, Daft's compensation soared to $74.2 million, up nearly 47% from the previous year.

The closer you look, the more you see executives reaping enormous rewards despite atrocious showings on the job. Incentive-based pay may well produce an incentive to earn a profit, but the truth is that it also produces an incentive to grossly inflate profits, or even to produce them out of thin air. In 1981 there were a grand total of three earnings restatements

SATAN'S STOCK PORTFOLIO

COMPANY	HIGH	LOW
Enron	$ 90.75	$ .08
Tyco	62.80	6.98
Global Crossing	61.00	.02
ImClone	169.13	5.85
WorldCom	64.50	.11
Xerox	124.00	4.50
Adelphia	87.00	.12
Martha Stewart Omnimedia	39.75	6.29
Qwest	64.00	1.07
Dynegy	89.00	.49
Sunbeam	52.00	.05

by American companies. By 1997, the figure rose to 49. And by 2002, there were over 1,000 restatements. The lack of clarity in financial reporting directly benefits CEOs because it offers countless opportunities for self-serving spin. When you're in charge of evaluating your own performance—and a positive evaluation can earn you millions of dollars—the urge to inflate your own grade can prove irresistible.

In corporate America, crime pays. Handsomely. Grotesquely, even. So the stomach-turning revelations of rampant corruption that have come to light are surely only the appetizer for a far larger banquet of sleazy scandals. WorldCom fabricates $7 billion in profits; Xerox suddenly realizes it inflated its earnings by $6.4 billion; George W. Bush can't recall why he waited more than eight months to disclose his incredibly timely sale of $848,560 in Harken Energy stock while sitting on its board of directors; Martha Stewart is so busy teaching the world how, with a few popsicle sticks, glue, and chintz, you can make a festive summer napkin holder that she can't figure out why her broker has no record of her stop-loss order; Arthur Andersen gets the rare corporate death penalty after shredding its credibility along with key Enron documents. If our rogue businessmen devoted half the energy to strengthening their companies that they do to devising elaborate swindles, a true economic boom—as opposed to the bogus nineties bubble—would inevitably follow.

Instead, their focus has been on finding the easiest way to enhance their company's bottom line, even if that means skirting the law. As a result, CEOs—aided and abetted by their cabal of financial gamesmen—have raised corporate deception to a fine art. Whether it's overstatement of profits (telecom giant Qwest sold network space to rivals, then bought back an identical amount in return, ingeniously using these "swaps" to inflate earnings), understatement of profits (believe it or not, as much as $1.5 billion of trading profit was actually hidden by Enron during California's energy crisis), or tax evasion (Dennis Kozlowski's art scam), there seems to be no end to the sleight of hand these boardroom tricksters will try.

Just how profitable has all of this corporate crime been? In the nineties the salary of the average CEO of a major corporation skyrocketed 571%. But this flood of good fortune did not, as is so often argued, lift all boats. In 1980, the average CEO made 42 times more than the average worker. In 1990, it was 85 times more. By 2000, CEOs were cashing paychecks a staggering 531 times larger than those of their average employee. Even in 2001, with the economy stalling and corporate profits falling by roughly 35%, pay for the typical CEO continued to climb—rising 7%, about twice the raise that the average worker received. This wildly out-of-whack corporate economic ratio makes about as much sense as paying extra at the market for rotten fruit.

Corporate Hocus-Pocus:
The Tricks of the Trade Revealed

In the 1980s the big innovation in corporate governance was linking executive compensation to performance by offering a bonanza of stock options. Only if the CEO and his executive suite came through with good company performance would they reap their rewards. Instead, aided and abetted by a gaggle of co-conspirators, the CEOs have devised ever more elaborate schemes for making those stock options pay off time and time and time again—performance be damned.

The mind-boggling case of Jones Apparel CEO Peter Boneparth is a perfect example of how companies are going to remarkable lengths to ensure their top executives get more than their fair share.

Boneparth joined Jones in 2001 and became its CEO the year after. Despite his short tenure, he quickly mastered the importance of becoming best buddies with the compensation committee. Witness his engorged compensation package, which included a salary of $1.5 million, rising to $2.5 million in 2004, along with $2 million in signing bonuses and options on 1.5 million shares of Jones stock. What makes this so incredible is that the board originally promised to give Emperor Boneparte—I mean, Boneparth—three million shares, or twice what the company owns. The company revised its executive compensation plan only after well-organized opposition from shareholders.

Now compare the options windfalls offered to executives like Boneparth with the paltry contributions companies made to the average employee's 401(k) plan. In 2000, the average 401(k) contribution was $1,322 per employee—2.8% of the employee's salary. Most CEOs, on the other hand, received options that more than doubled their salaries. And more than a few were the recipients of an embarrassment of riches known as an "option megagrant"—which, according to *The Wall Street Journal,* has "a face value of at least eight times an individual's salary and bonus."

Apparently, 111 business leaders were the lucky winners of these megagrants in 2001, up from 85 the year before. Among them was Kozlowski, who received a "megagrant" consisting of restricted shares worth $30.4 million and 1.4 million options initially valued at $21.8 million. The legal forms of abuse of stock-option plans are as infinite as the depths of CEO greed.

Stock options are also used to disguise the fact that, although CEO pay is occasionally slashed when companies suffer a downturn, the actual impact on executive bottom lines is usually negligible. John Chambers of Cisco is a prime example. In fiscal year 2001, as his company lost $1 billion and its stock fell 71%, Chambers saw his cash compensation decrease by over $1 million to a modest $268,000—giving the impression that he was suffering along with his shareholders. However, Cisco's board chose to reward his dismal performance with a special grant of 6 million stock options, which allowed the estimated value of his pay to rise 32% to $154 million, making him the highest paid CEO for that fiscal year. That's like giving a Barry Bonds–size contract to a pitcher who loses 20 games, or making Eddie Murphy the highest paid actor in Hollywood on the heels of *Pluto Nash.*

Ever the innovators, the leaders of corporate America have devised plenty of other creative new ways of lining their pockets. Citigroup's lavishly overpaid CEO Sandy Weill, for instance, has a clever provision in his contract that automatically reloads his stock portfolio with new options every time he cashes out. Unfortunately for Weill, his holdings are being replenished with

Citigroup stock, which was down 41% in the first nine months of 2002.

Not to be outdone by Citigroup, Merrill Lynch devised an especially intricate system for rewarding its head honcho. When Merrill's share value plunged nearly 24% in 2001, CEO David Komansky took a grandstanding pay cut of more than 50%. But due to some fancy footwork, he didn't wind up clipping coupons after all. While his 2001 cash bonus was limited to $1 million, Komansky was simultaneously rewarded by the company with the latest thing in stock-option gimmickry—the special restricted stock unit.

This new, supercharged type of stock option vests three times faster than regular options, meaning that Komansky could bank $2.2 million in 2003. Holders of the older, slower, less flashy restricted options cannot sell their shares for, typically, three to five years. According to Merrill's Management Development and Compensation Committee, the "special" units were created to help Komansky "bridge some of the gap between the $1 million cash bonus and what he could have received in a less challenging year." The question is why? Why should CEOs be protected from the consequences of a "challenging" year? Can't they withstand the gales of their beloved free market?

Stock Options:
The Gift that Keeps on Giving

More than just a way to pay off greedy CEOs, stock options have also proven to be a corporate accountant's wet dream—a versatile form of compensation that is not counted as an expense on company ledgers, and yet is fully deductible when it comes to chiseling the taxman.

Despite calls from John McCain, Warren Buffett, and others, and preemptive moves by the S&P 500 index, General Motors, Ford, Coca-Cola, Boeing, and General Electric, companies are still not required to treat stock options as an expense. So, while paying your CEO $100 million in cash reduces your income by $100 million, paying him or her with $100 million in stock options reduces your income by $0. Stock options are only accounted for when they are cashed in. By that time, with their value often considerably higher, they are actually treated as a business expense and the company can claim a large tax deduction. That's like a straight-faced loan shark writing off the cost of baseball bats and brass knuckles as a business expense in the course of collecting overdue loans. Well, not exactly, except that both examples are completely preposterous accounting propositions.

According to one estimate, the amount by which exercised stock options reduced corporate taxes may have as much as doubled between 1998 and 2000, from $28 billion to $56 billion. WorldCom, for example, used stock option deductions to trim $265 million off its tax bill between 1996 and 1998. And WorldCom's tax shenanigans look relatively modest compared to the $2.7 billion Microsoft saved, the $1.5 billion saved by Cisco, or the $1 billion that General Electric shaved off its tax bill through stock options.

A survey of the nation's largest and most profitable companies conducted by the Institute on Taxation and Economic Policy found that from 1996 to 1998 the top ten corporations saved $10.4 billion on taxes due to stock option deductions. That's money being stolen from the public coffers, helping to increase the once-again bulging budget deficit.

Options have also been used to grossly inflate reported earnings. The power of stock options to make a company appear healthier than it really is was underscored in May 2002 when Standard & Poor's announced that it planned to introduce much tougher standards governing the way it calculates corporate earnings, including counting stock options as a business expense. Under the new method, in 2001 Intel's profit would have plummeted from $1.3 billion to $254 million and Yahoo's loss would have shot from $93 million to $983 million.

Stock options are now the primary source of compensation for most executives. From 1992 to 2000, there was an eight-fold increase in the value of options granted by the 1,500 largest companies, raising the total value to $106 billion. Shifting the bulk of CEO pay off the company books helped boost average corporate profits by 16% over this eight-year period, which, in turn, caused stock prices to rise—and, as an added bonus, increased the value of the stock options held by the CEO. A wonderfully vicious little circle, don't you think?

Even the then-chairman of the Securities and Exchange Commission (SEC), corporate darling Harvey Pitt, admitted that, "If managers can reap profits from their options while shareholders are losing some or all of their equity stake, the options create conflicting, not aligned interests." He has suggested that executives "should be required to demonstrate sustained, long-term growth and success before they can actually exercise any of their options." In other words, CEOs should actually have to earn their mega-millions. What a revolutionary concept.

The Great 401(k) Illusion: Now You See It, Now You Don't

Of course, bloated stock-option packages aren't the only form of "stealth-wealth" that corporate bigwigs have cooked up. With CEOs increasingly under pressure to trim their own pay packets, they have begun to think outside the stock-options box, looking for—and finding—other ways to enrich themselves. Even after they've ridden off into the sunset of their golden years.

General Electric CEO Jack Welch's now notorious retirement package bestowed use of the company's aircraft for the rest of his life—and even found a way to compensate him *after* his life, with a special life insurance policy that provided benefits to his heirs free of estate and income taxes. But that's not all he got. Divorce papers filed by Welch's former wife, Jane Beasley Welch, revealed that Welch's gravy train into the sunset includes an $80,000-a-month Central Park apartment (I'm guessing at that price it probably has a park view), lifetime use of a company jet, maid service at his multiple homes, memberships at an array of country clubs, flowers, limos, phones, computers, furniture, and prime tickets to Wimbledon, the opera, the U.S. Open, and every New York Knicks home game.

What's really telling about the relationship between management and shareholders is that, were it not for the divorce, none of this would have been disclosed. All that was recorded in the company's 2001 proxy statement is that it would provide its departed CEO with "continued life-time access to company facilities and services comparable to those which are currently made available to him by the company." Welch said he decided that the company's shareholders should no longer have to foot the bill for most of the pricier perks because, as he put it in a column in *The Wall Street Journal,* "perception matters." In other words, he hadn't had a change of heart, just a change of PR strategy.

Welch, who seems to have a proclivity for bellying up to a midsection metaphor, having titled his self-aggrandizing autobiography *Jack: Straight from the Gut,* said that his decision to downsize his 24-karat golden parachute while continuing to defend its fairness and propriety "sure feels right in my gut." If that's truly the case, he needs to schedule an emergency appointment with a gastrointestinal specialist. The man from GE needs to have his GI examined.

As do his fellow overpaid brethren. It's gut-check time for all of corporate America.

Another retirement lottery winner is Terrence Murray, CEO of FleetBoston, who collected a $5.8 million annual pension when he retired at the end of 2002. He can thank his accommodating directors, who took a previous pension formula that would have given him a $2.7 million pension and helpfully doubled it, becoming the first major company to determine a pension plan partly on the basis of its CEO's stock-option gains. Neither figure, by the way, appears in any FleetBoston regulatory filing. I guess the company's directors believe in the old saw that the highest form of charity is charity given without recognition.

But while companies bent over backward to pay CEOs even after they'd stopped working, when it comes to the pension plan of the average working stiff, it's not the companies that are doing the bending. Big corporations don't seem to have any reservations about sticking it to the very employees upon whose labor their success is founded.

Take the great 401(k) illusion. Introduced with much fanfare in the 1980s, 401(k) plans were originally intended to be additional retirement income over and above a good solid pension. Instead, most companies have done away with pensions entirely and have foisted 401(k) plans on employees, requiring them to make the largest contribution to their retirement income themselves. Some companies have tried to prop their stock up by encouraging employees to buy more for their 401(k) plans, even while knowing the value was sure to drop.

Of the many offenses of Ken Lay and the Enron Gang, the massive dumping of their own shares while encouraging their employees and the public to hold onto theirs, and even buy more, is the most disgusting. "Talk up the stock and talk positively about Enron to your family and friends," Lay exhorted employees during a company-wide electronic town hall meeting in

September 2001, just four days before Enron closed out the worst quarter in its history. "The company is fundamentally sound," Lay said. In 2001 Lay sold over $100 million worth of Enron stock, $26 million of which was disposed of after Sherron Watkins informed her boss that the company was about to "implode in a wave of accounting scandals." Lay's successor Jeff Skilling sold $30 million worth of stock during the same year.

That the Enron Gang bankrupted its own company through poor judgment, fraudulent management, lies of omission, and lies of commission, is abhorrent enough. But even worse is the fact that these conscienceless goons nearly bankrupted thousands of their employees' 401(k) plans.

By law, plans like these have to be diversified, but many 401(k)s are nevertheless heavily weighted with company stock. The Profit Sharing/401(k) Council of America estimates that company stock accounted for, on average, 39.2% of 401(k) assets in 2000.

Although Enron's 401(k) plan was more inbred than most—58% of the plan was invested in Enron stock—it was nothing compared with those of Procter & Gamble (95%), Coca-Cola (81%), or General Electric (77%). These high percentages spell serious danger for employees—especially when combined with the limits and regulations the vast majority of plans impose upon the sale of 401(k) company stock. The most potentially damaging of these are blackout periods during which employees are barred from selling stock. Enron's last blackout period inconveniently—but not inadvertently—coincided with the stock's final plunge.

Sadly, Enron is not an isolated case. Just days after World-Com imploded, Judy Wilson Rambo, a former employee and a participant in the company's 401(k) plan, filed a lawsuit, claiming that WorldCom executives encouraged employees to buy stock "despite their knowledge that . . . [it] was not a prudent investment option." WorldCom employees' 401(k) retirement plan has lost more than $1.1 billion, not surprising when you consider that at one point, 55% of the plan was invested in the company's own stock. At 83 cents a share—the stock's price when trading was halted in late June 2002—the plan's WorldCom shares are now worth a mere $4.4 million. And, soon after Xerox announced it would restate its earnings by billions of dollars, employees filed a lawsuit against the company, alleging that the same reckless hawking of company stock had happened there.

CEO Loans:
Brother, Can You Spare a Billion?

Yet another fabulous perk CEOs treated themselves to was the company-financed loan. The gargantuan loans CEOs received from their companies include the $3.1 billion Adelphia Communications loaned to John Rigas and his kin, the $408 million WorldCom loaned to Bernie Ebbers, the $162 million Conseco loaned to Stephen Hilbert, the $88 million Tyco loaned to Dennis Kozlowski, and the millions upon millions in less ostentatious—but no less outrageous—raids on company funds by senior executives across the corporate landscape. When someone is being paid millions of dollars a year, with options for even more millions, how could he possibly need a $3.1 billion loan? What were these guys using all this money for, to buy themselves a continent or two?

And if you're thinking that, because they're called "loans," these arrangements bore any resemblance to the terms you and I would get from a bank, think again.

For starters, these loans were approved by corporate boards—boards more often than not beholden to the very same executives seeking the loans. It's like Tony Soprano getting his loan "approved" by Paulie Walnuts. Given the opportunity to select their own bosses, most CEOs obviously choose people who aren't likely to disagree with them very often. Quite frankly, CEOs would save everyone a lot of needless paperwork and time if they went down to the bank or the basement or wherever their company keeps its billions, and just took what they wanted. At least that's a more honest form of thievery.

For a CEO, going to a board to ask for a loan was a cakewalk. It was a great deal, if you could get it. But you can't. Those TV commercials for the Lending Tree and Ditech.com may make it look like applying for a loan is more fun than a Roman orgy, but, for most people, it's a highly stressful and onerous ordeal.

Let's say you want a loan. You go to the bank, fill out a few hundred forms, answer a multitude of questions, provide references and collateral, and then, after a month or so, you get turned down. Compare that with the experience of your average CEO who wanted to add a second polo field to his 100-acre spread in the Hamptons. He simply wrote himself a check and relied on a cooperative board to rubber stamp the transaction between rounds of golf. What these CEOs got weren't loans. They were very pricey gifts. And that's what they should have been called.

WorldCom, for instance, charged Ebbers just 2.3% interest on the $408 million he borrowed from the company. Before going under, Global Crossing—the basket case telecom operator that burst onto the financial scene in 1997 and grew into a fiber optics giant with almost $4 billion in annual revenues by 2000—made low-interest loans of $8 million to its then-CEO Tom Casey and $1.8 million to its president, David Walsh. Vivendi CEO Jean-Marie Messier, forced out of office in July 2002, was loaned $25 million by Société Générale, one of the company's biggest lenders. As part of the severance package requested by Messier—he can request his own severance package?—he asked that this loan be forgiven. It took two months for his request to be denied. In 1999 Denver-based Qwest communications forgave $575,000 that it had loaned to CEO Afshin Mohebbi. Three years later, in April 2002, it loaned him an additional $4 million at a 5.5% interest rate. Seem a little above CEO prime? Not to worry. I'm sure Qwest would have agreed to forgive that in due course as well.

And leave it to those endlessly imaginative book cookers at Enron to find a fresh and innovative way to pick shareholders' pockets: Ken Lay was given a $7.5 million line of credit, which he could then repay with company stock he'd been given or allowed to buy at a greatly reduced price. In other words, he was given money that he could pay back with stock that he had also been given. I think that's what the shifty bean counters at Arthur Andersen might have called a fiscally integrated deal.

And what happened if a CEO was unable to repay a loan? Never fear, that contingency had been taken care of, too. While homeowners who can't make mortgage payments must face foreclosure, CEO loan packages were routinely forgiven—written off as a corporate expense. Troubled E*Trade, for example, allowed CEO Christos Cotsakos to skate on the $15 million it had lent him—a move that didn't sit very well with shareholders, who raised such a stink that Cotsakos agreed to give back part of his 2001 salary. (Don't feel too bad for him, though, he could afford it. He was paid $80 million that year.) Senior executives at Home Depot, Compaq, and Maxtor were also loaned millions that they won't have to repay if they stay on the job for a few more years.

In the late nineties, Tyco's Kozlowski was loaned $19 million to help finance the building of his 15,000-square-foot house in Boca Raton, Florida. Not only was it at no interest, but, two years later, Tyco forgave the loan as part of a "special bonus" program. What about income tax, you ask? Well, that was covered as well. Kozlowski found himself the happy recipient of an extra $13 million from his company to cover his IRS tab. None of these "special bonuses," however, were disclosed to the public. Nor was the $25 million loan to Kozlowski the company secretly forgave in 1999.

Amazingly, companies even forgave the loans of executives who did a lousy job. Mattel wrote off a $3 million loan to its former CEO, Jill Barad, even though the toy company's stock plummeted by more than 50% during her three years on the job. And Kmart forgave the $5 million it lent to Chuck Conaway, whose shaky hand on the rudder steered the company to a Blue Light bankruptcy. The loans were given to them, apparently, just for being them.

Yet another important difference between insider loans and the kind an ordinary person would get is the level of disclosure required. The billions Adelphia loaned to the Rigas family were made public only in a small footnote in an earnings filing. And, if that wasn't shady enough, check out the opaque language used to supposedly divulge the arrangement: "Certain subsidiaries of the company are co-borrowers with certain companies owned by the Rigas family." Adelphia's accountants deserve every dime they got for figuring out how to make a smoking gun look like a bouquet of daisies. The footnote went on to assert —without even an attempt at an explanation—that even though the massive loan was not shown on the company's balance sheet, nevertheless, Adelphia (meaning, the shareholders) was on the hook for the $3.1 billion if it wasn't repaid. The Rigases clearly saw shareholders the way P.T. Barnum viewed circus goers.

Why not give this clever ploy a try next time you apply for a loan? When they ask you to list all your liabilities, just put a little asterisk next to the amount you list, and then down at the bottom of the form, in very small letters, write in: "Certain subsidiaries of my family—i.e. my wife and children—are co-borrowers with certain companies—i.e. credit cards, car, insurance, etc.—of certain assets that, if included on the family balance sheet, would result in a certain lack of positive cash flow, i.e. debt. Sort of."

So here is the question aching for an answer: How can this kind of thing be legal? How can corporate executives legally use the balance sheet of a public company as their personal bank? Don't the company's assets belong to the shareholders? And don't CEOs have a fiduciary obligation to them? How then can they write themselves checks for ridiculous amounts—often from companies that are troubled and can't afford it, and at the expense of shareholders who can't prevent it?

Millions of shareholders are waiting for a reply.

Pass the Coppertone, I'm Cutting My Taxes

Tax avoidance is another trick the corporate alchemists have refined into pure gold. And a golden tan—because the hot trend in corporate tax avoidance is moving your company to sunny Bermuda.

In fact, it's such an attractive proposition that I've decided to move there myself. But don't worry about getting me a house-warming present, because I'm not really going anywhere. I'll just do what the corporate tax fugitives do. I'll still live in America, earn my living here, and enjoy the protection, technology, infrastructure, and all the other myriad benefits of the land of the free and the home of the brave. I'm just changing my business address. Because if I do that, I won't have to pay for those benefits—I'll get them for free!

It's all perfectly legal. Dubbed "tax motivated expatriation"—which has a nicer ring than "sleazy tax-cheating loophole"—it's another megatrend in corporate America, with more and more U.S. companies reincorporating offshore as a way of slashing their tax bill by tens, and sometimes hundreds, of millions of dollars.

You see, Bermuda, along with sparkling turquoise water, beautiful pink sand beaches, a deep-water lagoon, and those picturesque policemen with the white hats, also has no income tax. None. Pop that into your Quicken and see how fast it fattens your wallet.

And setting up shop on the sun-kissed island couldn't be easier. A company "moving" to Bermuda doesn't actually have to move at all. It doesn't even have to have a local office or hold any meetings there. It just needs a PO box and someone to pick up the mail. Or it could just let the mail pile up and forget about having someone pick it up. There's another cost savings, right there.

It's a dirty—and, yes, highly profitable—accounting trick. This kind of paper relocation saved Tyco over $400 million in 2001. And Ingersoll-Rand, a venerable American company that made the jackhammers that helped chisel Mount Rushmore, avoids more than $40 million a year in U.S. taxes by slipping into its Bermuda shorts.

But the tax savings don't stop with sheltering overseas profits. Many companies that move to Bermuda also open a corporate beachhead in that financial Mecca of the Caribbean, Barbados, where, thanks to the magic of modern accounting and a sweetheart tax treaty, profits earned in America can be shipped abroad and transformed into a tax write-off.

The benefits of this offshore shell game extend well beyond a corporation's bottom line. Formerly red, white, and blue companies now sporting a Bermuda tan are also suddenly and conveniently immune to judgments against them in U.S. courts, less accountable to their shareholders, who are unable to file class action suits, and freed from a whole host of annoying government regulations.

Nobody is sure precisely how much this corporate exodus is costing us, but the IRS estimates that it's siphoning off at least $70 billion each year from the U.S. Treasury. And that number doesn't include the billions in taxes that corporations avoid paying by creating offshore subsidiaries. Enron, for example, had 881 of them and paid no taxes in four of the last five years. That's right, if you paid one dollar in taxes in those years, you paid more than this longtime fixture on the Fortune 500.

Even more galling is the fact that many of the same companies that are giving the taxman the finger as they shield themselves with their Bermuda zip codes think nothing of holding out their hand when Uncle Sam is shelling out government contracts. Ingersoll-Rand had more than 200 such contracts in 2001, while Foster Wheeler, another corporate émigré, is currently raking in $600 million in U.S. taxpayer-provided funds.

And how's this for irony: among the more than $1 billion in federal contracts held by Accenture, which relocated to Bermuda in 2001, is a five-year deal to redesign the IRS website. I wonder if it will include a special portal for those eager to avoid paying their fair share.

Also showing a flair for self-parody is Tyco, which established its Bermuda mail drop in 1997, and which since 2001 has also taken in $1 billion at the public trough—including $100 million for helping provide terror-related emergency response services. Very post-9/11 patriotic. Samuel Johnson's old saw that "patriotism is the last refuge of the scoundrel" may be due for an updating. Bermuda is the last refuge of the scoundrel. Patriotism comes in second.

In a Webcast to clients, Kate Barton, an Ernst & Young tax partner, didn't see any problem with this: "The improvement on earnings is powerful enough that maybe the patriotism issue needs to take a back seat to that." So why not sell arms to Al-Qaeda, while you're at it? They've got lots of money, and anything that creates a "powerful improvement on earnings" is presumably OK.

It's not just tax revenue that's being lost. Because of convoluted laws that allow profits funneled offshore to be invested in foreign countries without being taxed (as opposed to money that's brought back into the U.S., which is subject to taxes), we're also losing American jobs to cheap-labor havens like China and Mexico.

It all adds up to a pretty neat trick. Unfortunately, this tax dodge is not available to you and me—only to corporations that have powerful lobby organizations and make large donations to politicians in Congress, who just happen to create these fantastic tax loopholes.

Try telling the folks at the IRS that you're planning to relocate to Bermuda and would like to sign up for the zero tax rate and see how long it is before they stop laughing—and then lock you up. Even if you tell them you don't like paying taxes because they get in the way of "improving your earnings."

Despite the billions being lost to these offshore tax havens, however, Congress has shown little ardor for a policy change. On the other hand, if you're receiving the traditional sort of welfare, the meager check that arrives once a month for needy individuals, the president is determined to wean you from your bad habits. He doesn't want anybody getting a free ride from the government without accepting the responsibility that comes with it. At least anybody who's not a CEO.

It's a "two love" track: unconditional love for corporations, tough love for people.

Our MBA President and His CEO Sidekick

Of course, one of the main reasons the Bush administration has been so reluctant to rein in corporate America is because it is so much a part of it, with a vice president who was a CEO, three former CEOs who hold cabinet-level positions, two-dozen ambassadors who are former CEOs or company chairmen, a president who is the first commander-in-chief with an MBA, and a domestic agenda no deeper than tax breaks for friends.

Fittingly, then, both the president and the vice president were caught in the rising tide of corporate scandals that washed over the White House lawn in the summer of 2002.

The Bush crisis control team had an off day that July 31 when, in the space of 12 hours, it was revealed that both Harken Energy, while President Bush was on its board, and Halliburton, while Vice President Cheney was its CEO, had created subsidiary shell companies in offshore tax havens. The administration's attempt at what was supposed to be damage control did more harm than good.

First, Bush and Cheney's reps tried to argue that even though setting up shop in the Caymans is a favorite ploy of companies looking to avoid paying their fair share of taxes—remember Enron had 881 subsidiaries there—that wasn't the reason Harken or Halliburton had done it. Well, pray tell, what was? A desire to rack up frequent flier miles checking on the company headquarters/PO box? Exploiting all the oil under the Cayman Islands? Cheaper umbrella drinks for company meetings?

As if this half-hearted evasion wasn't lame enough, White House spokesman Dan Bartlett fell back on the classic Plan B: trying to make friends and win arguments by splitting hairs. Harken's offshore entity wasn't designed to evade taxes, explained Bartlett at the time, it was meant to enhance "tax competitiveness." And to his credit, Bartlett didn't even break out laughing after this claim. Probably waited until he got back to his office. Oh yeah, and, also, oral sex isn't—well, you know the drill.

White House press secretary Ari Fleischer even tried the ol' No Harm, No Foul defense, arguing that the reason Bush's company went Caribbean was a "moot question" because Harken never made any money on the Cayman venture. Memo to Fleischer: arguing that the crime didn't pay isn't a defense.

And by the way, thank you, Ari, for further evidence that our MBA president was an exceedingly poor businessman.

These wobbly spin doctors' task was, admittedly, made much harder by the fact that on the same day these tax dodge disclosures came to light, President Bush had spoken out with his usual Dudley Do-Right forthrightness against the very same practice. "We ought to look at people who are trying to avoid U.S. taxes as a problem," he said. Indeed we ought. So why don't we?

Let's start by looking at the problem of the vice president and Halliburton. During the Number Two's time as the company's Number One, there was a dramatic increase in the number of Halliburton subsidiaries registered in tax havens: from nine in 1995 to 44 in 1999. And it was accompanied by a no less spectacular drop in Halliburton's federal taxes: from $302 million in 1998 to less than zero—to wit, an $85 million rebate—in 1999.

At the same time they were hard at work stiffing U.S. taxpayers, Cheney and Halliburton were happily nursing at the public teat—the company received $2.3 billion in government contracts and another $1.5 billion in government financing and loan guarantees.

During the vice-presidential debate, Cheney scored points responding to a Joe Lieberman zinger about the millions Cheney had made during the Clinton-Gore years by boasting that "the government had absolutely nothing to do" with his burgeoning bank account. Only someone fully immersed in the corporate culture of our day could view $3.8 billion as "absolutely nothing."

It would have been nice to hear what Mr. Cheney has to say about all of this, but he began making himself very scarce—especially when it came to the media—right around the time in May 2002 when reports first surfaced that the Securities and Exchange Commission was looking into Halliburton's Cheney-era accounting practices.

His vanishing act was so effective that many started to wonder if Cheney has returned to his "secure, undisclosed location." If he had, it was only because the mountain hideaway was filled with fat-cat donors. It turned out that the vice president had been talking after all—but only to those ready to write a hefty check to the GOP.

Cheney headlined more than 70 fundraising events leading up to Election Day 2002. At one such event, donors who ponied up $25,000-per-couple were allowed to take part in a 45-minute roundtable discussion with Cheney. So it seems that if the White House Press Corps wants to get any serious face time with the vice president, it's gonna cost them. $277.50 per minute. I wonder if Connie Chung and Chris Matthews or Mike Wallace and Morley Safer can team up and get the couples' rate?

Of course, Cheney's reluctance to talk to reporters is understandable, given what has come to light about his heretofore highly touted tenure at Halliburton, including the questionable accounting, the offshore subsidiaries, and the revelation that the company did business with Iran, Libya, and—despite Cheney's denials—Iraq. It's his very own "Axis of Profits."

But, to be fair, under Cheney, Halliburton did end up giving a little something back to America—in the form of $2 million worth of fines for consistently overbilling the Pentagon. In one case they charged $750,000 for work that actually cost them only $125,000. Despite all this, the company has continued to be awarded massive government contracts, including a 10-year deal with the Army that, unlike any comparable arrangement, comes with no lid on potential costs. I guess it really does help to have friends—and ex-CEOs—in very high places.

During a fund-raising appearance last summer, Cheney lauded the White House's commitment to "more accountability for corporate officials." I'd love to know if richly rewarding corporations that have defrauded taxpayers is the kind of "accountability" he was referring to.

If you happen to find yourself at a GOP fund-raiser, would you mind asking him?

Pink-Slip Pig:
"Chainsaw" Al Dunlap

Probably no breed of business leader is more lauded than the hit man "turn-around artist." For a hot-shot CEO taking over a troubled company, mass firings are the ultimate quick fix, the accounting equivalent of crack: cheap, easy to score, instantly gratifying, and highly addictive.

Working overtime to prove his contention that "downsizing is a way of life in America," the most crack-happy hatchet man in recent memory was "Chainsaw" Al Dunlap. He's the kind of guy Verdi would have written an opera about if he'd ever had the misfortune to meet him. As he mowed down employees like a boardroom Rambo, Dunlap reveled in his arrogance ("I'm a superstar in my field, much like Michael Jordan in basketball and Bruce Springsteen in rock 'n' roll") and his lack of charm (of one nosy reporter he said, "If he were on fire, I wouldn't piss on him"). Star-struck investors ate up his schtick.

When Dunlap took the reins at Lily-Tulip, a paper cup manufacturer, in 1983, he fired all but two of the company's senior management. And that was just on his first day. He was immediately hailed as a hero by the Wall Street cost-cutting cult.

Dunlap's combo-pack of a prickly disposition and blatant incompetence had gotten him fired from Max Phillips & Son, a waste management company, nine years earlier. According to court testimony from Max Phillips, Dunlap not only bad-mouthed the company to such a degree that he actually cost it business, he also neglected his duties so egregiously that Phillips was obliged to fire him after just seven weeks.

Not to be daunted by such a minor setback, Dunlap landed on his feet at the Nitec Paper Corporation just six months later. In his third year there, the company reported a sudden spike in profits, for which he, of course, took full credit. Despite this apparent success, Dunlap's personality was such a problem that Nitec's owner also eventually fired him. Although no specifics were given about the personality clashes, George Petty, Nitec's principal owner, observed that, "There were growing and increasing personal difficulties between Dunlap and the other senior members of Nitec's management. . . . These difficulties had become so serious that virtually all of Nitec's senior management below Dunlap threatened to resign en masse if Dunlap remained at Nitec."

Just a few weeks after he had been ushered out with a very generous severance package, a routine auditing of Nitec's books exposed a bombshell. Instead of the $5 million surge in profit claimed by Dunlap, the company was actually $5.5 million in the red. Chainsaw Al had learned the value of creative accounting—according to Nitec's financial vice president, expenses, inventory, and cash on hand had all been adjusted on Dunlap's orders to make windfall profits out of pitiful performance.

Incredibly, even while Nitec was taking Dunlap to court for his malfeasance, he was offered yet another top job, at Scott Paper, the sort of comatose manufacturer just screaming for Dunlap's brand of shock therapy. True to form, he laid off one-third of the company's workforce (about 10,000 employees) and 71% of its headquarters staff in his first year. And he cut costs in other beneficent ways. Before Dunlap took over, Scott gave about $5 million annually to charitable causes. Afterward, they gave nothing. "You're in business for one thing," Dunlap croaked. "To make money."

Then, at the height of his celebrity as Wall Street's cost-cutting centerfold, Dunlap was tapped to head Sunbeam, the beleaguered small appliance manufacturer based in Boca Raton, Florida. If ever a company needed better management, this was it. But instead of actually analyzing the company's problems, Dunlap resorted to his tried-and-true slash-and-burn tactics. He immediately fired 6,000 employees, fully 50% of the workforce, closed or sold 18 out of 26 factories, and cut 80% of the product line.

This time, however, his bloody bag of tricks didn't work. Profits wouldn't budge. If he couldn't actually make the company profitable, Dunlap decided, he could at least make it look profitable on paper. With a little help from the corporate criminal's best friend, the master chefs of book-cooking at Arthur Andersen, Dunlap used illegal accounting tricks to shift revenue around, which had the effect of increasing Sunbeam's reported losses under previous management. Millions of dollars of expenses incurred in 1997, his first full year at Sunbeam, were charged to 1996 instead. Dunlap then dipped into this artificial reserve to inflate accounts and "increase" earnings. Here's how an SEC spokesman later described Dunlap's scam: "You load up the cookie jar with improper reserves and then when you need a sugar jolt, which in this example is positive earnings, you reach into the cookie jar."

When Dunlap gobbled up the last cookie in the jar, the scheme collapsed, along with $5 billion of shareholder value. The company went bankrupt. These days, a share of post-Dunlap Sunbeam will cost you about a nickel, down from $12.50 when he arrived. So much for the power of management by Chainsaw.

Did Dunlap's vaunted reputation crash and burn along with the company? Was he excoriated for his gross incompetence, and did he grovel to keep his job? Far from it. When the SEC finally investigated his Sunbeam shenanigans and he was summoned by the Sunbeam board to explain himself, Dunlap threw one of his trademark tantrums, shouting, "I'm much too rich and much too powerful to have to take this shit from you!" I'm sure it would have sounded even better if Verdi had set it to music.

He was fired, but he still received a $27 million severance package. Investor lawsuits, however, ultimately ate it all up—and $8 million more of his ill-gotten gains.

Then at the beginning of September 2002, without admitting any wrongdoing, Dunlap agreed to pay a $500,000 fine to the SEC to settle charges that he misrepresented Sunbeam's accounts. And $15 million more to settle yet another shareholder lawsuit. Dunlap also accepted a lifetime ban preventing him from ever serving as a director or an officer of a publicly owned company. Thousands of shareholders, no doubt, breathed a heavy sigh of relief.

FUN FACT QUIZ

1. Which of the following statements is true?
    a. George W. Bush has been arrested four times.
    b. George W. Bush is the first president with an MBA.
    (*Answer:* "b." Bush has been arrested only three times: once for drunk driving in 1976, and twice while a student at Yale—for ripping down the goal posts after a Princeton/ Yale game and for stealing a Christmas wreath from a hotel. He managed to avoid arrest at Harvard Business School, from which he graduated in 1975.)

2. Which jobs did Bernie Ebbers have prior to becoming CEO of WorldCom?
    a. Gym teacher, milkman, and bar bouncer.
    b. Bookkeeper, shoe-shine stand operator, and paper cutter.
    (*Answer:* "a." Bookkeeper, shoe-shine operator and paper cutter were all jobs held by Al Capone.)

3. *True or False?* In the mid-nineties, indicted former CEO John Rigas put his home phone number on Adelphia's cable bills.

   (*Answer:* True. It is not true, however, that he asked customers to check a box on their bill if they'd like to donate one dollar to the "John Rigas Bail Fund.")

4. Which of the following is a job previously held by Martha Stewart?

       a. Cancer drug developer

       b. Stockbroker

       c. Bail bondsman

   (*Answer:* "b." Bail bondsman is probably the most recent addition to her Palm Pilot. As for cancer drug developer, I'm sure she wishes she'd never met one.)

5. Which of the following is true of former Tyco CEO Dennis Kozlowski?

       a. In 2002, he was arrested and charged with evading millions of dollars in tax on art purchases he made.

       b. In 2002, he was invited to be Florida Atlantic University's Business Leader of the Year.

   (They're BOTH true. And, in a speech to the graduating class at St. Anselm's College in New Hampshire, also in 2002, he said, "You will be confronted with questions every day that test your morals. Think carefully, and for your sake, do the right thing, not the easy thing.")

6. Which of the following are actual suggestions made by former WorldCom CEO Bernie Ebbers to save money at the company's headquarters?

       a. Lower the thermostats.

       b. Let office plants die to save on water.

       c. Count coffee bags to make sure they aren't stolen.

       d. Switch to AT&T for long-distance service.

(The answers are "a," "b," and "c." It is not true that to stay warm, Ebbers asked employees to snuggle by the space heaters on especially cold days.)

7. Why did John Rigas refuse to carry porn films on his cable systems?
   a. It offended his sense of morality.
   b. Securing broadcast rights was too convoluted.
   c. He was reserving the channel space for family programming.

   (*Answer:* "a." Pocketing $3.1 billion from Adelphia shareholders, however, didn't weigh on his conscience one bit.)

8. *True or False?* According to *USA Today,* 82% of 401 high ranking corporate executives admit to being less than honest on the golf course.

   (*Answer:* "True." And the other 18% were probably lying to the person taking the poll.)

9. What percentage of the Fortune 1000 is managed by female CEOs?
   a. 5%
   b. 9%
   c. 1%

   (*Answer:* "c." There are only 11 women CEOs. And none of them has been indicted in the recent spate of accounting scandals.)

10. Which of the following events did Sunbeam's "Chainsaw" Al Dunlap *not* attend?
    a. A single Sunbeam Board meeting
    b. The funerals of his parents
    c. His own colonoscopy

    (*Answer:* "b." The story that Dunlap forced a junior Sunbeam manager to have his colonoscopy for him because he was too busy firing people seems to be just a rumor.)

Of Pink Slips and Profits

Al Dunlap is hardly the only CEO who downsized his way to the top—and into the hearts of Wall Street. Jack Welch, the legendary former CEO of General Electric, who for years was regarded as corporate America's reigning management wizard, built his reputation—and his fortune—by deploying a neutron bomb strategy that vaporized workers while leaving GE facilities intact.

When Welch took over GE in 1981, the company had 285,000 employees in the United States. By the time he retired in 2001, that figure had been slashed by more than 45% to 158,000.

But isn't all this tough-guy cost-cutting—what John Chambers, Cisco's CEO, calls "workforce optimization"—good for business?

The sheer size of certain layoffs—30,000 at Boeing, 26,000 at Daimler-Chrysler—makes it hard to believe they're not carried out recklessly, rather than to creatively reshape a company. The insensitivity with which firings are often conducted also seems to be deliberately designed to maximize indignity and resentment. The problem isn't just that the line between responsible downsizing and careless butchering is being crossed more and more frequently—it's that saving jobs isn't even seen as a worthy goal anymore.

One of the most galling developments in the frenzy of firings that accompanied the recession was the erosion of what little decency remained in the process. In December 2001, the *Boston Globe* reported that the traditional taboo prohibiting firings during the holiday season had gone the way of the wassail bowl and neighborhood Christmas caroling. In the grim final months of 2001, already darkened by the shadow of September 11, almost a million people lost their jobs.

Former Enron employees were fired at mass meetings or, even more heartlessly, with a message left on their voice mail. But, for the employees the company actually valued, things were very different. Two days prior to Enron going belly-up, the company gave $55 million in bonuses to senior employees while simultaneously coming out against additional help for the 4,500 workers unceremoniously fired. And—in a colossal act of hubris—the bankruptcy plan protected these senior employees from having to return any of their money. What could that possibly have to do with healthy capitalism? Mercifully, a bankruptcy judge reversed this provision in the plan.

When CNN laid off 400 workers in 2001, their computers were rendered inaccessible even before they had returned to their desks. At Amazon.com, fired workers were warned that if they talked too loosely about their time at the company, they would lose their severance benefits. So, apparently along with profits and consumer confidence, Amazon's executives also lost their copy of the Constitution. Last time I checked, in America you're not supposed to be punished for speaking your mind, for telling people your office cubicle is too small, or that they can get books cheaper at Barnes&Noble.com.

And after all of this pain, it turns out that massive layoffs may not even reap the intended rewards. Even after giving out 9,400 pink slips for Christmas 2001, Motorola has continued to tank. Along with waving goodbye to over 30% of its workers, the company has said farewell to over 60% of its value.

Professor Wayne Cascio of the University of Colorado at Denver has been studying downsizing strategy among the Standard and Poor's 500 for the last 18 years. His conclusion? "Layoffs don't work." After comparing the stock price and profitability of companies that made layoffs with those that didn't, Cascio determined that, "Companies that institute layoffs don't outperform their industry, and they don't outperform more stable employers who haven't done layoffs. . . . You can't shrink your way to prosperity."

In fact, Cascio's study validates the opposite approach to the showy "lean and mean" tactics Jack Welch, Al Dunlap, and so many others built their reputations on. Companies that expand and evolve—"even in hard times"—are the ones that do best by, as Cascio puts it, "creating new assets, finding new sources of revenue, innovating." But innovation takes ingenuity, creating new assets takes strategic planning, and finding new sources of revenue takes good old-fashioned hard work. Firing people is just so much easier, especially if you do it over the phone—or, better yet, via e-mail. That way, you can dispense with any uncomfortable human interaction.

Unfortunately, a monkey-see, monkey-do mindset afflicts CEOs with an even greater virulence than it does teenagers. So layoffs remain wildly popular despite all the evidence that bad management, not excess employees, is what's plaguing American business.

And when bad management drives the company into the ground, the upstairs/downstairs double-standard continues to reign supreme. In June 2002, following the first announcement of its multi-billion-dollar accounting fraud, WorldCom began laying off thousands of workers worldwide. Those losing their jobs at WorldCom's Clinton, Mississippi, headquarters were informed by a mass-produced form letter and then escorted off the premises with local police officers hired specially for the purpose. But for about 200 of WorldCom's top performers, the so-called "Inner Circle," June was a very good month indeed. On the same day WorldCom stunned the world with the magnitude of its accounting fraud, the Inner Circle began an extravagant all-expenses-paid vacation at the Grand Wailea Resort Hotel and Spa in Maui.

The Grand Wailea is sited on 40 lush acres and features a 2,200-foot-long pool and Hawaii's largest spa. And they don't call it the "Grand" Wailea for nothing. Rooms rent from $435 to $10,000 a night. The Inner Circle guests were also treated to a dinner at Nick's Seafood Restaurant, which WorldCom rented out for $20,000. A *New York Times* reporter was unable to ascertain the exact mood of the WorldCom guests but determined that they were "trying to make the most of their time at the resort." And why not? There are much more important things than a colossal accounting scandal, after all—like not getting seconds on the bacon-wrapped scallops, for one thing.

The fun didn't end at the Grand Wailea. In August of 2002 the unreconstructed party animals at WorldCom planned a much-needed "Global Implementation and Support Event" at an "off-site location." In other words, senior employees in the New York office (minus the two who had been arrested the day before) were going on an all-night open bar booze cruise on the *Cloud Nine*, a luxurious party boat. The menu for the event included Norwegian salmon, filet mignon, prime rib, roast filet of ostrich and hand-dipped chocolate strawberries.

After the *New York Post* published details of the trip, WorldCom was forced to cancel the event, although it defiantly went ahead with an outing to a Yankee game for top performers. Whether the top performers in question were top performers in hiding debt was not disclosed.

The Corporate Bacteria Culture

We've spawned a business culture that has made gods of those doing the easy thing—whether it's ripping-off shareholders, avoiding taxes, or slicing and dicing workers—instead of the right thing. Turning it around is going to take more than noble commencement speeches and toothless presidential lectures. Although Kozlowski, Rigas, Waksal, Fastow, Sullivan, and who knows how many other corporate execs appear to have crossed the line into outright criminal activity, countless others have pulled off elaborate schemes and plundered their companies without needing to break the law.

That is why reform will be so hard. It will take actual oversight by the Securities and Exchange Commission, as opposed to its whimpering pleas for compliance; real accountability on the part of auditors and accounting firms; corporate boards that don't kowtow to unscrupulous, profit-hungry CEOs; and throwing every corporate crook in jail.

But even all this won't be enough. Because CEOs don't act alone.

Like an overflowing honeycomb, the corporate beehive is buzzing with eager worker bees and drones—company directors, Wall Street analysts, K-Street lobbyists, and politicians—who, with the syrupy nectar of profits or campaign contributions dribbling from their lips, enthusiastically service the needs of the King Bee.

IN A RICH MAN'S WORLD

I'm tracking a new phenomenon called "scandal fatigue." It sets in when the corporate crime rate gets too high and the numbers being bandied about become too boggling to get your mind around.

For instance, I was plenty angry when WorldCom announced that it had misstated its earnings by $3.7 billion. I couldn't really get a handle on what a figure like that meant—but I knew it was a pantload. Then they looked through the books again and realized that, oops, the amount was actually $7 billion. Was I supposed to be twice as ticked off? Or were there just too many zeros to grasp?

The reason our eyes start to glaze over at a certain point is that we lack what T.S. Eliot called "an objective correlative"—a way of relating to something as abstract and conceptual as a seven followed by nine zeros.

With that in mind, I've done a little research in an effort to offer up some perspective on the magnitude of these crimes. My hope is that when you see a number like $100 million—the amount Jeff Skilling pocketed from Enron before abandoning the sinking ship—expressed not in dollars but in terms we can all identify with, your outrage meter will be set to the proper scale.

Here goes.

The total amount of sweetheart insider loans doled out to John Rigas (Adelphia), Bernie Ebbers (WorldCom), Stephen Hilbert (Conseco), Dennis Kozlowski (Tyco), and Ken Lay (Enron) was $3.9 billion.

With $3.9 billion, you could:

- Fund Habitat for Humanity to build 83,691 homes at a cost of $46,600 each for America's homeless.

- Send 35,583 poor but deserving students to Harvard Business School.
- Buy 390 million tickets to see *Harry Potter and the Chamber of Secrets*. Or one medium popcorn and soda.
- Rent Mariah Carey's mega-bomb *Glitter* 977 million times from Blockbuster. Although there are quicker ways to drive yourself insane. For instance, watch just five minutes of *American Idol 2*.
- Buy the estimated one million homeless American children the Denny's world-famous Grand Slam Breakfast ($2.99) every day for three and a half years.
- Pay Dick Cheney's vice-presidential salary of $174,475 a year for 22,000 years. Or his hefty Halliburton retirement package twice over.
- Loan United Airlines the $1.8 billion it says it needs to avoid bankruptcy—twice. Or you could just flush the money down the toilet. The results will be the same.
- Foot the bill for you and the 195 members of your high school class you really liked to ride a Russian rocket into space.
- Finance 39 equally priced sequels to Eddie Murphy's $100 million flop, *Pluto Nash*. You could . . . but please don't.
- Buy every WorldCom shareholder a Xerox copier, some aspirin from Rite Aid, a year of long-distance service from Qwest, and a share of Enron stock (suitable for framing).
- Build 97 identical buildings to the Empire State Building, whose original cost was just $40 million. That assumes, of course, that you'd have a time machine set for 1930. And that it actually works.
- Buy 195,000 Vietnamese mail-order brides at $20,000 each. While it includes the cost of visa and airfare, it does not include the wedding invitations or cake.
- Have a cable TV box installed in every room in your house, assuming your house had 156 million rooms and your

cable company offered no discount on the $25 dollars per installation.

- Fund the SEC's new, increased, annual budget for five years.

Still having a little trouble with the figures? Well, consider this: According to *Fortune* magazine, the total amount of money raked in by corporate executives selling company stock even while their companies crashed and burned was roughly $66 billion.

With $66 billion, you could:

- Fund the annual budget of the FBI, corporate crime-fighting included, for 16 years.
- Give 74 times what America currently gives in foreign aid to all of sub–Saharan Africa.
- Cover the entire $25 billion America has spent fighting the war against terrorism in Afghanistan. And still have enough left over to give all Afghans more than two times their average yearly income.
- Spend 132 million nights with Julia Roberts at the nightly rate she charged as the hooker in *Pretty Woman*.
- Buy 355 brand new 747s from the Boeing Corporation. And even then, during beverage service, the stewardess would only give you half a can of Coke.
- Buy 3.3 billion copies of *Who Moved My Cheese?* But even if you read each and every one, you still couldn't explain why it's been a best-seller for over two years.
- Pay President Bush's $400,000 salary for 165,000 years. Although, if he's anything like his dad, you'll only be on the hook until 2004.
- Pay the $1.08 million sales tax on Dennis Kozlowski's artwork and still have $65.99 billion left to buy every masterpiece in the Metropolitan Museum of Art's Impressionist collection at its assessed value.

I hope your blood is really boiling now. But perhaps still not enough to take action.

Then try these numbers on for size:

The total loss in market value of WorldCom, Tyco, Qwest, Enron, and Global Crossing was $427 billion.

With $427 billion, you could:

- Fund the United Nations for the next 263 years and still have $164 billion left over for unforeseen famine relief and peacekeeping missions.
- Get Argentina back on its feet by paying off its external debt three times over.
- Give $356 to every man, woman, and child on the planet living in poverty.
- Build and deploy 2,702 comet-hunting Contour satellites. The cost to track them down is extra.
- Buy 61 billion packs of cigarettes, now $7 each in New York City. Or you could transplant the lungs of 1.7 million patients—at $250,000 each—suffering from irreversible emphysema.
- Order 34 billion prime cut filet mignons from Omaha Steaks. Baked potato not included.
- Pay the combined salaries of every player in baseball for the next 237 years. Although I don't know why you would.
- Build an underground tunnel connecting Fort Lauderdale, Florida, to Montego Bay, Jamaica. The best part? It would only take 145 years to complete, and you'd have $160,870,968,150 left over to spend at the Half Moon Club.
- Pay Texas Ranger Alex Rodriguez's $25 million a year salary for more than 17,000 consecutive years.

THE BLOODLESS COUP

The Corporate Takeover
of Our Democracy

"There can be no effective control of corporations while their
political activity remains. To put an end to it will be neither a
short nor an easy task."

THEODORE ROOSEVELT
(August 31, 1910)

"THE MEN MAY BE the head of the house," says Lainie
Kazan in an oft-quoted line from *My Big Fat Greek Wedding*, "but the women are the neck and they can turn the head
any way they want." In the same way, our political leaders may be
the head of the country, but the greedy horde of special interests
is the neck that turns our politicians' gaze this way and that—
including away from corporate abuses. Oh sure, official Washington thumped its chest loudly after the WorldCom story
exploded and hastily passed a corporate responsibility bill it had
labored for months to scuttle. But the web of corruption is far
too tightly woven to be unraveled with the few modest reform
measures put in place so far.

The financial scandals of our time were made possible by an
unprecedented collusion between corporate interests and politicians that, despite all the breast-beating about reform, is still going
strong. Together, these two powerful groups tore down hard-won

regulations that restrained the worst capitalist excesses, leaving in their place a shaky edifice of feckless self-policing and cowed regulators, powerless to prevent the corporate Chernobyls.

Because corporations are such generous campaign donors and such demanding patrons, they have been coddled and cuddled and humored by lawmakers until little remained of a regulatory regime dating back to the last great era of capitalism run amok, the 1920s. Like teenagers insisting they are mature enough to look after themselves, the corporate pigs whined furiously about laws and regulations they viewed as onerous—laws and regulations we had already learned the hard way were essential to control the forces of greed. But they didn't just whine, they put their money—and their considerable political muscle—where their mouths were.

Once corporate America got the keys to the car, Mom's credit card, and the free run of the house, it threw a drunken pool party the likes of which even Hugh Hefner has never seen. With government regulators forced to butt out, a wave of what Kevin Phillips, author of *Wealth and Democracy,* calls "financialization" swept the economy. "The processes of money movement, securities management, corporate reorganization, securitization of assets, derivatives trading, and other forms of financial packaging are steadily replacing the act of making, growing, and transporting things," Phillips wrote. In this financialization fun house, real profits aren't necessary; you can simply make them up. Financial shenanigans are so much easier than actually making a company work.

Corporations get their way in Washington by traveling a long-established highway of corruption—with well-stocked gift shops at every exit. Lobbying in America has become a $1.55 billion business. There are 38 lobbyists for each and every member of Congress. Lobbyists from just one industry alone, the hyperactive pharmaceutical business, outnumber actual members of Congress by 623 to 535. Get those guys a dose of Ritalin.

This is the nexus of corporate corruption; the source of all the swill. The unseemly link between money and political influence is the dark side of capitalism. It was this link that prompted a full-court-press by key members of Congress against crucial reforms proposed by ex-SEC chairman Arthur Levitt in the nineties, reforms that might have prevented some of the bloodletting of the last year.

It was also this link that gave Enron and Kenneth Lay their aura of power, and made Lay a principal shaper of the administration's energy policy and an intimate FOG (Friend Of George). This aura didn't come cheap. Enron and its executives doled out $2.4 million to federal candidates in the 2000 election and were among George W's biggest donors. Lay and his wife alone have donated $793,110 to the GOP since W's dad was in office. Enron has also spent big bucks lobbying Congress and the White House: $4 million in 1999 and 2000 alone. The money had bought the company a bipartisan who's who of Washington insiders—including James Baker, Mack McLarty and Gore 2000 fundraising director Johnny Hayes—to help push its corporate agenda.

In exchange for his unwavering support, "Kenny Boy" was given unprecedented input into the makeup of the Federal Energy Regulatory Commission (FERC), the agency charged with regulating Enron's core business. Lay bragged to one potential nominee about his "friends at the White House." He also personally put the screws to FERC chair Curtis Hebert in an effort to change his views on electricity deregulation. Hebert didn't oblige, and was soon the former chairman of FERC, replaced by Enron ally Pat Wood. Wood actually insisted that the collapse of Enron "doesn't seem to be tied too much to deregulated energy markets." You know that something is rotten in Washington when the top energy industry regulator is so unabashedly anti-regulation.

We also now know why the White House was willing to go

to court to fend off congressional efforts to find out who Vice President Cheney met with for input on his Energy Task Force. Turns out the VP and his staff had at least six meetings with representatives from Enron—including two with Chairman Lay himself—the last of which occurred just six days before the company revealed that it had vastly overstated its earnings, signaling the beginning of the end for the energy giant.

The Morally Bankrupt Bankruptcy Act

The link between money and policy is also all too evident in the Bankruptcy Reform Act—yet another glaring case of legislation crafted specifically for business interests at the expense of the public. Faced with scrambled nest eggs, sinking pension plans, shaky health coverage, and a gloomy job market, millions of average Americans are taking it on the chin—and in the wallet. Indeed, one out of every sixty-nine U.S. households filed for personal bankruptcy in the year ending March 2002.

And it's important to note that only 3% of these filings are by people who abuse the system by living extravagant lifestyles and then leaving their creditors holding the bag. The majority are actually low- to middle-class people who can't pay their bills because they've lost their jobs or been hit with crippling medical expenses or been enticed into running up unmanageable credit card balances by easy-credit come-ons and here-today-gone-tomorrow "teaser" interest rates.

The Bankruptcy Act would make it much harder for average Americans to start afresh after they declare bankruptcy, while, not coincidentally, adding billions of dollars to the bottom line of banks and credit card companies.

Why, then, were our elected representatives so eager to pass the legislation? Perhaps it has something to do with the

$28 million the finance and credit industries have contributed to political campaigns since 1990—including over $4 million in the 2002 election cycle. Credit card giant MBNA, a major proponent of tougher bankruptcy standards, was the top individual contributor to President Bush's 2000 campaign—while two other big credit card issuers, Citigroup and Morgan Stanley, were among his top-10 donors.

For an especially sleazy example of how this Beltway quid pro quo works, look no further than the case of Representative Jim Moran, the chief Democratic sponsor of the bankruptcy bill and, not coincidentally, the founder and co-chair of the New Democratic Coalition—the corporate money wing of the party dedicated to bringing Democrats more in thrall to big business. It seems that back in 1998, Moran was on the verge of being buried under an avalanche of hefty credit card balances he couldn't pay off. Things looked grim for the Congressman—until he was bailed out by a sweetheart loan orchestrated by the folks at MBNA. The same folks later claimed that they had offered the loan to Moran not realizing that he was a member of Congress and that he might be involved in the bankruptcy bill. Instead, a spokesman said the loan "made good business sense."

It sure did, because, in a move as shameless as it is despicable, Moran then turned around and helped craft a bill that will pay back his loan to MBNA many times over—and make it harder for average consumers who find themselves in the same jam he was in to get out of debt. Do you think MBNA will ride to their rescue as well? Or will it do everything in its newly fortified power to exact its pound of flesh?

It is particularly ironic that Congress was wrapping up its billion-dollar gift to the banking industry during the same week executives of Citigroup and J.P. Morgan Chase were lambasted on Capitol Hill for helping Enron defraud shareholders to the tune of $8 billion. Only in Washington could a pair of companies be publicly raked over the coals—branded as bald-faced liars and criminal accessories—on a Tuesday and then blown an all-is-forgiven make-up smooch on Thursday.

So once again big donors get a kiss on the lips and little guys get a kick in the rear. And those trying to dig themselves out of a mountain of debt are not likely to be given a boost by a contracting job market with more people seeking unemployment benefits than at any time in nearly 20 years.

The Mandarin Class

The sad truth is that we've produced a mandarin class in this country; a special breed of swine that feeds on the handouts from corporate America and in turn does its bidding in the corridors of political power.

Let's take a closer look at the dirty work of some of the more illustrious of the Beltway's blue-ribbon influence-peddlers.

The Very Model of a Modern Major Lobbyist

Ed Gillespie is the archetype of this power porker class. You probably won't recognize the name. Like vampires, grave robbers, and the people who host infomercials, lobbyists prefer to work in the dark. That's why *The New Republic* described Gillespie as "the most important operative you've never heard of in the Bush presidency." Gillespie's Oval Office access rivals that of cabinet secretaries and White House advisors—even approaching the entree of the president's personal syntax coach. Of course, Gillespie's sage considered opinions have one crucial difference from those of the president's more visible advisors: they

GILLESPIE'S CLIENTS: A SAMPLER

Enron	The energy company hired Ed Gillespie's firm for around $700,000 to lobby the president on his energy plan. Dick Cheney and the staff of his Energy Task Force had at least six meetings with Enron representatives, including two with Ken Lay himself.
National Association of Realtors	Gillespie successfully persuaded Treasury Secretary Paul O'Neill to postpone a proposal that would have allowed banks into the real estate brokerage business.
Daimler-Chrysler	In March 2002, higher fuel efficiency standards were yanked out of Bush's energy bill, a victory for the automobile industry.
The Steel Industry	Gillespie succeeded in persuading the Bush administration to abandon its free-market credentials, and impose tariffs on imported steel.
Americans for Better Education	This phony grassroots organization raised over $1 million to lobby for Bush's education bill, and was run from Gillespie's Washington office.
21st Century Energy Project	A coalition of Gillespie's clients used the Project as a front to lobby for Bush's energy bill. Both Enron and Daimler-Chrysler contributed $50,000 to the Project. The energy bill that passed the House in August 2001 contains about $33 billion of tax breaks for the energy industry.

are bought and paid for by corporations and special interest groups.

Take a peek at Ed Gillespie's résumé and he starts to seem like the evil genius behind every bit of unpleasantness we've endured in the past decade—Woody Allen's *Zelig* crossed with Hannibal Lecter. As the program chairman of the 2000 Republican convention, Gillespie spearheaded the effort to portray W as "a different kind of Republican." Having written much of the Contract with America for Newt Gingrich, Gillespie was now busily rewriting it, keeping the party's right-wing ideologues out of the limelight and turning over the convention stage to such well-known Republican thinkers as Chaka Khan and The Rock.

Ed Gillespie could have had his pick of jobs inside the administration. At one time or another during the 2000 campaign, he had worked for each member of the Bush camp's ruling troika—Andrew Card, Karl Rove, and Karen Hughes—and he was buddies with dozens of lower-level staffers, like his campaign trail roomie, Ari Fleischer.

But Gillespie decided he would rather become the best-connected lobbyist since Moses interceded with God on behalf of the Israelites.

Never Can Say Goodbye

While many of the mandarin class like Ed Gillespie glide smoothly through the revolving door connecting the public and private sectors, the positions they hold are usually either appointive or party posts. Not so for an elite group of former elected officials who have, either by their own choice or by the will of the voters, made the move to the padded green pastures of corporate lobbying.

FAZIO'S CLIENTS: A SAMPLER

General Electric	As a Congressman, Fazio accumulated an impressive record on environmental issues, fighting for toxic waste clean-ups at military installations, clean water projects in California, and against the expansion of offshore drilling. But, in June 2000, lobbyist Fazio quickly turned into the environment's Mr. Hyde by having an EPA-ordered clean-up around power plants owned by his client GE shelved for "further study."
AT&T	On AT&T's behalf, Fazio fought to prevent the Baby Bells from providing high-speed access in the long-distance market.
Schering-Plough	Fazio attempted to extend the patent of the highly lucrative allergy drug Claritin for his client, Schering-Plough, the company that was fined $500 million by the FDA for repeatedly violating quality-control regulations.
American Meat Institute	In its ongoing efforts to defeat proposed legislation banning meatpackers from owning the hogs and cattle they kill, the meatpacking industry hired Vic Fazio in early 2002, a decision which in part led Senator Chuck Grassley (R-Iowa)— one of the chief sponsors of the legislation—to comment, "We anticipate a very difficult battle."

Vic Fazio, for example, spent 20 years in the House of Representatives, becoming chairman of the Democratic Caucus in 1995. After leaving office in 1999, he joined the Washington office of the New York public affairs firm Clark & Weinstock, partnering with an old buddy, former Representative Vin Weber, a Republican from Minnesota who had left public life under the massive black cloud of the House check-kiting scandal.

Fazio, a "shoulder-rubber extraordinaire" according to *California Journal,* wasted no time in signing up as clients Microsoft, AT&T, MidAmerica Energy Holdings, grain-trading giant Cargill, the Edison Electric Institute, Freddie Mac, and Sallie Mae.

Northrop, which had donated generously to Fazio when he was in Congress, also appointed him to its board of directors in 2000. As a Northrop director Fazio received an annual retainer of $32,000 in 2001, and was paid $1,000 extra for every board and committee meeting he attended that year. What, the job didn't actually require showing up for work? On top of that, Northrop directors also receive $1,000 a day for performing "extraordinary services" for the board. Would that include letting huge executive pay raises slip through unnoticed? Turning a blind eye to stock crashes? Approving multi-billion-dollar loans? Or are those just "ordinary services"?

The Big Double-Dipper

Former Montana Governor Marc Racicot is a Beltway pioneer, part of a new breed of lobbyist not content to shuttle back and forth between political posts and private sector jobs. Boldly going where no one had gone before, Racicot figured, why not do both at once?

After being elected chairman of the Republican National Committee, a powerful post with control of the party's purse strings, Racicot announced that he would continue to work his other gig as a high-powered lobbyist. I guess the thinking was, Why have only one job where you can exploit your business and personal relationships for wealth and power, when you can

RACICOT'S CLIENTS: A SAMPLER

Enron	Racicot was on the payroll of Bracewell & Patterson, whose largest client was Enron. In May 2001, Racicot sent an e-mail to Governor Jeb Bush requesting information about pending bills regarding new power plants: "I would like to know what they do, how they would help, if at all, and what the predictions are that either one will be passed by the Legislature."
National Electric Reliability Coordinating Council	This industry trade group hired Marc Racicot, who promptly met with Cheney and Cheney's energy director Andrew Lundquist to discuss EPA requirements that old power plants update their air-purifying equipment. Cheney's energy task force later recommended to the Justice Department that it drop lawsuits it had already brought for violations.
American Forest & Paper Association	Racicot was hired to lobby on the Association's behalf when environmental legislation affected the use of timberlands.

have two? To hear Racicot tell it, he just couldn't make ends meet on the $150,000 a year that the RNC chairmanship pays. And Republicans wonder why they are perceived as being out of touch with the needs of ordinary Americans.

After a few highly visible Republicans—notably Senator John McCain, William Safire and Bob Novak—intimated that they would prefer a party chairman who was devoting his full-time energy to the job rather than moonlighting as a highly paid shill, Racicot sulkily decided he would continue to work, not exactly as a lobbyist, but rather as a member of the politically connected Bracewell & Patterson law firm. Under that cover, he would draw less fire but could still have his cake and eat it, too.

The Grand Old Man of the Grand Old Party

Like Racicot, Haley Barbour, the éminence grise of corporate grease, also served as chairman of the RNC—although Barbour at least chose to put his lobbying business on hold during his term. Officially anyway. From his current inside/outside perches as finance chairman of the Republican Senatorial Campaign Committee and a lobbyist with Barbour Griffith & Rogers, he is the acknowledged master of an especially brazen form of lobbying that connects suggestible politicians directly with deep-pocketed donors.

As finance chairman, Barbour hits his clients up for donations to the party. As a lobbyist, he urges those same companies to donate directly to Republicans in need. Barbour multiplies his influence further when he distributes the Republican Senatorial Campaign Committee's cash, nearly $50 million in the 2002 election cycle.

BARBOUR'S CLIENTS: A SAMPLER

Big Tobacco	Haley Barbour has fought especially hard on behalf of Big Tobacco. Having lost his heroic rearguard action against the landmark tobacco settlement, Barbour is still struggling manfully to keep the Food and Drug Administration's hands off tobacco. In 1998, the key year for the industry's battle against the comprehensive tobacco bill, the three largest tobacco companies gave Barbour's firm $1.5 million for its services.
Nestle & Ralston Purina	Both companies hired Barbour as their lobbyist at a time when they were trying to get their merger approved by U.S. regulators. On December 11, 2001, the merger was approved.
Lockheed Martin	Lockheed is currently using Barbour's services to help extend its federal contract to manage Sandia National Laboratories in New Mexico, with 7,700 employees and a $1.7 billion budget. Lockheed's contract runs out in September 2003 and, rather than decide the issue immediately, the Department of Energy wants to grant Lockheed an extension on the contract.
Microsoft	The computer software giant paid Barbour's firm $540,000 in 2000, and $440,000 in 2001, using Barbour's skills to ease its way through its battles with the Department of Justice.

Bristol-Myers Squibb	The company, which was concerned that Medicare might trim the gargantuan margins on prescription drugs, hired Barbour, who helped deliver congressional inertia. The 107th Congress once again failed to pass prescription drug legislation, including a simple provision that would have enabled low-income seniors to get a 30% discount on their prescription drugs.
BellSouth	Barbour lobbied on behalf of the company during its battle against AT&T to allow it to go long distance. In May 2002 BellSouth began offering long distance in Georgia and Louisiana and is expected to be granted permission to offer long distance in five additional southern states.

Barbour's firm is an anomaly in the lobbying world. Unlike Gillespie's company and most others, Barbour Griffith deals only with Republicans. The all-male staff of lobbyists is 100% Republican, as are the receptionists, secretaries, and boys in the mailroom (I believe Dante referred to something like this as the Fourth Circle of Hell). With $10.8 million in lobbying revenues, Barbour's company was ranked #1 in influence by *Fortune* magazine in 2001.

The Senate's leading Republican Trent Lott is a particularly close friend of fellow Mississippian Barbour, which may have something to do with the millions of small, green, bill-fold-sized portraits of George Washington that Barbour has given Lott over the years. Listen to Lott speak and you wind up asking yourself, What has Haley put him up to this time?

All in the Family: Lobbying's Crown Princes and Royal Consorts

---

Many lobbyists have ties to the government officials they lobby that go far beyond an ordinary business relationship. Many are former colleagues, old friends, or holders of other people's debt in the enormous favor bank that is Washington, D.C.

There's a reductionist take on the headlines that holds that tribal loyalty is the most powerful force in the world. When we look at the earth's chronically bruised trouble zones, from Northern Ireland to East Timor, we see people acting on some ancient imperative of shared heritage instead of in accordance with their nobler instincts as individual human beings. Politicians and corporate executives also display caveman-like tribal loyalties that transcend their sense of right and wrong.

For CEOs, the tribal response is played out in the board-room where fellow executives are reluctant to blow the whistle on their peers. Inside the Beltway, tribalism is manifested in the courtesy extended to former elected or appointed officials who have, reluctantly or not, returned to the private sector—as lobbyists. Like the children or spouses of colleagues, these ex-officials have any number of open doors awaiting them along the corridors of power.

With the going rate for access in Washington as high as it is, these refugees from public life become corporate hirelings even before their names have been painted out on their Capitol Hill parking spaces. Paul Wellstone, whose progressive voice was so tragically silenced, once explained the high demand for this specialized breed of lobbyists this way: "Their value is that I don't think anybody in the Senate ever says no to anybody who served. It's just kind of the unwritten rules, out of courtesy."

But some lobbyists have ties to key legislators that are

even stronger. Chet Lott, a Domino's pizza franchisee, recently decided to give up the glamorous world of pepperoni and extra cheese and get into the lobbying game. Now, Chet Lott did not go to Washington to lobby in areas of his actual expertise—to propose stiff jail terms, for example, for pranksters who order a dozen pizzas delivered to a stranger. Instead he took up the causes of BellSouth, the National Thoroughbred Racing Association, Day & Zimmerman, a munitions maker, and Edison Chouest Offshore, a boat chartering company that has no connection to pizza except that its clients like it.

For BellSouth, Lott weighed in on one of the most intensely lobbied issues of modern times, the Tauzin-Dingell Bill, which would allow the Baby Bells to compete with phone companies to provide long-distance service. Because the bill is ideologically neutral (Democrats and Republicans don't fall neatly on opposite sides) and there was scant interest from voters, legislators could sell their votes with little fear of the consequences. As a result, the interested parties spent more than $32 million in campaign contributions between 1999 and 2001. Since the bill has passed the House but not the Senate, senators, at least, can count on the phone companies reaching out to touch them with fat checks for years to come.

On behalf of the Racing Association, Lott is keeping an eye on a pending bill banning Internet gambling, which track owners fear could start a horse race to regulate their own industry. For Day & Zimmerman, he and his partner, former Representative Larry Hopkins (R-Ky.), have been consulting on defense issues, and for Edison Chouest, Lott is doing his level best to make sure that Edison continues to be the government's number one supplier of special-purpose vessels. Don't ask me what the government needs so many special-purpose vessels for.

And don't ask Chet Lott either.

Despite the protests of his clients, one suspects that young Lott has been hired not for his expertise in dealing with sophisticated legislative matters but because his dad just happens to be Senator Trent Lott. Both men deny any impropriety, of course, and a BellSouth spokesman says that the accident of Lott's paternity has nothing to do with his hiring. "They just have to accept my word," the spokesman said. Which I guess explains the recent spate of job applicants at lobbying firms whose previous job experience was "pizza delivery guy."

But someone is definitely getting ripped off here. Either Lott's clients paid good money for access that the good consciences of Lott *père et fils* forbid them to deliver or the public's interest has been trumped by the powerful bond between father and son. Either way, in a modern parable, it would be only just if Lott's son—rather than Lot's wife—were turned into a pillar of salt.

Nudging Chet Lott at the K Street trough is Joshua Hastert, eldest piglet of Representative Dennis Hastert (R-Ill.). After extensive experience owning a record store called Seven Dead Arson, Hastert Jr. came to Washington to work for Federal Legislative Associates (FLA), a lobbying firm that represents a number of diverse interests like FirstPlus Financial Group, American Airlines, and some high-tech firms like MP3.com. "The fact that he is the speaker's son was certainly a factor," said David Miller, managing partner at FLA, "but he's really cool." I know plenty of cool twenty-somethings who couldn't land that job based on their coolness alone.

The sons of senators Harry Reid (D.-Nev.), John Breaux (D-La.), Orrin Hatch (R-Utah) and Ted Stevens (R-Alaska) are lobbyists too, as is Senator Mary Landrieu's (D-La.) aunt. Linda Daschle, Senator Tom Daschle's wife, also has her snout in the feed, plying the lobbying trade for Baker, Donelson, Bearman, and Caldwell. Linda Daschle has numbered among her clients American Airlines and Northwest Airlines (bailouts and regulatory issues), Boeing (the usual), the American Trucking Association (fighting the loosening of trade restrictions), United

Technologies Corporation (defense contracts), drug maker Schering-Plough (patent extensions etc.), and the American Concrete Pavement Association (hey, I'm all for concrete and pavement).

Two of Linda Daschle's clients illustrate the potency of the nexus both defensively and offensively. Loral Space and Communications paid $460,000 to Baker, Donelson for the services of Mrs. Daschle and four other lobbyists after it was fined $14 million for illegally selling classified missile technology to China. And L-3 Communications hired Daschle and her company to fight to have the FAA approve its airline-baggage bomb-screening equipment even though the airlines overwhelmingly preferred the more accurate device made by rival InVision. But shortly after Linda Daschle was hired, Congress ordered the FAA in—according to the *Washington Post*—an "unusually explicit directive" to buy one machine from L-3 for each one it bought from the other company.

Another congressional spouse willing to get down in the mud with the corporate swine is Anne Bingaman, wife of Senator Jeff Bingaman (D-N. Mex.). Mrs. Bingaman was paid a total of $2.5 million to lobby for Global Crossing, before it went bankrupt, making $57 billion of shareholder equity disappear. Global Crossing's chairman Gary Winnick played the Washington game with unsurpassed mastery, signing up Anne Bingaman as a lobbyist; Bill Clinton's defense secretary, William Cohen, as a board member; and gifting both George Bush the elder and Terry McAuliffe, the chairman of the Democratic National Committee, with insider deals on Global Crossing stock. Former President Bush made $4 million from his and McAuliffe walked away from the smoking wreck with $18 million.

Family ties also extend into the corporate boardroom, with a handful of congressional spouses sitting on the boards of

ALL IN THE FAMILY

Everywhere there's lots of piggies,
Living piggy lives.

           — **"Piggies," The Beatles**

Lobbyist	Relation-ship	Politician	Position in 107th Congress
Chet Lott	Son	Sen. Trent Lott (R-Miss.)	Senate Minority Leader
Linda Daschle	Wife	Sen. Tom Daschle (D-S. Dak.)	Senate Majority Leader
Joshua Hastert	Son	Rep. Dennis Hastert (R-Ill.)	Speaker of the House
Scott Hatch	Son	Sen. Orrin Hatch (R-Utah)	Ranking Member, Judiciary Committee
Phyllis Landrieu	Aunt	Sen. Mary Landrieu (D-La.)	Appropriations Committee
John Breaux, Jr.	Son	Sen. John Breaux (D-La.)	Chief Deputy Whip
Key Reid	Son	Sen. Harry Reid (D-Nev.)	Majority Whip
Anne Bingaman	Wife	Sen. Jeff Bingaman (D-N. Mex.)	Chairman, Energy and Natural Resources Committee

big corporations. Susan Bayh, the wife of Senator Evan Bayh (D-Ind.), sits on the board of E*Trade and Ruth Harkin, Senator Tom Harkin's (D-Iowa) wife, sits on the board of Conoco. Bill Allison of the Center for Public Integrity calls board appointments for congressional spouses a "growing phenomenon," and cautions that "it gives corporations the kind of access to a politician that's above and beyond what a normal lobbyist has." Members of Congress only have to disclose if they or their spouses receive more than $1,000 for sitting on corporate boards, not how much they actually make.

Hey, Big Spender:
Lobbying's Ten Most Wanted

The best source of cash flow for Washington's influence peddlers are corporate bullies and bad boys—companies that can't possibly get what they want legitimately because it is so clearly contrary to the public good.

Here are the top ten big spenders over the period from 1997 to 1999, a list of business behemoths that have paid handsomely to circumvent the public interest.

It's no surprise that tobacco pusher Philip Morris is number one. After all, any industry that kills 400,000 Americans every year is bound to have a bit of a public relations problem. To counter the bad publicity spreading from cancer wards across the land and the periodic calls for greater regulation from some busybody agency head or legislator who hasn't sold out, Philip (they've spent so much trying to get me to like them, I feel we should be on a first-name basis) spent $54,216,000 on lobbying between 1997 and 1999. And that doesn't include the boatload of cash they spent trying to make kids think cigarette smoking is "cool." Phil is also the largest source of campaign contributions among the tobacco giants, giving over $13.5 million to nicotine-stained congressmen since 1996.

In 1998, Big Tobacco increased its spending on lobbying by over $30 million from the year before as it battled a broad array of anti-smoking initiatives, from curbing tobacco advertising to increasing the price of cigarettes to giving the FDA authority to regulate nicotine. With the four largest cigarette makers laying out more than $100,000 on lobbying each and every day Congress is in session (plus another $250 a day on teeth whiteners and breath fresheners), the smoking industry's flair for bribery and coercion will ensure that Big Tobacco, unlike its customers, isn't going to die any time soon.

Number two is Verizon's predecessor, Bell Atlantic, which spent a whopping $41.9 million on lobbying (plus $7.5 million in campaign contributions since 1996) primarily on anti-trust matters. In the nineties, phone companies developed an overpowering urge to merge. The understandable concern that this might lead to monopoly pricing and indifferent service was pooh-poohed more than 41 million ways by companies like Verizon, crazed with lust for corporate intercourse. The end result? Yep, monopoly pricing and indifferent service. Every time Verizon's lobbyists pooh-poohed, the public got poohed on.

Next up is ExxonMobil Corporation, which bought $34.1 million worth of lobbying services between 1997 and 1999 (and, since 1996, Exxon and Mobil [later ExxonMobil] have given a combined $4 million in campaign contributions). And you might say they got a bargain since the government okayed their controversial, competition-cooling merger in 1999. ExxonMobil, along with the rest of the oil industry, has also battled to maintain relaxed standards on pollution and global warming, to be permitted to drill for oil wherever it feels like—even if it's in one of the last pristine wildernesses on Earth—and to keep America dependent on dirty, scarce fossil fuels instead of switching over to renewable, environmentally friendly sources of energy.

Number four is Ford Motor Co. with a lobbying bill of $29.5 million (and, since 1996, a campaign contribution tab totaling over $2.5 million). Ford threw most of its dollars at the successful effort to hold back regulations mandating higher fuel economy standards. In particular, Ford circled its wagons around its highly profitable SUV business to prevent the soccer mom's urban assault vehicle from being held to the same emissions standard as a car. Currently treated as light trucks, SUVs consume so much fuel that they have become a secret weapon for Saddam Hussein and the other oil-bloated tyrants of the Middle East.

Making a smooth landing at number five is Boeing, America's largest airplane manufacturer. Between 1997 and 1999, Boeing spent over $26.6 million on lobbying. The company's actions in the wake of September 11 offer a perfect example of the kind of self-serving agenda that money was used to promote. Boeing wasted no time calling Washington for favors after the attacks, pestering the Department of Defense to restart stalled negotiations that would allow the company to lease 100 new 767 jets to the Air Force for conversion into aerial refueling tankers. Estimated to cost the nation $26 billion during the next 10 years, it's a seriously pricey big-business bailout. And Boeing is well-equipped to ensure that more money comes its way. Its Washington office is headed by Rudy F. de Leon, Clinton's last deputy secretary of defense, and it employs over 80 in-house and outside lobbyists.

Parked in the number six spot is the world's largest carmaker, General Motors, with $26.3 million in lobbying expenditures from 1997 to 1999. Killing the Kyoto Protocol—the global warming initiative that would have reduced carbon dioxide emissions worldwide—was the primary objective of GM's D.C. minions. As with so many anti-reform efforts, you have to ask yourself: if GM and the other automakers put as much time, money, and ingenuity into increasing fuel efficiency as they do into lobbying the government for special dispensation, don't you think they might be able to have a kick-ass non-polluting car in the showrooms next week?

AT&T, number seven on Washington's speed dial with $24.6 million in lobbying expenses and nearly $10 million in campaign contributions, had a giant "squeeze-the-little-guy" merger with the nation's second-largest cable company, TCI, to protect. Once the merger was complete, AT&T immediately began behaving exactly like the bullying monopoly that merger-opponents feared it would become. The company lobbied frantically to keep Internet service providers from using its newly acquired cable TV lines—something that would have saved the public a lot more than "a buck or two" in service fees.

Clearly not suffering from insufficient funds, number eight, Citigroup, paid $24.1 million (and, together with Citicorp, over $6.3 million in campaign contributions since 1996) to help speed the passage of the Financial Modernization Act, a bill which yielded billions in dividends by permitting commercial banks to engage in investment banking and vice versa. The bill nailed shut the coffin of New Deal regulations designed to protect consumers and safeguard banks from their own excesses. Delighted securities bankers danced on the grave.

As the parent of NBC, General Electric knows a little something about the value of making *Friends*—which is why the conglomerate, number nine on our list, spent $23.3 million to keep the pressure on Washington to do its bidding. As a major polluter of New York's Hudson River, GE has fought tooth-and-nail—and spent millions of dollars—to prevent the Environmental Protection Agency from handing it the bill for the cleanup. GE's Washington operatives have successfully forestalled any clean-up of the carcinogenic PCBs (polychlorinated biphenyls) the company dumped not only in the Hudson but elsewhere around the country. One of those operatives is the ubiquitous global peacemaker—and one-time environmental crusader—former Senator George Mitchell. As the *Boston Globe* asked in March 2002, "Has Mr. Integrity Sold Out?"

Finally, rounding out the list at number ten is telecom titan Sprint, weighing in with $22 million (and, since 1996, $3 million in campaign contributions). Sprint has shared interests with AT&T and Verizon including deregulation, broadband access, and Internet gambling and taxation, and true to its name, it's catching up to the big guys fast.

REAL/FAKE
PRESSURE GROUPS QUIZ

There are thousands of political organizations. Some are grassroots mom-and-pop operations, some are giant lobbying interests that represent the titans of industry and commerce. But, no matter their size, or their make-up, they all have one thing in common: an earnest-sounding name that either perfectly illuminates the group's agenda, or cleverly hides it. For example, a group called "People Against Stuff That Sounds Bad" is probably genuinely opposed to bad-sounding stuff, although there's a slight chance it's actually for it. On the flip side, "People in Favor of Things Every Sane Person Supports" is, in all likelihood, ardently opposed to these popular things. So, what's in a name? For political pressure groups the key to getting their wolves in the door is to dress them up in sheep's clothing. Take a look.

1. Two of the following political organizations are real. Can you spot the fake?

a. Americans for Better Education
b. Women's Action for New Directions
c. Citizens Against Government

(*Answer:* "c." Although, there actually is a group known as "Citizens Against Government Waste," which presumably also supports puppies, sunny days, and pretty flowers.)

2. Which of the following is a real political organization with powerful lobbyists and the ear of the president?
   a. Stand Up For Steel
   b. Fight Fiercely for Forestry
   c. Cooperate for Corn
   d. Dance for Dairy
   e. Tango for Toast

(*Answer:* "a." And it actually succeeded in overcoming the administration's professed belief in free trade.)

3. Listed below are the names of four political organizations. Three are fake and one is a lobby group funded by Philip Morris to stub out anti-smoking legislation in Florida. Which is the real Philip Morris-supported political organization?
   a. Institute for Reasonable Reaction
   b. Center for Feasible Choice
   c. Consumers for Responsible Solutions
   d. Association of People and Policies

(*Answer:* "c." After spending $360,000 in 2002 to gather signatures, the group was disbanded when word of its patron was leaked to the press.)

4. Fill in the blank. Which of the words below completes the name of this real political organization: "_____ for Common Sense"
   a. Taxpayers
   b. Institute
   c. Stand Up

(*Answer:* "a." And, according to its website, it was instru-
mental in saving taxpayers $4 million by putting the
kibosh on the NASA Russian Space Monkey program.)

5. Fill in the blank. Which of the following words completes
the name of this real political organization? "Friends
of _____."
    a. Stuff that Explodes
    b. Drugs and Alcohol
    c. Tobacco
    d. Dick Cheney

(*Answer:* "c." Someone did try to organize a group called
"Friends of Dick Cheney," but neither of his hunting
buddies could make the meeting.)

6. What is the name of the largest and most influential trade
organization representing the opinions and interests of
the frozen-food industry to government, the media, and
consumers?
    a. The American Friends of Delicious Frozen Food
    b. National Association for the Advancement of
       Frozen Food
    c. American Frozen Food Institute
    d. The Fresh Food Sucks Association

(*Answer:* "c." And they're working hard. According to its
website, during the 1990s, the FDA proclaimed that
frozen fruit and vegetable products have nutrient profiles
equivalent or superior to their fresh food counterparts.)

7. According to its website, what is the motto of "Citizens
for a Sound Economy"?
    a. Lower taxes, less government, and more freedom.
    b. Less talk, more rock.
    c. Stronger government, lower taxes, less regulation.
    d. We'll beat anyone's advertised price or your mat-
       tress is free.

(*Answer:* "a." And, according to its website, with a donation of $50 or more, you'll get a polo shirt with its logo on it. Donations are NOT tax deductible.)

8. There are two legal organizations listed below. Can you guess which one is supported by Ralph Nader?
   a. Center for Study of Responsive Law
   b. Institute for Legal Reform

(*Answer:* "a" is the Ralph Nader organization; "b" is an incorporated affiliate of the U.S. Chamber of Commerce that works to protect corporate wrongdoers from lawsuits.)

Scoring

7–8 correct answers: You should definitely make something other than C-Span the default page on your web browser.

4–6 correct answers: One morning a week you should listen to Howard Stern on the ride to work instead of NPR.

2–3 correct answers: You should be pleased that you're smart, but not a wonk.

0–1 correct answers: It wouldn't kill you to flip over to *The West Wing* during the commercials on *The Bachelor*.

Want to start your own political organization, but can't find a name that sounds important yet really says nothing? We can help. Just choose one word from columns A, B, and C, print up letterhead, and off you go . . .

A		B	C
Center	(for)	Economic	Fairness
Coalition	(for)	Reasonable	Solutions
Institute	(for)	Sensible	Resolution
Consumers	(for)	Social	Justice
The Society	(for)	Equitable	Equality
Americans	(for)	Spirited	Accountability
Leaders	(for)	Desirable	Alternatives

The Matrix

As impressive as the arm-twisting efforts of the Top Ten are, when it comes to pushing the lobbying envelope nobody did it quite like Enron. Over the course of its now infamous life, the energy company turned the art of lobbying into a science.

Enron did this through an ingenious piece of computer software it called "The Matrix." Like the one in the movie, Enron's matrix sought to control other people—you know, members of Congress and presidential candidates—with a simple computer program. Every time a potential change in federal regulations loomed on the legislative horizon, a team of Enron statisticians, programmers, and public affairs officers, led by economist Gia Maisashvili, would input the relevant data into the Matrix. After some high-tech number crunching, the Matrix would put a price tag on the cost of that change to Enron. If the number was not to Enron's liking, the company's Washington team of lobbyists and well-funded legislators would swoop in like marauding Huns.

"We were the pioneers," Maisashvili said. "It was a new thing to be able to quantify regulatory risk." A new thing but not necessarily a good new thing. After Maisashvili quit in 2001, he said, "They could not have cared less if that was a good thing [for the public] or not. They cared only if this was good for Enron."

Forfeiting Our Future

No lobbying effort by Enron reveals the insidious way in which the company wielded its power in Washington as well as its successful promotion of the Commodity Futures Modernization Act of 2000. The act would have more aptly been called the Commodity Futures Do What You Want Act because this obscure measure opened the floodgates for Enron to play fast and loose in the arcane world of derivatives trading, a $95 trillion industry.

Trading in derivatives—financial contracts promising payments based on an estimated future price of a certain commodity—was one of the many schemes by which Enron kept millions in debt off its balance sheets, and one of the primary reasons for its eventual downfall.

The Commodity Futures Modernization Act exempted over-the-counter derivatives from regulation and gave Enron Online, a private commodity exchange, a leg up on competitors such as The Chicago Board of Trade and The New York Mercantile Exchange, which, as quasi-public entities, were subject to far more regulatory scrutiny. This wildly profitable advantage didn't come about by accident. The energy company had campaigned tirelessly for the bill knowing that the smudging of black-and-white rules would provide all kinds of cover for the financial maneuvers that were its bread and butter.

An especially rancid aspect of the passage of the act is the key role played by the Gramm family. In 1993, while chairing the Commodity Futures Trading Commission, Wendy Gramm helped pass a set of rules that exempted much of Enron's energy trading business from governmental oversight—effectively allowing Enron to cook its books outside the view of government regulators. Six weeks after shepherding this process, Gramm left "public service" for a cushy, well-paying seat on Enron's board of directors, a fitting reward for special services provided.

Seven years later, those same rules were on the verge of being enshrined into law as part of the Commodity Futures Modernization Act when the scheme hit a glitch. Of all people,

Wendy Gramm's husband, Senator Phil Gramm, was holding the bill up. But it wasn't because the good senator had any objections to Enron getting its way—after all, Ken Lay's company had given him $100,000 worth of campaign donations over the years. No, the delay came about because Gramm was hard at work tweaking other provisions in the bill that were important to his even bigger buck sponsors in the banking industry. And you know what they say about the difficulty of serving two masters.

Once the senator was able to mold the legislation to the bankers' liking, however, he quickly allowed the bill to proceed to the Senate floor, where, to Mrs. Gramm and Mr. Lay's mutual good fortune, it passed unanimously.

Who said romance is dead? The sordid setup makes you wonder if, on their wedding day, the Gramms took a vow to "love, honor, cherish, and profit from Enron—till death, or bankruptcy, do us part."

How the Pigs Stopped Reform

The Commodity Futures Modernization Act was but one in a series of victories the corporate class tallied over the forces of rational restraint. And the reason for the winning streak is one borrowed from Latin American soccer: The referees were on the corporate payroll. So not only were they sure to look the other way when a low blow or rabbit punch was delivered—they'd even toss in a cheap shot of their own now and then. Just look at what happened when regulators tried to rein in stock option abuses in the early nineties, nearly a decade before the issue would gain notoriety as the source of so much financial corruption.

The year was 1993. After a great deal of study, the Financial Accounting Standards Board (FASB) decided that there was something wrong, even dishonest, about the excessive use of stock options by so many companies. The board was especially concerned by the way options were being concealed in financial reports. Its solution? A rule instructing auditors to begin putting options where they belonged: on the expense side of the ledger.

Seems sensible enough. But all hell broke loose.

The corporations mobilized a massive retaliatory strike led by Connecticut Senator Joe Lieberman, who proudly labels himself a "pro-business Democrat." And business seems to be quite pro-Lieberman. Between 1997 and 2002, he received $371,867 from bankers, brokers, and accountants. No wonder Lieberman got out front early to protect stock options.

Speaking on the Senate floor, he actually tried to turn stock options into a Joe Six-Pack issue, claiming: "What's on the line here really is the future of jobs in this country." Jobs washing CEOs' Jaguars and BMWs? Mowing the lawns of their six vacation homes? Linking options to jobs is a bit like linking the price of caviar to the stability of the U.S. economy.

Even now, after all the revelations of options excesses, Lieberman claims that it is "intellectually irrational" to try to expense something the value of which is not known until it is sold. The problem with that somewhat more rational-sounding argument is that, as Lieberman well knows, businesses routinely place a price on all kinds of things with more or less intangible value on the balance sheet.

And Lieberman did more than just speak out, he actually introduced a bill instructing the SEC—the agency in charge of enforcing accounting standards—to ignore anything FASB might recommend about expensing options. He then enlisted a diverse political cast, ranging from Democrats Barbara Boxer and Bill Bradley to Republicans Connie Mack and (surprise, surprise) Phil Gramm to help him pass it.

The clamor didn't stop there. Silicon Valley's high-tech

options groupies—zealously defending the massive windfalls stock options were bringing them as the Internet craze heated up—soon waded into the fray, holding a 4,000-strong anti-FASB rally in March 1994, complete with T-shirts featuring anti-FASB slogans. They also inundated their representatives in Washington with thousands of letters.

As the opposition movement gathered steam, a number of lobbying groups became involved. Chief among them was the Coalition for American Equity Expansion, which worked closely with congressional staffers on the wording of Lieberman's bill.

After rounding up 600 CFOs to sign a letter critical of FASB's proposals, the Coalition raised the stakes even further by installing a key Lieberman staffer—stock options expert Kenneth Glueck—as its director of Tax and Finance Policy. Joining in the anti-FASB lynch mob were the Council of Institutional Investors, the United Shareholders Association, the Financial Executives Institute, and dozens of pension funds.

In the face of this alarmist furor you'd think the besieged Accounting Board could at least count on its own kind to acknowledge the wisdom of reform, right? Guess again. The Big Five accounting firms weighed in on the side of the anti-reform extremists, selling their souls to their clients rather than upholding the venerable traditions of their trade. As one former SEC employee put it: "The accountants were going beyond good accounting. They were advocating a business position. They wanted to keep their customers happy. It was quite unseemly."

Astonished at the vehemence of the opposition, Arthur Levitt, then chairman of the SEC, told FASB to back off. He feared that if FASB continued to push, Congress might abolish the standards board altogether. It was, he recalls, his "biggest mistake." Ultimately, Lieberman's Senate resolution to condemn the reform was passed by 88–9 and FASB caved. Instead

PHONY GRASSROOTS CAMPAIGN

One of the most useful tools in the lobbyist's bag of dirty tricks is the phony grassroots campaign. It works like this:

Step 1: Take out alarming full-page ads in national news-papers that enrage people by wildly exaggerating the effects of some legislation pending before Congress: "The Federal Government is trying to steal your car!!!"

Step 2: Include a list of phone numbers of congressmen or, better yet, a single toll-free number that ordinary citizens can call to express their opinion on the issue at hand. "Call your congressman immediately and tell him/her it's un-American for the government to steal your car, and he or she should vote against HR 1342 because it's a slippery slope. Next, they'll be stealing our babies!"

Step 3: Include a sneaky little clip-and-mail coupon at the bottom that can be sent to your congressman's office.

So, let's turn the tables on these grassroots harvesters and send the coupon below to your representative, senator, governor, or the president. A comprehensive list of their names and addresses can be found at www.congress.org.

Dear Representative/Senator/Governor/President/Other _____,

As a concerned citizen of *(your town and state),* I am writing you to ask that you refrain from making important decisions based on phony write-in campaigns like this one. Please determine your positions using the best available information, the advice of impartial experts, and, most of all, your own conscience. Please ignore suspicious deluges of mail or phone calls which are often solicited dishonestly by lobbying firms.

Thank you in advance. God bless America (optional),

(Your name)

---

of real reform, the agency passed an insipid rule requiring the cost of stock options to be disclosed—but only in tiny footnotes—while continuing to allow corporations to place options on the wrong side of the balance sheet.

The options cancer was thus allowed to metastasize. Even more destructive to the body politic, the success of this no-holds-barred approach to killing reform emboldened the nexus of corruption to use it again and again in the years leading up to the current corporate scandals—and, in the process, build the house of cards of the New Economy.

The Shareholders Be Damned!

One of the more flagrant displays of hypocrisy by our representatives during the regulation-busting nineties was the passage of the Private Securities Litigation Reform Act. Part of Newt Gingrich's Contract With America, it was designed to protect auditing companies from shareholder lawsuits. With this piece of legislation, Newt and his friends did away with crucial protections against exactly the kind of accounting gimmickry that has robbed billions from the pension funds and 401(k)s of hard-working Americans.

Before Congress handed this gift to the securities industry, auditors could be held liable for all the damages arising from a case of fraud—a powerful deterrent to such behavior. Now an audit company can be found liable only if the victims can prove the firm had an intent to defraud—a notoriously difficult legal hurdle to clear. So, with the stroke of a pen, Congress made it easier for corporate thieves to plunder public companies without fear of being sued.

As a justification, the bill's defenders trotted out the usual tired arguments. Mark Gitenstein, a lobbyist for the bill, said that it would "get rid of frivolous, merit-less" lawsuits and screen "the marginal cases from the serious ones." The bill passed after heavy lobbying by the accounting industry, especially from Arthur Andersen, which—clearly fearful of a raft of shareholder lawsuits resulting from the books it was merrily roasting—brought in a high-powered securities lawyer to plead its case. His name was Harvey Pitt.

So strong was the magnetic pull of corporate largesse that the bill even survived a veto by President Clinton, with 89 House Democrats and 20 Senate Democrats voting to side with big business, rather than the president. Bill sponsors senators Christopher Dodd (D-Conn.) and Pete Domenici (R-N. Mex.) were, not coincidentally, major recipients of Andersen donations: Dodd has received $54,843 from the firm since 1991. Almost half of that was given between 1995 and 1996, the same time period in which the bill was under consideration. Domenici, meanwhile, has received $16,300 since 1989 from Andersen. Two-thirds of that was deposited in his account between 1995 and 1996.

James Chanos, a leading hedge-fund manager, and one of the first to question Enron's soaring profits, calls the reduced liability that the Litigation Reform Act made possible "one of the major, major contributors to this rise in corporate chicanery." For his part, James Cox, a professor of securities and corporate law at Duke University, bitterly denounced the bill as "the ultimate in special interest legislation," declaring that, in one fell swoop, Congress had reversed "eighty years of federal procedure."

Modernization Madness

The other key item pushed through as part of the deregulation frenzy was a little number called the Financial Modernization

Act, passed in November 1999. This progressive-sounding measure would supposedly "modernize" the financial services industry. Seems like a good thing, doesn't it? Kind of like installing updated software on your computer. But what this act really did was demolish many of the rules and regulations that had been put in place after the spiritual grandfathers of the current crop of corporate pigs caused the Crash of '29. Those rules had kept the nation's banks secure, and—give or take a savings and loan scandal or two—reasonably honest, for 65 years.

Specifically, the Financial Modernization Act abolished the separation of investment and commercial banking, doing away with restrictions that kept investment banks, commercial banks, insurance companies, and securities firms far enough away from one another's business to prevent the blatant conflicts of interest that fueled so much of the recent spate of fiscal crimes. The centerpiece of those New Deal–era regulations, the Glass-Steagall Act, has long been the Moby Dick of financial companies—the elusive prey the expansion-crazed Captain Ahabs were determined to land no matter what the consequences to the unsuspecting American public.

With Glass-Steagall finally harpooned, they set out on their great adventure on the high seas of financial double-dealing.

Tauzin Tramples Levitt

By the end of the nineties the signs of gross abuse were visible to anyone who bothered to look. At the SEC, clear-eyed Arthur Levitt decided to make a move, and it was a bold one. Deeply troubled by the conflict of interest created by accounting firms also offering consulting services to their clients, Levitt proposed a fundamental reform to the industry: separating auditing from consulting, for real. The chairman might have thought he'd felt

ARIANNA HUFFINGTON

the full wrath of the accounting industry during the FASB fiasco, but, as he was soon to discover, he hadn't seen anything yet.

In the time since the accounting industry helped pummel Levitt and FASB in 1993 over regulation of options, the industry had undergone a miraculous process of reverse metamorphosis—devolving from a monarch butterfly floating above the corporate fray into a larval grub crawling around in the political muck.

Between 1998 and 2000, the Big Five accounting firms invested almost $15 million in lobbying. And they doled out so much campaign cash that more than 50% of current House members and 94 out of the 100 senators have pocketed money from accountants. As for the other six, perhaps they've hidden the contributions by calling them "miscellaneous other pro-curements."

The big accounting firms had become so adept at getting their way in Washington they even opened up their own lobby-ing divisions to help other companies pervert the democratic process. Well, you know what they say: diversify, diversify, diversify.

Washington Council Ernst & Young, a division of Ernst & Young, is now one of the ten largest lobbying firms in Wash-ington, with billings of about $11 million annually, while Price-waterhouseCoopers' lobbying arm rakes in around $10 million. As accounting professor Bob Jensen colorfully describes the accounting businesses, "They say they're for motherhood, but they're selling prostitution."

So when, in 2000, Levitt suggested separating auditing from consulting, the accountants knew they were powerful enough to pick, and win, a fight. They were damned if they were going to lose so much revenue—by this time income from consulting was more than triple the income from auditing.

Levitt recalls the reaction of the heads of the accounting firms this way: "We're not with you, Arthur. This is going to be war. We're going to fight you all the way. We'll fight you in the

Congress, and we'll fight you in the courts." It was practically Churchillian. And it was no idle warning. After all, one of the accountants' best friends in Congress was Rep. Billy Tauzin, the Ragin' Cajun who, as chairman of the powerful Committee on Energy and Commerce, had significant power over the SEC thanks to his ability to squeeze its budget.

Tauzin, together with representatives Michael Oxley and Thomas Bliley, sent a four-page letter to Levitt. Its message was clear: slow-track the issue, or else. Making sixteen requests for additional information, the letter reached its crescendo in a lightly veiled threat. Reacting to an auxiliary proposal of Levitt's that would limit the ability of accountants to own shares in companies that they audited, the gang-of-three asked Levitt to "estimate the number of violations that would exist if the stock restrictions applicable to the accounting profession were to be applied to the SEC and its staff."

Tauzin, who had banked $280,000 in campaign contributions from the green eyeshade set, threw himself into the fray with the same vigor he would disingenuously display just a few years later when leading the chorus of outrage against Arthur Andersen and Enron during congressional hearings.

But, back in 2000, it was still more profitable for Tauzin to demagogue *for* the accountants. And he had plenty of company. Besides Tauzin, the accountants mobilized a rapid response squad that included 46 other congressmen and a lobbyist A-Team including such longtime Beltway fixtures as Vic Fazio and the ultra-smooth former Clinton White House counsel Jack Quinn. They also brought in Dan Brouillette, a Tauzin aide turned lobbyist, turned assistant energy secretary in the Bush administration. And a steady stream of letters— including one signed by 10 U.S. senators—began flowing into the SEC, beseeching Levitt to back down.

Levitt refused, launching a last-ditch effort to build popular support for the reforms by traveling across America, holding

BUYING CONGRESS

Total Campaign Contributions from the Accounting Industry, 1989–2001

SENATE TOP FIVE	GRAND TOTAL
Christopher J. Dodd (D-Conn.)	$482,453
Charles E. Schumer (D-N.Y.)	340,006
Phil Gramm (R-Tex.)	204,185
Ron Wyden (D-Ore.)	166,340
Rick Santorum (R-Pa.)	146,868

HOUSE TOP FIVE	GRAND TOTAL
W. J. "Billy" Tauzin (R-La.)	$286,593
E. Clay Shaw Jr. (R-Fla.)	232,759
Martin Frost (D-Tex.)	205,154
Sherrod Brown (D-Ohio)	198,565
Christopher Cox (R-Calif.)	156,759

hearings on accounting abuses. But the torrent of congressional pressure—which included threats to slash the SEC's budget if Levitt continued to insist on auditor independence—finally became too much for him to handle. Once again, Levitt gave in and compromised. Accountants could keep their consulting money, he decided, but would have to inform their own internal audit committees of the income. Kind of like a heroin addict having to tell his fellow junkies where he scored his smack. Looking back on the debacle, Levitt is rueful: "That was a compromise that I would not make today," he sighs.

Senator Sarbanes' Comatose Bill
Shocked Back to Life

You'd think that once the Enron mess hit the proverbial fan in November of 2001, our spineless representatives in Washington would have snapped to the task of instituting reforms—if only to provide cover for their scandal-exposed rear ends. But, no, they merely bobbed, weaved—and played to the camera—as usual. Tauzin made a particularly good show of it, publicly running roughshod over his former foxhole buddies at Andersen and Enron.

One of the few Beltway insiders to push for corporate reform in the immediate aftermath of Enron's collapse was Senator Paul Sarbanes. But, in the time-honored Congressional tradition by which sleaze overwhelms sagacity, his attempts to strengthen the SEC, restrict accounting firms' ability to double-dip as consultants and auditors for the same client, and impose stringent conflict-of-interest rules on the investment banking world were met with unbridled resistance.

By the spring of 2002, Sarbanes' bill lay in a deep coma and was not expected to survive, having been beaten within an inch of its legislative life by a goon squad made up of lobbyists for the financial industries and their No. 1 Senate enforcer, Phil Gramm.

Fresh from a meeting at which Gramm urged them to "stall, stall, stall," the lobbyists brought out the rhetorical brass knuckles, issuing an "Action Alert" to the effect that Sarbanes' bill would result in a "de facto government takeover" of the accounting profession and "serious, harmful consequences for capital markets and American business." The warning on a pack of cigarettes is less alarmist. Then the dutiful, can't-retire-soon-enough Gramm pulled out his well-thumbed copy of Robert's Rules of Parliamentary Obstruction and went to work, pressing Banking Committee Chairman Sarbanes to hold more hearings on the bill—even though the Committee had already held ten—and offering 41 last-minute amendments. Fellow Republican committee members added another 82 amendments for good measure—a few extra kicks in the gut of the grievously wounded bill. It was democracy at its worst.

Accounting industry lobbyist John Hunnicutt explained the strategy: "Once the excitement and the glare fades," he said of reform efforts on the Hill, "people really start to think about it." Translation: he and his friends were keeping all their fingers and toes crossed that, "once the excitement and the glare fades," people would forget about the lies, the fraud, the cooked books, and the document shredding and just lose interest.

And, for a time, it looked like they just might get their wish. "It is unlikely," said Senator Jon Corzine, a Banking Committee member championing reform, in May 2002, "that we will get strong reform unless there is a new event that captures the public imagination." Think about that: the largest corporate bankruptcy in history—up to that time—and the parade of revelations of corruption that followed weren't exciting enough to do the trick.

Then along came WorldCom, which didn't merely capture the public imagination—it grabbed it by the throat. In short order, Sarbanes' comatose initiative was shocked back to life and quickly passed. The passage of the bill and the broadcast-ready perp-walks of Adelphia's John Rigas and WorldCom's Scott Sullivan were supposed to send to us all a clear message that a new age of corporate responsibility had begun.

But the worst problems plaguing our corrupted system remain unaddressed by what is now the Sarbanes-Oxley Act. Stock options, tax havens, and the Chinese wall between research analysts and investment bankers are not dealt with at all in the Act and even the possibility of accounting firms double-dipping as auditors and consultants is only restricted, not banned.

But it's not just that there's a long list of vital reforms still needed. The corporate crimes that have so sickened us are only symptoms of a much larger—and much more insidious—crisis. In a bloodless coup, our government by, for, and of the people has been replaced by the dictatorship of the corporate dollar.

Why Washington Should File for Moral Bankruptcy

"It's just the tip of the iceberg."

That was the mantra of the moment in the second half of 2002, as soothsayers from think tanks, the media, politics, academia and even the business world assessed the wave of corporate scandals.

I disagree. I think those scandals are actually just the tip of the tip of the iceberg because, beyond the financial frauds that have endangered jobs, retirement funds and the stock market, corporate America's profit *uber alles* mindset is also endangering the health and safety of the American people.

The general public is up in arms—and rightly so—about the kind of corporate greed that leads to massive shareholder rip-offs. But shouldn't we be even more irate about corporate greed that puts not just our pocketbooks but public safety and our lives at risk?

"In the long run," said President Bush in a finger-wagging speech to Wall Street in the midst of the scandals, "there's no capitalism without conscience"—an assertion that makes you wonder if his severance package from Harken Energy included a pair of rose-colored glasses. Of course there's capitalism without conscience, Mr. President dear. We're up to our necks in it.

Market forces have no intrinsically moral direction, which

is why, before he wrote *The Wealth of Nations,* Adam Smith wrote *The Theory of Moral Sentiments.* Ethics should precede economics. But it doesn't have to. And it's not inevitable that it will. We know this because we've seen the results of capitalism without conscience: the pollution of the air we breathe, the water we drink, and the food we eat; the endangerment of workers; and the sale of dangerous products—from cars to toys to drugs. All in pursuit of ever-greater profits.

The public good is being auctioned off to the highest bidder.

9/11: When the Pigs Turned into Vultures

No lobbying campaign in history reveals the depths of the corruption of corporate America as hauntingly as the one that followed September 11.

The speed with which corporate America reacted to the glimmer of future profits in the smoldering aftermath of the national crisis was simply atrocious. Before the fires were even out in New York, the lobbyists had swooped down on Capitol Hill to make sure they got their piece of the overstuffed pie they were certain would be served up.

It is now painfully clear that our leaders—both in the current administration and its predecessor—knew that a terrorist attack on American soil would almost surely happen at some point. So, why didn't they do more to protect us? Could it be because the public interest didn't have a gaggle of lobbyists patrolling Congress and the White House offering cash incentives to protect the American people from fanatics and madmen?

If counterterrorism had been an industry doling out large contributions, our political leaders would surely have leapt into action—pushing through legislation to ensure our airports were secure and our intelligence operations were actually collecting intelligence. Instead, the attacks exposed not only how vulnerable our airports are but how vulnerable our system of government is when policy priorities are determined not in response to the public interest but in response to the best-funded interest groups.

In the absence of a flush lobbying organization representing the public good, Congress began its 107th session by tuning its fiddle for the burning of Rome with deeply essential matters like the bankruptcy reform bill. Making its friends in the banking industry happy was clearly a higher priority than homeland security.

Indeed, the nexus of corruption was one of the few aspects of American life not shaken to its foundation by the events of 9/11. The airline industry, for instance, didn't miss a beat in dispatching its lobbyists to take advantage of the national trauma. In deep financial trouble long before the attacks, the airlines were nevertheless able to wrangle a gargantuan $15 billion bailout package from Congress—secured by an army of lobbyists including Linda Daschle. So the $50 million a year the airline industry spends on lobbying, and the $6.8 million it contributed to both parties last election, turned out to be pretty smart investments. As for the actual economic victims of the attacks, the billions did nothing to shield airline workers from massive post-bailout layoffs: 30,000 at Boeing, 27,000 at American Airlines, 20,000 at United, 12,000 at Continental, and 11,000 at US Airways. Nor did they stop US Airways from declaring bankruptcy.

The pharmaceutical industry was equally eager to mine our national suffering for nuggets of gold. Of course, to hear the drug companies tell it, they were as patriotic as Patrick Henry, as generous as Andrew Carnegie, and as selfless as Mother Teresa. Which would be true if Patrick Henry had proclaimed, "Give me liberty or give me profits," Mother Teresa had enlisted Calcutta's lepers as lobbyists, and Andrew Carnegie had spent millions on self-aggrandizing full-page ads.

In a slew of high-level meetings in October and November of 2001 with the likes of homeland security czar Tom Ridge, HHS Secretary Tommy Thompson, and even the president himself, the pharmaceutical industry's chief executives eagerly exploited the panic surrounding the anthrax attacks to make their lifelong legislative dreams come true: lower drug approval standards, less oversight, less regulation and immunity from lawsuits.

This rancid lobbying campaign was sweetened with the cherry-flavored rhetoric of munificent patriotism. The comments of Alan Holmer, the head of PhRMA, a drug industry lobbying group, were particularly Orwellian. "This is not about profits. It is not about patents," he said of efforts to boosts profits by enhancing patents. "It is about making sure we have an adequate supply of medicines available to the American people."

In those dark days, as the country dreaded the delivery of the next suspicious envelope, Peter Dolan, chief executive of Bristol-Meyers, proudly claimed: "We are part of the nation's defense system. As an industry, there is a real opportunity for us to give our resources in a time of great need." Mr. Dolan must have been using a different dictionary, because mine defines "giving" as "making a present of"—not "figuring out a way to make a ton of money while taking advantage of the nation's bioterrorism fears."

Which is exactly what the industry did. Who remembers the headline-grabbing deal that Bayer cut with HHS Secretary Thompson to provide Cipro to the government at the special price of 95 cents a pill, marked down from its previous special price of $1.77? It sounded good—until it came out that it costs Bayer about 20 cents to make a Cipro tablet. The company would still be making hundreds of millions of dollars off the anthrax attacks—to say nothing of the priceless free publicity the rush on Cipro brought. "There will be so much trust," predicted Bayer CEO Helge Wehmeier at the time. "We'll benefit greatly from this." I'm sure America's anthrax victims—the ones still alive, at least—were very happy to hear that.

As if this jagged little pill wasn't hard enough to swallow, it turned out the Federal Trade Commission was investigating charges that Bayer conspired to keep a low-cost generic version of Cipro off the market by illegally paying three of its competitors a total of $200 million.

Think of that: at the very moment the public was freaking out about whether there was going to be enough of the life-saving drug available, Bayer was actually paying other companies hundreds of millions of dollars not to produce it. And the fact that the company just happened to have a spare $200 million sitting around for corporate payola proves how insanely lucrative the drug business is.

Joining the shameless mob of business interests smelling blood in the water after 9/11 was Big Steel. Wrapping themselves in the flag, steel industry lobbyists descended on Washington in search of new tariffs on imported steel. They insisted that the controversial levies were a matter of national security.

Senator Rick Santorum, the Pennsylvania Republican, who is a major recipient of Big Steel donations, said after the attacks: "This is an industry with significant national security implications. It's important from the whole basic concept of maintaining manufacturing in this country. It's important to have a vibrant domestic source of steel." Notice the emotional appeal to some vague "basic concept." Like agribusiness, steelmakers like to tap into America's image of itself as a country that makes stuff and grows things, even though the less manly service sector actually constitutes 80% of our nation's economy.

Of course, President Bush was calling steel "a national security issue" even before the War on Terror. Proving himself a true Man of Steel, in August 2001, having already ordered a review of steel policy, he ranted and raved to an appreciative crowd of steelworkers in Pittsburgh, demanding that foreign producers cut their own exports, and repeating the national security canard.

In truth, this national security argument is red, white, and blue rubbish. Calling it "absolute baloney," Robert Crandall, a steel expert at the Brookings Institution, says that one or two mills could provide all the steel needed for national defense in any conceivable emergency.

While all these special interests reacted to 9/11 with an outstretched hand, the food industry responded with a closed mind. Its lobbyists—including trade groups like the National Food Processors Association, the Food Marketing Institute, and the American Frozen Food Institute—fought a guerilla campaign to stall the Public Health Security and Bioterrorism Bill, which included increased inspections of imported food, a requirement for food manufacturers to register with the government and authorizing the FDA to seize suspect food without having to obtain a court order.

But as bald-faced as each of these groups was in its post-9/11 special pleading, our political leaders outdid them.

Far from it disrupting their normal run of unabashed corporate toadying, the war on terrorism enhanced it. Indeed, it gave our leaders cover to put forward their favorite answer to many a problem America faces: a massive corporate giveaway. And they even had the gall to call it patriotism. Others, using the English language more rigorously, called it war profiteering.

The so-called economic stimulus package that passed the House just over a month after September 11 would have been scurrilous in times of prosperity. But in a time of national calamity it was, quite simply, grotesque.

The stimulus package was little more than a rehashed corporate wish list, doling out $115 billion in tax breaks to big business and the wealthiest taxpayers, and a comparatively measly $14 billion to poor and moderate-income families in the form of tax rebates and unemployment benefits. And while the tax cuts for the haves were permanent, those for the have-nots were good for only one year.

What's more, the money given to corporate America was given without conditions—not tax credits tied to investments, but handouts more likely to end up in CEOs' compensation packages than back in the economy.

All you really needed to know about the true nature of the economic stimulus package could be found in a largely unnoticed provision that made permanent a gaping tax loophole that was about to expire. It allowed multinational corporations such as GE and Ford to preserve forever a key weapon in the corporate tax dodger's armory: the freedom to shift profits overseas. Tell me, how exactly is providing incentives to keep money out of our economy supposed to stimulate our economy?

The House bill was so outrageous that even some top GOP officials balked. In a rare slip from the party line, Treasury Secretary Paul O'Neill colorfully criticized it as "show business." Representative Greg Ganske (R-Iowa), one of seven Republicans who voted against the bill, labeled it "an early Christmas card" for "already profitable corporations." And the president's ornery budget director, Mitch Daniels, informed the nation in a poetic outburst that "the corral gates" have been blown open and "the animals are running loose." The galloping beasts in this case were corporate lobbyists and their chums on the Hill.

The juiciest goody in this box of corporate bonbons was a retroactive repeal of the corporate alternative minimum tax, a treat that would lead to $25 billion in instant corporate rebate checks to needy companies such as IBM (slated to get $1.4 billion), GM ($833 million), and GE ($671 million).

Of the $25 billion refund, over $6.3 billion was earmarked for just 14 corporations. Predictably, these 14 lucky winners were regular and generous political donors. Over the last 10 years, they've poured almost $15 million in soft money into the national committees of both parties. And, as always, investments made in politicians are never wasted.

Such a blatant quid pro quo is so indefensible that even the main champions of the stimulus package—the grandly named Economic Security and Recovery Act—didn't try very hard to justify it. Take Representative Dick Armey's wan effort on *Meet the Press*. There he was, half-heartedly trying to convince Tim Russert that we needed these massive tax cuts because the last round of massive tax cuts were not geared to stimulating the economy. Really? Wasn't that him at a House subcommittee hearing a few months earlier, selling the last tax cut bill as "just the shot in the arm that this economy needs"? But if something isn't working, why try more of it?

Armey then treated Russert and the rest of us to a lecture on how big corporate giveaways are the best way to create new jobs. Unfortunately, the facts don't bear him out. The $15 billion Congress handed the airline industry didn't keep it from laying off over 150,000 workers. Armey went on to promise that the new stimulus package "will create 170,000 new jobs next year alone." At the time of Armey's hopeful pronouncement 7.8 million were unemployed in the country; by fall 2002 that figure had risen to more than 8 million.

So let history record that, after September 11, our leaders brought the nation together and decided to fight the war on terrorism by making business lunches fully tax-deductible, offering billions to panhandling American businesses, and levying no taxes on corporate profits patriotically funneled offshore. Call it Operation Enduring Avarice. It's enough to put a lump in your throat.

Washington's consistent siding with the wealthy and the influential over the public has led to a fundamental breakdown of our democracy. What follows is a closer look at four stunning examples: corporate America's fight to end environmental protections and the craven corporate gluttony of the pharmaceutical, steel, and farming industries.

The Nexus vs. the Environment: Dirty Politics

How have President Bush and his corporate backers worked to undermine the environment? Let me count the ways. . . . Um, I better go get my calculator.

Since January 2001, the president and his energy-industry-friendly appointees (an understatement akin to calling mosquitoes "blood-friendly") have trashed the environment through dozens of actions. They have (take a breath, through a gas mask, if you've got one) abandoned a campaign promise to regulate carbon dioxide emissions, suspended an executive order preventing repeat polluters from obtaining government contracts, proposed reversing a ban on road building in 60 million acres of national forest, canceled a deadline for automakers to develop prototypes for high-mileage cars, rolled back safeguards for storing nuclear waste, shifted Superfund hazardous-waste cleanup costs from polluters to taxpayers, blocked a program to stem the discharge of raw sewage into America's waters, undermined protections for national parks and national monuments, and put forward a plan to reduce the likelihood of forest fires by allowing the timber industry easier access to federal lands in order to chop down trees. And that's just a partial list.

From arsenic in our water to carbon dioxide in our air; from undermining Kyoto to promoting drilling in Alaska; from refusing to raise auto mileage standards to handing the keys of our energy policy over to corporate interests, this administration has done exactly what Big Business wanted it to do.

Nowhere is this more evident than in the president's flip-flop on carbon dioxide.

During his run for the White House, candidate Bush made an unequivocal pledge to—read my lips—"require all power plants to meet clean air standards in order to reduce emission of sulfur dioxide, nitrogen oxide, mercury and carbon dioxide."

But soon after assuming office, responding to pressure from energy industry lobbyists, the president removed a line about carbon dioxide and the importance of clean air from his maiden speech to a joint session of Congress. The question became: Was this merely a rhetorical concession or a preview of a full-scale surrender to anti-environmental zealots?

The answer became all too clear when it was revealed there was an e-mail circulating among members of the energy crowd's "Cooler Heads Coalition" high-fiving themselves on this "famous victory"—i.e. convincing the president to abandon his one major pledge on the environment.

The president claimed that in executing his CO_2 flip-flop he was "responding to realities" and taking care "not to take actions that could harm consumers." But there in black and white in the e-mail was the "reality" he was actually responding to: "President Bush and Vice President Cheney have made the right decision . . . with *a little good advice from their friends.*"

The gloating was nauseating, but not nearly as nauseating as the vice president's claim that Bush's campaign position on carbon dioxide was a mistake because carbon dioxide isn't really a pollutant. By way of a reply, one can't do better than quote David Doniger of the Natural Resources Defense Council: "If carbon dioxide isn't a pollutant, maybe ketchup is a vegetable after all."

It's worth noting that when faced with a similarly vociferous campaign of opposition from the energy industry, the president's father had the guts to resist and do the right thing, signing an acid rain program into law as part of the Clean Air Act of 1990. But where "41" stood firm, "43" caved. The younger Bush's enemies might say it's the difference between a decorated WWII pilot and an AWOL Air National Guardsman. But others know it's simply the fact that campaign contributions from the energy industry to the Grand Old Party have amounted to an astounding $185,022,044 since 1989.

The assault on the environment continued. Limits on arsenic cramping your profitability? No problem. Gone. No more arsenic limits. Regulations about how to dispose of toxic waste putting a dent in your annual report? Say no more. Toss it wherever you'd like. That handy river, for instance.

This president's record, both in Austin and in Washington, clearly demonstrates that he puts the profits of industry ahead of the health and safety of people—no matter how devastating and long-term the consequences. Just talk about how the science "isn't conclusive," cite a few "experts" on the industry payroll, and mention jobs a lot. Besides, the consequences of such policies—you know, leukemia, brain tumors, auto-immune diseases, workplace accident rates—probably won't show up until after the next election.

As governor of Texas, Bush signed an "audit privilege" law that allowed companies to "keep secret all information about toxic chemical releases, spills and other environmental problems"—even from state regulators and citizens trying to sue. If it's the people's air, water, and health, how can one possibly assert "privilege" in violating them? But, then, Bush and his cronies are used to taking privilege for granted.

If California had had an audit privilege law, then the thousands of people poisoned in the case made famous by Erin Brockovich could never have sought and received legal redress. In Los Angeles, Chromium 6—the same carcinogenic chemical that had a starring role in the film—was detected in the water system at levels that spurred scientific debate over safety limits. The Brockovich case involved hundreds of victims; those affected by contaminated water in the L.A. Basin could number in the hundreds of thousands.

That's why the public's right to know is so fundamental—and so strenuously resisted by the chemical industry. When a group in Ohio, for instance, spent $150,000 trying to pass a right-to-know ballot measure in 1992, Big Chemical poured in $4.8 million to defeat it. Such victory-at-any-price tactics have proved extremely effective—the last right-to-know initiative to pass was in California in 1986.

Of course, if they're not doing anything wrong, why would they care so much if the public, through its regulatory agencies, double-checked? I guess "trust but verify" doesn't apply domestically. More like "trust and drink up."

The industry has been equally effective at preventing government regulation of any kind for all but a small fraction of the 80,000 synthetic chemicals that have been created in the last 50 years. Instead, we rely on the industry's "self-regulation." The problem is, the honor system never works with people who have no shame.

To try to keep profits soaring, the chemical industry has stepped up its toxic contributions to our political class. After all, the right to pollute our air and water system isn't free. It requires that you first pollute our public policy system. A 1980 industry memo fretted over the polluters' "political muscle, how much we've got, and how we can get more." Clearly, they found out. Since then, the industry has doled out $122 million in political contributions—and has been flexing its political muscle since dollar one.

In March 2001, Bill Moyers, one of the Fourth Estate's preeminent defenders of true democracy, produced *Trade Secrets*, an explosive PBS documentary that used a million pages of internal chemical industry documents to expose the long-term cover-up of the poisonous effects of various chemicals on unsuspecting workers and consumers. Most of these chemicals are still unregulated.

Obtained by lawyers representing Elaine Ross, whose husband died of brain cancer at the age of 46 after working at a chemical plant in Louisiana for 23 years, the documents—many of them stamped "secret" and "strictly confidential"—conjured up a terrifying moral universe in which deadly hazards to human life were nothing more than impediments to ever healthier bottom lines. Unfortunately, it's also the universe our political and corporate leaders are forcing most of us to live in, whether we want to or not.

The Chemical Papers, as the documents at the heart of *Trade Secrets* were called, are the toxic twin to the infamous Tobacco Papers. With any justice, they should have turned the chemical companies they've exposed—including Dow, DuPont, Shell, Conoco, and B.F. Goodrich—into the political pariahs that tobacco companies have become. But justice is the one thing the industry has been happy to ban.

Consider a 1959 Dow Chemical memo which conceded that extended exposure to one of the company's products was "going to produce rather appreciable injury," then shockingly added: "As you can appreciate, this opinion is not ready for dissemination yet, and I would appreciate it if you would hold it in confidence." In other words, this stuff causes cancer—but keep it under your hat.

When I met with Moyers shortly after the documentary was aired, he spoke with authority and passion about the "vast chemical experiment" being shamefully conducted on our children.

"I was walking in Central Park with my grandson," Moyers told me back then, "and he asked, 'How old are you, Pa?' I told him that I was 66. Then he looked up at the sky and asked:

'What is the world going to be like when I'm 66?' And the truth is, I couldn't tell him. We just don't know." And we even have to fight for the *right* to know.

But what we do know is that breast cancer, brain cancer in kids, testicular cancer in teens, infertility, and learning disabilities are all on the rise. And that this isn't just a coincidence. We also know that if we ended the noxious collusion between the chemical industry and our political overlords, Bill Moyers' grandson would have a better chance of getting to see what the world will be like when he's 66.

And these anti-environmental zealots are no longer just throwing cash in from the outside, influencing policy from industry-sponsored think tanks. They're now directing policy much more comfortably—from right inside the administration. Take Lynn Scarlett. Before being tapped by Bush for assistant secretary at the Department of the Interior, she was CEO of the Reason Foundation, a think tank promoting less regulation. Before becoming an environmental regulator, Ms. Scarlett described environmental regulations as a form of "Green punishment." It's unclear whether "green" means "environmental" or "monetary." Although to Ms. Scarlett the two are probably one and the same.

Then there's John Graham, named to head the Office of Information and Regulatory Affairs after a heroic career dedicated to fighting public health and safety rules. As head of the Harvard Center for Risk Analysis, he argued against the EPA's efforts to regulate dioxin. And pesticides. And radon. And second-hand tobacco smoke. And, of course, asbestos. His arguments have invariably been based on a perverse cost-benefit analysis that somehow "proves" that everything that is bad for you is actually good. (Though I wonder how many asbestos milk shakes or radon-laced cookies Mr. Graham whips up for his own children.)

And the president apparently believes it, too. What else can explain the front-page stories in April 2001, trumpeting the Bush administration's decision to end mandatory testing for salmonella in hamburger meat served in federal school lunch programs? Such was the outpouring of indignation and incredulity that, within 24 hours, the decision was reversed and blamed on— who else?—a subordinate at the Department of Agriculture. "Somebody made a mistake," said department spokesman Kevin Herglotz.

But even in the incredibly unlikely event that it was just "a mistake," it was a revealing one. And it was entirely in keeping with this administration's ethos that perceives all environmental and public health regulations as government coercion designed to interfere with the free market. Why else would you even consider abandoning a policy that saw a 50% drop in salmonella contamination in the ten months before Bush decided to reverse it? And why else would you target the Environmental Protection Agency for a $300 million budget cut?

This decision didn't happen in a vacuum. There was one other factor: intense lobbying by the meat industry to ditch the testing—even though salmonella causes 1.4 million illnesses and 600 deaths a year. The industry's business-friendly alternative included irradiating the beef to kill the bacteria—which would have put a whole new spin on that cafeteria classic, "mystery meat." Today's special: Nuke Burgers and Toxic Joes.

The Energy Task Force

Then, of course, there's the sorry excuse for administration outreach known as Dick Cheney's Energy Task Force. In early 2002, after more than a year of stonewalling by the administration, the membership of the taskforce was finally disclosed. It was instantly clear that it was the oil, coal, and gas lobby that had been doing all the thinking, taking over both long-term policy-making and day-to-day environmental decisions. The result has been a massive regulatory rollback and juicy profits for industry fat cats. Cheney effectively privatized the nation's energy policy.

Along with doing everything in its considerable power to find a way to realize its obsessive dream of drilling in the Arctic National Wildlife Refuge, the Bush administration, cheered on by an all-star team of lobbyists, has also worked tirelessly to promote an energy plan that is long on building new power plants but pathetically indifferent, even hostile, to the idea of conservation. It doesn't even address the single most obvious and effective step we can take to conserve energy: increasing auto fuel-efficiency standards.

Instead of supporting the effort by senators John Kerry (D-Mass.) and John McCain (R-Ariz.) to gradually increase fuel standards over the next 13 years, in March 2002 the White House and 62 senators joined in an unholy alliance with carmakers and autoworker unions to kill the plan, which would have saved about 2.5 million barrels of oil a day. That, roughly, is the amount we currently import from the entire Middle East. Isn't the terrible cost of our oil dependency on the Middle East obvious enough to justify standing up to the auto industry?

Remember the wide-eyed walk the president took in 2001 through a Department of Energy showcase of energy-saving devices, including that triumph of American ingenuity, a state-of-the-art cell-phone charger? After the tour, he grandly announced over $85 million in grants to encourage the development of renewable-energy technologies. Sure, it sounded good, but it was classic Bush zero-sum grandstanding—it simply restored the $85 million in funding for renewable energy the president had previously recommended cutting. It was like a carjacker wanting the key to the city for returning one of the two cars he just boosted.

It was also a drop in the bucket when compared to the roughly $1 billion in tax incentives, credits, and other deductions handed out to the president's buddies in the oil, coal, nuclear, and gas industries since he took office. To announce those, by the way, there was no press conference.

It's more than a little ironic that, in his private life, President Bush is actually a leader in consumer conservation. His Crawford, Texas, ranch has been described as "an environmentally sensitive showplace" designed with "state-of-the-art energy efficiency." The house is filled with energy-saving devices, while the lawn and orchard are irrigated with recycled water.

Isn't it time that Bush starts preaching to the nation what he practices back at the ranch? And isn't it time that the members of Congress who betrayed the health and safety of their country are punished? On election day, voters have the opportunity to elbow aside the lobbyists. If Washington insists on importing its thinking, we need to make sure the ideas aren't stamped "Made by Big Business."

The Other Chapter 11

Though the reform-free "Bankruptcy Reform Act" would make it much harder for the average person to declare Chapter 11, it's all the rage on Wall Street these days. All the best corporations are doing it. But there is a different kind of Chapter 11, and one that poses a real danger to our democracy.

The "other" Chapter 11 is an obscure clause buried within the 555-page North American Free Trade Agreement, the trade treaty that encompasses the United States, Mexico, and Canada. In theory, the clause is designed to compensate companies from the three countries that signed the agreement if one of the two other governments seizes a company's property. But we don't live in a theoretical world.

In the real world, the lawyers who helped draft NAFTA inserted language that makes it possible for companies to seek compensation from any one of the other two signatory nations if regulations cause a dip in their future bottom line. So, for example, a U.S. company can sue the Canadian or Mexican government for compensation if it's losing money in Canada or Mexico because of government regulations in that country.

About two dozen companies have already cashed in, or are in the process of trying to cash in, on this other kind of Chapter 11. In Mexico, when a U.S. firm's efforts to reopen a toxic waste dump south of the border were thwarted by local citizens convinced that the noxious landfill had led to a boom in cancer cases in the region, the company, Metalclad, a waste-management company from California, invoked Chapter 11 and was awarded $16 million in compensation from the Mexican government.

And because this is an international treaty, American companies aren't the only ones allowed to rob the till. Methanex, a Canadian corporation, sued the U.S. government for $970 million because California had the temerity to phase out a cancer-causing gasoline additive the company produced. The NAFTA panel asked for more conclusive evidence that the ban was unjustified, but did not dismiss the case. And the threat of such lawsuits continues. As they say, no good energy industry regulation goes unpunished.

What this ludicrous provision really does is give multinational corporations the right to undercut the public interest, do an end-run around our justice system, and jeopardize our health and the safety of the communities we live in.

Taxpayers would be forced to pay off the polluters who are giving them cancer. And since the cases are ruled on behind closed doors, by a secret NAFTA tribunal whose decisions are not subject to appeal in U.S. courts, we may never know the full extent of the damage done.

That giant sucking sound you hear is the public good being slurped up by voracious corporate interests.

Even when it's not fully exploited, this provision works its magic. The mere threat of these mega-buck claims is now all that's needed to intimidate state and local government officials considering new regulations. In *Trading Democracy*, his disturbing documentary on the subject, Bill Moyers reveals how big tobacco used its high-powered lobbyists and the threat of a massive Chapter 11 lawsuit to bully the Canadian government into backing off on its plans to regulate cigarette packaging. These kinds of legal strong-arm tactics are not exactly earning us a lot of good will abroad.

As William Greider, author of *Who Will Tell the People*, put it: "If you're a civil servant, or even a political leader, you've gotta think twice when a corporate lawyer comes to you and says, quite forcefully, we're gonna hit you for half a billion dollars if you do this."

The Nexus and the Pharmaceutical Industry: Money Is the Drug

But, hey, even if we have to pick up the tab for being poisoned and sickened, at least once we're diagnosed we can always take some new high-tech drugs to make us better, right? Wrong. If the disease doesn't get you, the cure might. The toxic marriage of money and political influence doesn't end once it's made us sick—it continues right into the ostensible healing stage, too. Each year, tens of thousands of people are killed by the giant drug companies, whose wanton disregard for human life is only matched by the tobacco companies and firearms manufacturers.

With more than 100 deaths linked to its best-selling cholesterol drug, Baycol, Bayer was finally forced to pull it off the market. Though not until Baycol earned Bayer profits of

$720 million in 2001 alone. Bayer was earning $7.2 million for every death its product caused by leaving it on the shelves. Or, depending on the way you look at it, a few more deaths were just the price of doing business.

But what about the F.D.A., the agency whose mission it is to protect us against just this very thing? Not to worry. Thanks to mega-millions spent on campaign contributions and lobbying, the pharmaceutical industry—Washington's longtime 800-pound gorilla on steroids—has been able to skirt government oversight of its patent-extending and price-gouging schemes by muscling politicians into doing its bidding. For every disease the drug-companies cure by developing a new drug, they develop a new way to contaminate our political system.

But nothing they've done in the U.S. compares to their handiwork in Africa. There the U.S. drug companies deliberately allowed the deadly AIDS epidemic to spread while they waged a legal battle to keep low-cost versions of life-saving anti-AIDS drugs from the millions dying of the disease. In 2001 the public outcry about these dirty deeds finally reached critical mass, shaming the drug companies' Washington lickspittles into looking at their shoes when their longtime patrons came calling for more favors. The industry was forced to relent, dropping its lawsuit and begrudgingly lowering the price of AIDS drugs to poor countries. At least they were able to make millions of dollars in profits first. Too bad about the hundreds of thousands of people who had to die. But maybe that's the Gloomy Gus way to see it, and the pharmaceutical executives are glass-half-full kind of people.

They'd have to be, considering their latest scheme. At a cost to consumers of billions of dollars, the drug companies are using American courts to stall the sale of generic versions of some of their most popular and sorely needed products. Here's how it works: When a drug's patent is about to expire, the patent-holding company wards off the oncoming competition by filing numerous costly frivolous lawsuits against anyone who even thinks of making a low-cost, and perfectly legal, version of the pill. The drug company doesn't really expect to win, but the suit can delay the generic version from hitting the market for years—allowing the patent holder to rake in billions in additional, competition-free sales. Of course, to the more than 41 million people uninsured, the lack of an available generic version of a drug means the lack of the drug altogether. And the beautiful part (at least to the glass-half-full crowd) is that the public gets to pay twice: we pay for unnecessarily high-priced drugs, and we pay for the court system the drug companies are exploiting to keep us paying the high price.

A bill to put a stop to this outrageous abuse of our legal process was introduced by senators John McCain and Charles Schumer and passed the Senate with 78 votes. Originally considered a long shot, the legislation gained momentum, helped, ironically, by the support of a number of other corporations that have recognized that this kind of patent thievery is actually costing them hundreds of millions of dollars in over-inflated health care costs. And in a rocky economy, little things like hundreds of millions of dollars get noticed. Executives at General Motors, for instance, figured out that the drug manufacturers' maneuvering to maintain market exclusivity on five top-selling drugs—including Paxil, Prilosec, and Wellbutrin—after the patents had expired had cost GM over $200 million.

For the first time, it's not just voiceless millions in Africa or poor people on Medicaid who are feeling the sting of the drug companies' shameful ability to bilk the system. It's powerful corporations that pay top dollar for receptive ears in Washington.

Not only has the pharmaceutical industry brought on the wrath of other businesses, it's now finding itself where no business wants to be: in the crosshairs of federal investigators. No fewer than 20 drug companies—including Bristol-Myers, Eli

Lilly, Pfizer, and Bayer—are being investigated by government agencies, including the Justice Department, the Food and Drug Administration, the Federal Trade Commission, and the Department of Health and Human Services.

One company, TAP Pharmaceutical Products, has already been fined $875 million for "fraudulent schemes for pricing, sales, and marketing" of its prostate cancer drug Lupron—the largest health-care fraud settlement in history.

If signing off on a false balance sheet will soon be enough to supposedly land a CEO in the slammer for 20 years, what should the sentence be for allowing liver damage and deaths in the service of milking a few extra months' worth of profits out of a defective, deadly product, as Wyeth did with its drug Duract? Or how much time should executives do who sign off on working conditions that lead to 56,000 deaths a year from on-the-job accidents or work-related illnesses such as black lung and asbestos poisoning?

Unfortunately, there is not yet a vaccine to immunize our elected watchdogs in Washington against the drug companies' money and clout. Outright removal of the infected politicians is often the only option, but that can be very expensive. The pharmaceutical industry spent a whopping $177 million on lobbying in just the last two years. And of their 623 registered lobbyists, more than half are former members of Congress or former government employees. Which is nice, because if you're a young politician selling off your vote and your integrity, it's easier if there's a seasoned veteran involved who was once in your shoes to smooth the process. It's kind of like a Big Brother program.

And it works the other way, too. For instance, Defense Secretary Donald Rumsfeld was formerly CEO of drug giant G.D. Searle, and White House Budget Director Mitch Daniels was a senior vice president at Eli Lilly. It's all one big happy family—and one with lots of family gatherings, called political fund-raisers.

KEEP AWAY FROM CHILDREN . . .
AND ADULTS

Both the number and the rate of product recalls have been rising steadily. According to the Consumer Product Safety Commission, which has jurisdiction over more than 15,000 types of products, there were more recalls in 2001—344—than in most years during the previous decade. The Agriculture Department, which regulates foodstuffs, and the National Highway Traffic Safety Administration, which does the same for vehicles and associated products, also report sharply rising numbers of recalls. In a single week in the spring of 2002, 919,000 child car seats; 124,000 children's soap-making kits; 23,000 pounds of turkey meat; 14,000 bottles of a nutritional supplement; and 7,500 exercise machines were recalled for being unsafe.

COMPANY	PRODUCT
Johnson & Johnson	Stopped selling its heartburn drug Propulsid in March 2000 after it had been connected with 80 deaths.
Wyeth	Pulled painkiller Duract off shelves after it was linked to liver-related deaths. Despite a 2002 study revealing that women using Prempro, Wyeth's highly profitable hormone replacement drug, displayed an increased risk of breast cancer, heart attacks, strokes, and blood clots, the company continues to market the drug.
Bayer	In August 2001, Bayer withdrew its popular—and highly profitable—cholesterol drug Baycol from the market. Over a hundred deaths have been linked to the drug.

Schering-Plough	Alleged to have produced asthma inhalers that didn't contain asthma-fighting medication—an omission linked to 17 deaths, including that of a 10-year-old boy.
ConAgra	Recalled nearly 19 million pounds of ground beef in July 2002 contaminated with the E.coli bacteria. The tainted meat has been connected with 47 cases of illness in 14 states, and one death in Ohio.
Pacific Gas & Electric	Starting in the 1950s, PG&E dumped carcinogen-laced water into unlined ponds, from where it was able to seep into Hinkley, California's water supply. Residents of the town were not told about the contamination until the late 1980s. In 1996 PG&E made a $333 million settlement with them and the story later became *Erin Brockovich*. Since then a broader case has been filed against PG&E in other towns, and fifty people have died, lawyers allege, from cancer, kidney and liver diseases and respiratory problems.
Graco	Recalled nearly one million child car seats because metal hooks and bars that link the seat to the base may be missing and could fail in a crash or sudden stop. The recall occurred weeks after Graco removed the seat from stores without informing consumers of the problem.
Tyco	35 million indoor fire sprinklers were recalled because they may not work in an actual fire.

Kmart	Recalled about 24,000 Martha Stewart Everyday brand tea kettles because boiling water could be expelled from the spout.
Honeywell	In October 2001, Honeywell agreed to pay a civil penalty of $800,000 to settle allegations that Duracraft Corp.—which Honeywell purchased in 1996—failed to report problems with a number of its products to the Consumer Product Safety Commission in a timely manner.
Roche Pharmaceuticals	Although Roche warns that Accutane can cause serious birth defects, between 1982 (the year Accutane hit the market) and 2000 nearly 2,000 women became pregnant while using the drug. Most of those pregnancies ended in abortion, but of the 383 babies born, nearly half had birth defects.
Bridgestone	The company pulled 6.5 million Firestone tires in 2000 after road safety authorities linked the tires to 271 deaths and over 750 injuries.
American Home Products	American Home Products finally settled a $3.75 billion lawsuit in January 2002 to resolve claims that its wildly popular obesity drug combination, Fen-Phen, was connected to heart-valve disease. Over 6 million people took the drug before it was withdrawn from the market. The FDA has linked Fen-Phen and Redux, another diet drug made by the company, to over 300 deaths.

Daisy Manufacturing	In October 2001 the Consumer Product Safety Commission filed a lawsuit against Daisy in an attempt to compel the company to inform consumers that two of its airgun lines are defective and pose considerable risk of injury or even death. Daisy has refused to voluntarily recall these guns.

Standing Up for Steel

"Stand Up For Steel." That was the slogan of Big Steel's recent campaign and, as silly as it sounds, it worked. Goaded by super-lobbyist Ed Gillespie, Congress and President Bush did stand up for steel. In fact, they practically jumped up and down, raising tariffs on imported steel by 30% in March of 2002. Gillespie's old boss, Commerce Secretary Donald Evans, served as point man on steel protection. Evans' primary challenge was to overcome the warnings of Bush's economic advisors that the president's much-ballyhooed—not least by Bush himself—free trade credentials were now in laughingstock territory.

But Gillespie, aided by other major-league lobbyists like former GOP Representative Vin Weber, and his partner, former Democratic Representative Vic Fazio, carried the day. A representative of the steel industry even gushed, "What Ed did was play a role we needed and which the White House needed. He had the confidence of both parties. He was the bridge." Which, translated, means: "He lied to the president, inflated our concerns and invented a crisis on our behalf." "The bridge" was a big money-pit boondoggle granted by the president to the moribund steel industry. Think of it as a Bridge to the Nineteenth Century.

But getting such a useless hulk built wasn't easy. The battle to limit lower-cost steel imports pitted powerful interests, and their lobbyists, against one another. Arrayed against the old-line steel companies like Bethlehem Steel, the US Steel Group of USX Corp, and Wheeling-Pittsburgh and the steelworkers union were small, more efficient companies, like Nucor, known as mini-mills, and representatives of the many industries that consume steel, like automakers and producers of heavy machinery.

Going by the numbers, the steel users had the leverage. Almost 12 million people work in their factories, as opposed to just 160,000 for traditional Rust Belt steel makers. The government bailout of the floundering steel companies will inevitably cost jobs in other industries—as many as eight for every steel job saved. Higher steel costs, of perhaps 10% or more, will inevitably be passed along to ordinary consumers when they buy a car, a toaster, or a new house.

But all endangered workers, it's clear, are not created equal, at least in the eyes of the gods of Washington. Big Steel happens to be concentrated in several key swing states like Pennsylvania, Ohio, West Virginia, and Indiana. It wouldn't take much to tilt the balance of power in these places in 2004.

The steel industry's startling success in hustling the Bush administration into doing its retrograde, anti–free trade bidding was due to a robust Beltway strategy honed over twenty years of trading money for favors. The efforts of lobbyists like Gillespie and Weber, who stage-managed the kind of stunts that impress election-minded lawmakers—like organizing a protest march of 25,000 steelworkers and their supporters in Washington and arranging for the president to attend a steelworkers' picnic shortly before Labor Day—cost the industry $5 million in 2000 and $2.7 million in the first half of 2001.

The lobbyists were also on hand to help Bush frame his position in politically justifiable terms. Of course, it wasn't the truth—his position couldn't be justified by the truth. What they did was provide him with the most politically acceptable lie. Which was, as the president said repeatedly, that some action was necessary to counter an "import surge," even though imports have actually declined 27% in the last five years. Bush, and the industry behind him, know that the lie might be noted here and there, but, after a day of bad press, the press moves on. The subsidies and the bad policy, however, stay for good.

What's more, old line steelmakers are ill-suited to any defense role when compared with the more flexible and modern mini-mills, which produce as much steel as the dinosaurs do with their Jurassic technology. And at a far lower cost.

There were also, the president said, national security consequences to the steel welfare plan. True enough—but they just weren't the ones he cited. Key allies in the war on terrorism in Europe and Asia howled in protest at the new tariffs. Countries like Russia, South Korea, and Japan will all take an enormous hit from higher prices on imports here, while European countries have agreed to forgo retaliatory tariffs in exchange for "exemptions" for about 60% of European steel imports adversely affected by the tariffs. And all this interventionist back and forth from an administration whose leader vowed during the campaign: "I would be a free-trading president."

Anne O. Krueger, deputy managing director of the International Monetary Fund, noted in her report on the industry: "The American Big Steel industry has been the champion lobbyist and seeker of protection. It provides a key and disillusioning example of the ability of special interests to lobby in Washington for measures which hurt the general public and help a very small group."

Raising Pigs for Fun and Profit

On May 13, 2002, President Bush signed the Farm Security and Rural Investment Act, and thereby reneged on a campaign pledge to wean farmers from subsidies. If the understandably low-key event had been any more dour, after signing the bill into law those in attendance might have expected the president to read some type of eulogy.

As well he should have. The Farm Bill, which will cost taxpayers around $190 billion over the next ten years, was the latest victory of an unlikely band of corporate hogs who have long been glutting themselves as the recipients of America's largest welfare program: farmers. But these aren't Ma and Pa Kettle, *Green Acres,* or *Grapes of Wrath* farmers. These are enormous, politically savvy and powerful corporations—like ConAgra, Cargill, and Smithfield Farms—that are riding a subsidy-funded wave of consolidation. In agribusiness as elsewhere, the rich just keep getting richer. And thus more powerful. And thus more subsidized.

The top 10% of the farming business receives two-thirds of all farm aid, which amounted to $29.8 billion in 2000. The bottom 80% of farmers get less than a sixth of the subsidy pile, and 60% of America's farmers get no aid at all. In 2000, 154 farms got checks from Uncle Sam for more than $1 million. Fifteen Fortune 500 companies, including Chevron, Dupont, John Hancock Mutual Life Insurance, and Westvaco, were among the million dollar jackpot winners. At least 12 members of Congress also got crop support money, as did poor struggling sons of the sod like David Rockefeller, Charles Schwab, and Ted Turner. Even newsman Sam Donaldson, a fearless tilter at the windmills of political hypocrisy, collected a total of just over

$100,000 between 1993 and 1995 for his mohair goat ranch in New Mexico.

Expanding Corporate Welfare
As We Know It

The overarching interest of the unholy alliance is to pad the pockets of the business elite at the expense of the public. And that has not been changed by either the events of September 11 or by the shock waves of the financial scandals. There is no greater irony—or hypocrisy—than the hard line taken against welfare for the working poor by the same people who don't bat an eyelid at hundreds of billions of dollars doled out in corporate welfare.

In the spring of 2001, President Bush breathlessly made the release of his new budget sound like a watershed event. "This budget offers a new vision for our nation," he proclaimed. "It also represents a new way of doing business in Washington, and a new way of thinking."

Apparently, Representative Tom DeLay and Speaker Denny Hastert didn't get the memo.

According to complaints filed with the Federal Election Commission and the Justice Department by Judicial Watch, DeLay solicited potential donors—just days before Bush's announcement—with the opportunity to "be invited to meetings with top Bush administration officials, where your opinions on issues like tax reform will be heard."

For his part, Hastert dangled the promise of donors becoming "special advisors" on tax policy who would be "introduced to the who's who in Washington"—including Vice President Cheney. Hastert even threw in Budget Director Mitch Daniels as a bonus (limit one per customer). No mention of whether that special (interest) blend of White House coffee would be served.

Indeed, this "new" way of doing business has taken Washington by storm, despite Bush's boast that "this budget funds our needs without the fat." Every lobbyist on K Street—and every member of Congress who has been on the receiving end of corporate largesse—has been fighting, quite successfully as it happens, to ensure the "fat" remains in the budget.

So what's become of the White House declaration of war on corporate welfare? To test the accuracy of Bush's boast, take a look at the corporate "Dirty Dozen," 12 of the most galling government giveaways targeted back in 1997 by a broad-based alliance of activists and members of Congress calling themselves the Stop Corporate Welfare Coalition.

Most of the 12 are still doing just fine—fat, sassy and continuing to gorge themselves at the public trough.

Witness the Market Access Program, a pricey corporate-assistance program that fritters away taxpayer dollars to promote the products of hard-luck cases such as Dole, Sunkist, and Ocean Spray. When word leaked out that MAP was in the White House's crosshairs, some well-connected nexus member must have called off the hit because, lo and behold, here it is alive and well—with its $90 million budget due to more than double by 2006. So much for the war on corporate welfare.

But take heart, there has been at least one cosmetic change: the money no longer goes directly to the impoverished corporations but is laundered through trade associations such as the National Watermelon Promotion Board, the American Peanut Council, the Catfish Institute, and Asparagus USA.

Then there's the Partnership for a New Generation of Vehicles, which poured $1.5 billion into the pockets of needy domestic automakers like Ford, General Motors, and Daimler-Chrysler to develop a "Supercar." And for that, they obviously needed some supermoney. President Bush has abandoned the eight-year effort—which has failed to put even a single vehicle, super or otherwise, on the road—in favor of the Freedom Car, a partnership between the federal government and Detroit's Big Three automakers with a 2002 budget of $127 million and a requested budget for 2003 totaling over $150 million. As the Natural Resources Defense Council put it: "We can't afford another research program that just gives billions of dollars in subsidies to the automobile industry with no commitment from it to actually produce advanced vehicles for consumers to buy." Especially since we already have electric and hybrid car technology. Indeed, when I'm driving my Toyota Prius—a hybrid car—I know that there is no reason not to have millions of fuel-efficient cars on the road right now.

One of the dirtiest of the Dirty Dozen, the ironically named Clean Coal Technology Program, not only survived the sham chopping block but is getting a major funding bump, earmarked to receive $2 billion over the next 10 years to continue to do what it's failed to do so far—and what environmentalists contend cannot be done: produce coal that burns without releasing large amounts of carbon dioxide and toxic chemicals.

What the coal producers can do quite well is burn up public money. To keep the furnace full, the coal industry gave $3.6 million to federal candidates in the last election. And unlike Wall Street, there is no bear market in Washington—a $3.6 million investment begets a $2 billion return. Not bad.

In Bush's utopian Beltway, his massive but somehow "just right" tax cut would be accompanied by a "just right" spending increase of 4% and a principled elimination of all budgetary fat. But reality is not nearly so obliging: corporate welfare is expected to cost the taxpayers $80 to $100 billion a year, and lobbyists will continue to fight to put back even what little fat is liposuctioned from the budget.

The American Shipbuilding Association, for example, has gotten its friends in Congress—including senators Trent Lott,

Ted Stevens, and John Breaux—to intercede on its behalf to try and reinstate the federal loan guarantees given to purchasers of American-built oil tankers and cruise ships. The guarantees were increased to $33 million in 2002, and the House has voted to appropriate $50 million for 2003.

"When Republicans refuse to cut corporate welfare," Stephen Moore, president of the Club for Growth, told me, "they expose themselves as fiscal hypocrites who only want to cut government programs that don't benefit their own donors. Some of the biggest Republican donors are the biggest recipients of unwarranted federal grants and subsidies."

So, far from there having been a reordering of the nation's priorities, we still have the same old pecking order. Billion-dollar corporations continue to ride first class on the government gravy train while, even in the middle of a recession, desperate measures like temporary welfare assistance for needy families have been given the boot. The president's first budget proved that Aid to Dependent Corporations is a lot more resilient than Aid to Dependent Children.

Too bad the vulnerable children and their parents and grandparents couldn't afford to respond to DeLay and Hastert's kind invitation to hobnob with Washington's who's who and offer their "special advice" on the president's budget. Maybe they'll run into Mitch Daniels down at the free clinic.

THE ENABLERS

A Conspiracy of Thousands

———◆———

"The love of money as a possession—as distinguished from the love of money as a means to the enjoyments and realities of life—will be recognized for what it is, a somewhat disgusting morbidity, one of those semi-criminal, semi-pathological propensities which one hands over with a shudder to the specialists in mental diseases."

—JOHN MAYNARD KEYNES

WHO FILLED THE TROUGH? Who laid the table at the banquet of greed? Who made it possible for the pigs to gorge themselves on ludicrous quantities of stock options, grossly inflated pay packages, and a dazzling array of perks so indulgent they make Donald Trump look puritanical? As in a country house murder mystery, the servants at this corporate bacchanal have their own stories of lust and deception, just as colorful as those of their masters.

These decorative accessories to corporate crimes, these enablers of the pigs' excesses, did not start out as groveling slaves. At one time, not so long ago, they were charged with impartial oversight. Or, at the very least, objective analysis. But, as executive pay went through the roof, anyone with even a passing interest in the corner office was dragged in by the irresistible undertow of easy money. Not only did the enablers turn a blind eye to the machinations of excess, they all-too-frequently bent over backward to grease the wheels. The watchdogs had become lapdogs.

Alan Greenspan:
From Hero to Goat

In the go-go boom of the nineties, market experts went nuts, high as kites on the decade's Internet opium.

In 1998 Federal Reserve Board Chairman Alan Greenspan had praised the country's economic performance, calling it "as impressive as any I have witnessed in my nearly half century of daily observation of the American economy." Greenspan claimed that the country was bound into a "virtuous cycle" of low unemployment, low inflation and soaring stock prices. Wall Street's insiders fell over themselves in their rush to salute this powerful prophet of wealth. "Alan Greenspan has probably been one of the greatest benefactors to the American people over the last few years," exulted William Cheney, chief economist at the John Hancock Life Insurance Company. "If you had to pick out one single person for the economy's remarkable performance, his name is atop that list," concurred Richard Yamarone, director of economic research at the Argus Research Corporation in New York. "He's responsible for this historic economic expansion."

But Greenspan sounded a note of caution the next year that fell only on the deaf ears of the hear-no-evil, giddy new economy crowd. "History tells us that sharp reversals in confidence occur abruptly," he warned in scholarly tones. "A bursting bubble is an event incontrovertibly evident only in retrospect."

Two years later, in 2001, with the "sharp reversal" picking up steam, the tide of Wall Street opinion, amazingly, had turned against him. With the first stomach butterflies of impending panic starting to flutter, the mood in the market turned to one of kill-the-messenger. Merrill Lynch told its clients that the Federal Reserve was "behind the curve" with Greenspan at its helm. John Makin, an economist at the American Enterprise Institute, called the Fed's attitude "disconcertingly complacent," and commentator Bill O'Reilly quite simply dismissed the Fed's chairman: "The financial markets no longer trust him, and millions of Americans don't, either." While O'Reilly may have been right, the markets were clearly wrong.

Greenspan had suffered from fickle affection before. In December 1996, just after he made his infamous remarks about the "irrational exuberance" of the stock market, Senator Trent Lott weighed in with his own irrational ignorance. "I would be almost willing to bet that he wishes now that he had not used the words that he did," Lott sulked. Democratic Senator Tom Harkin called Greenspan's comment "very ill-advised."

The very people who put Greenspan on a pedestal when he was saying what they wanted to hear, were quick to knock him off as soon as he brought them a message of caution. He was a guru only as long as he delivered upbeat messages. Despite many signs that the market was grossly inflated, the very people who should have been advising their clients that they might want to consider moving some of their hard-earned savings into more secure investments were actually doing the opposite. In September 1999, Jim Glassman and Kevin Hassett published *Dow 36,000*, espousing the belief that the stock market would reach that level in three to five years. Three months earlier David Elias had gone a little further in his book *Dow 40,000*. The same month that Glassman and Hassett predicted 36,000, Charles Kadlec and Ralph Acampora blew both books out of the water with *Dow 100,000: Fact or Fiction*. (Even though the Dow has experienced a drop of more than 30% since Glassman and Hassett's book was published, Glassman is unapologetic, arguing in *The Wall Street Journal* that the market will eventually prove him right. He's just not saying when.)

In October 2002, Greenspan was awarded an honorary knighthood in Great Britain for his "outstanding contribution to global economic stability." But when Greenspan started bursting bubbles in 1999, no one in the market wanted to hear what he had to say. And at the head of the bull market herd were the glorified glamour boys (and girls) of greed, the research analysts.

Schizophrenics in Suits, Part One: The Analysts

"I have been buying stocks since I was eleven years old," Warren Buffett said. "Maybe when I was eleven or twelve I paid attention to Wall Street research, but not since." Supposedly, analysts are the shrewd, can't-fool-me guys of Wall Street, able to see past the smoke-and-mirrors of corporate confabulations to perceive the underlying strengths and weaknesses of the market and the individual companies of which it's composed. The assumption that their assessments are warts-and-all objective pictures of a company's financial health is the bedrock of the investment banking community.

Well, that's how it's *supposed* to work. But that's not the way things have been working. Even though analysts were paid fabulously well for their advice—Salomon Smith Barney's Jack Grubman earned $20 million a year, Merrill Lynch's Henry Blodget a mere $12 million—those high salaries didn't seem to be enough. In the gonzo nineties the analysts reached for the skies.

For years after the great crash of 1929, legislation passed by FDR to keep banks clean—specifically, the Glass-Steagall Act—did a pretty good job of ensuring that analysts weren't subject to coercive influences by separating the investment banks that handle stocks, bonds, options and the like from the commercial banks that hold depositors' money.

As little as a decade ago, investment banks employed a small number of highly professional analysts who offered shareholders independent and objective advice and, to a large extent, served them well. The mid-nineties soon put an end to that arrangement, as merger-mania spawned the monolithic monsters that exist today. Commercial banks began offering mutual funds and investment banks offered checking accounts. The distinctions between the commercial banking industry and its investment banking sister became blurred.

This alone should have made the financial press wary. When investment banks were smaller, competing on the accuracy and quality of their stock picks, the field was more level. After consolidation, the much larger stock-picking departments of the big Wall Street firms and the resources that they could command steamrolled over the little guys, beating the smaller banks on the sheer volume of their stock picks, if not on their quality.

The analysts were now employed by the same executives who were in charge of all the other departments, including handling mergers and acquisitions, capital markets, as well as the money-making powerhouses of the investment banking industry: the sales and trading divisions. "Seeking out conflicts of interest in investment banking," wrote the *Economist,* "is like peeling an onion. It could go on and on until there is little or nothing left."

To offer investors some kind of protection, Chinese walls were erected between departments, procedural barriers intended to prevent analysts, working in the research department, from crossing over to the sales department and abusing their priestly impartiality.

The Internet boom blew big holes through those walls. As the nineties roared on, more and more Internet start-ups were going public, offering shares in Initial Public Offerings.

Although IPOs are only one of the services covered by investment banks, in the Internet era it sometimes seemed as if they were the only game in town. Income from investment banking shot up as the bubble of the dot-com IPO craze and tech-industry boom inflated.

The real trouble started when someone, his name lost to the ages, realized that the small army of analysts who work for investment banks—Merrill Lynch alone employs 800—could also be salesmen for the infant stock of newborn IPOs. After all, they spend their days telling investors which stocks to invest in and which to avoid—why not get them to talk a whole lot more, in always positive ways, of course, about the companies the bank is taking public or which it is preparing for a merger?

Are you about to merge with a company and are worried about the prospects for your stock? Get one of the banks' star analysts to talk up your shares on the morning chat shows. Are you an investment banker trying to sign a client and need a "research report" promoting the favorable conditions for a public offering? No problem. Research will willingly oblige. Have you bedded your dream client only to see his IPO's value start to fall? Just hop back over that meaningless Chinese wall and get an analyst to issue a "buy" recommendation.

In the early nineties, "buy" recommendations outnumbered "sell" recommendations by 6 to 1; by the end of the decade, that ratio was almost 100 to 1.

Like chicken pox in a kindergarten, the highly infectious concept of analysis as sales tool swept Wall Street. No institution was left unmarked, and the Chinese wall had become merely a speed bump, barely registering on the surface of the speedway that now connected research and banking. The firm that had the largest research department suddenly found it had the largest marketing department with the added bonus that, like all skillful sales efforts, this one operated on the sly. After all, investors still assumed that analysts were independent, voicing support or concern for newly issued stocks regardless of who had overseen their birth.

As the many ways in which compromised research could be so helpful were discovered, and the influence of the analysts grew, the once nerdy numbers guys turned chic. A group of elite salesmen arose from the serried ranks of researchers. Their names—Henry Blodget, Jack Grubman, Mary Meeker, Abby Joseph Cohen—assumed totemic status.

Analysts had become glamorous, even hip. I'm pretty sure I heard one guy on CNBC say, "I highly recommend this company, dude." They used to be the bottom-dwellers of the Wall Street food chain, but now, there they were, camera-ready every morning for their regular appearances on the financial channels, lunching with next-big-thing dot-commers, lording it over the bankers in the afternoon, and heading out on the town or home to count their money in the evening. Suddenly, analysts were celebrities.

By the late nineties, Merrill Lynch's star analyst Henry Blodget had been so inflated by the same gassy optimism that was filling the market bubble itself, that when he arrived late at a Manhattan lunch event, the speaker announced that, "Elvis has entered the building." *Fortune* magazine reported that a pair of investors once sneaked into the grounds of Morgan Stanley analyst Mary Meeker's Palo Alto home just to peek into the rooms and stick their fingers in the swimming pool of their superstar idol. Barbra Streisand, Reggie Jackson, and Saudi Prince Alwaleed sought her financial counsel. So obviously she was good. Viacom sent a corporate jet to fly her out to Bermuda for a ninety-minute meeting and Chinese bankers begged Morgan Stanley executives to send her out to meet them. Meeker ended up being the first stock analyst to become a household name. The only things she didn't have were endorsement deals with Nike ("Just Buy It"), her own brand of breakfast cereal ("Meekers!" They're Magically Delicious!), and her own television show

(*Who Wants To Be a Billionaire?*). The next thing would have been Tyco selling Mary Meeker action figures. "Pull her string and she blows smoke up your ass."

Variously dubbed the eternal bull, the perennial bull, the perma-bull, or Queen of the Bulls, Goldman Sachs' analyst Abby Joseph Cohen personally briefed Alan Greenspan and appeared at a New Economy conference with President Clinton. Global Crossing Chairman Gary Winnick would describe Salomon Smith Barney's golden-boy analyst Jack Grubman as "the Bruce Springsteen of telecom."

All of this, of course, came with hefty compensation, and the more investment banking dollars analysts helped generate for their firms, the bigger their paychecks grew. Blodget and the other hot analysts were rewarded with salaries that were directly tied to the amount of investment trade they brought in. Between December 1999 and November of the next year, Merrill's Internet group was involved in deals that were worth approximately $115 million. And that meant that Blodget saw his pay package increase from $3 million to $12 million.

The analysts' new power was like a drug, and it went straight to their heads. They had become so confident in their own God-like vision that the rest of the market watchers fell into line. In May 1999, when Meeker upgraded America Online, its value rocketed almost 10% in just one day. Only a few weeks later, it dropped by 5% when Henry Blodget warned that growth was slowing. In November 1996, rumors that Queen Bull Abby Joseph Cohen was turning bearish caused the Dow to fall 50 points. The drop was halted only when she convened a press conference to say she had not changed her tune; the market turned around and closed higher than it had opened.

Trips across the Chinese wall became just another stop on the analysts' daily commute. Before they merged with Salomon, analysts at Smith Barney were given an end-of-the-year statement breaking down their compensation so that they could clearly see just how much of their pay had been "earned" the new-fashioned way. Euphemistically labeled a "helper fee," this bonus should have been called a "help yourself fee."

Just in case any of the analysts didn't catch on to the new M.O., Merrill Lynch's management sent out a memo in late 2000, inviting them to enumerate their contributions to investment banking that year. "Please provide," the memo solicited, "complete details on your involvement in the transaction, paying particular attention to the degree that your research coverage played a role in origination, execution and follow up." In the past, this would have been the most egregious violation of banking ethics; in these ethics-free years, it became the tune to toot your horn to.

For Mary Meeker, being an analyst was "like being a Gumby. You're pulled in a lot of different directions." But, unfortunately, not the right directions. Like the one where she would, say, give objective analysis that would lessen the likelihood of people losing their retirement savings.

Did these people have their morals and their judgment surgically removed?

Some analysts seemed to lose all sense of how to honestly evaluate a company's prospects and put the English language through remarkable contortions in order to justify their inevitable "buy" recommendations. Relentlessly hyping the value of dot-coms making absolutely no profits, and with no profitability threshold in sight, Meeker came up with a number of ingenious and bizarre valuation strategies. One was a zany technique called "discounted terminal valuation," which supposedly allowed one to see five years into a company's (invariably profitable) future. She was also a master of rationalization for the lunatic assumption that "page views" and "eyeballs" equated with dollars and cents. Meeker filled voluminous reports with tidbits like this one from an evaluation of Yahoo (entitled "Yahoo, Yippee, Cowabunga . . ."): "Forty million unique sets of eyeballs and growing, in time should be worth nicely more than Yahoo's current market value of $10 billion."

And even though the tech bubble burst long ago, Mary Meeker's a bubble-half-full kind of gal. Of the 15 stocks she was analyzing in 2001, only two didn't have a "buy" or "out-perform" recommendation. For instance, Meeker gave both Yahoo and Priceline a bullish "outperform" rating even as the two darlings of the Internet were losing 96% of their value. As nuclear winter descended on the NASDAQ, a reporter for the *New York Times* finally asked a Morgan Stanley official if Meeker's "nonstop optimism had anything to do with the fact that most of the companies had engaged Morgan Stanley as an investment bank." The official answered, in an equivocation that would have done Bill Clinton proud, "It is what it is."

Other Internet analysts also found it hard to kick their bullish habits and to free themselves from their addiction to empty speculation. In the six months after Abby Joseph Cohen told clients in late 2000 that "the backdrop for tech investments is favorable," the NASDAQ dropped 43%. With either moxie or mendacity, in early 2001, she advised clients to up the percentage of stocks in their portfolio from 65% to 70%.

The supposedly brilliant analysts who were infatuated with so many of the Bright New Companies, which were so "creative" and "aggressive," were also infatuated with silly sales gimmicks like sock puppets (Pets.com) and upper-crust English butlers (AskJeeves.com).

But that was just crazy Internet nonsense, you say? Well, ask yourself what the financial world learned from the excesses of the Internet debacle. Judging by the more recent set of scandals, not much. Enron, Global Crossing, WorldCom, Qwest—they're Yahoo, Netscape, and Priceline all over again, only with even more investor money down the drain.

Portrait of a Pig:
Jack Grubman

In the first year of the new millennium, the analysts were still playing fast and loose, still relishing their influence and power, still living the high life. While Meeker and Blodget confined themselves largely to the Internet sector that had mainly disappeared in the tech crash, former Salomon Smith Barney analyst Jack Grubman was deeply involved with today's criminal headliners. Before resigning in ignominy in August 2002, the high-flying telecom power broker, who pulled in $20 million a year owing to his well-developed abilities to navigate the stretch of road connecting research and sales, was eloquent in his disavowal of ethics.

"What used to be a conflict is now a synergy," Grubman cheerfully explained, before the telecom bubble he helped create burst. "Someone like me who is banking-intensive would have been looked at disdainfully by the buy side fifteen years ago. Now they know I'm in the flow of what's going on." You know, the flow of money from hardworking average investors into the pockets of snake-oil salesmen in expensive suits and Italian leather shoes, with Wall Street offices and Park Avenue penthouses.

In June 2002 we learned a bit more about just how much of that flow Grubman diverted, with reports that he acted as an unofficial consigliere to Global Crossing Chairman Gary Winnick, a role undisclosed to the investors he hawked Global Crossing stock to. Apparently, at the same time Grubman was offering supposedly objective analysis of Global's fortunes, he was advising Global on everything from merger deals to major hiring decisions as well as offering special allocations of hot IPO shares to favored Global Crossing executives, including

Chairman Winnick and CEO John Legere. And it turns out that his relationship with WorldCom's disgraced CEO Bernie Ebbers was equally tight. He sat in on WorldCom's board meetings and offered Ebbers preferential access to valuable IPO stock. That's conflict turned into synergy, all right.

And if you think that Grubman's only motivation was money, you underestimate him. He also liked the glamour. The stuffy old-guard may have disdained him in 1985 when he left AT&T for Wall Street, but when he was hanging out with Winnick, he found himself at the center of an international elite. At a lavish dinner hosted by Winnick at Claridge's in London, Grubman dined on tournedos of Aberdeen Angus with, among others, King Constantine of Greece, Baroness Thatcher, and then-Secretary of Defense William Cohen, who had flown 16 hours from Chile. Perhaps it was this brush with political power that taught Grubman the ABCs of political back scratching. Or perhaps it was just a coincidence that on the day he was subpoenaed by the House Financial Services Committee, he donated $100,000 to the Democratic Senatorial Campaign Committee.

This check-to-cheek relationship cost investors who relied on Grubman's opinion dearly—$57 billion, to be precise—when Global Crossing went belly up in January 2002. Would an objective analyst have maintained a "buy" rating on Global Crossing, as Grubman did, even as its stock price plummeted from a high of $61 to $1.07? Although, in Grubman's defense, when the stock hit $1.07 he did finally change his recommendation . . . to "neutral."

Would an objective analyst have waited until the day before WorldCom announced one of the world's biggest accounting frauds to cut his rating to a massively understated "underperform?" When might he have recommended that investors "sell"? The day the company auctioned off its conference tables and cubicles on eBay? Of course, back when he was Master of the

Telecom Universe, Grubman had derided the very notion of objectivity, scoffing: "Objective? The other word for it is uninformed." Translation: Only fools, suckers, and outsiders play fair.

The truly shocking thing is that most of what Grubman did, while certainly sleazy, isn't against the law. Grubman tiptoed along the edge of illegality by refraining from writing about Global Crossing during the times he was counseling them on specific deals. But, as with so many of the rules "governing" Wall Street, those concerning so-called blackout periods are filled with loopholes and open to wildly divergent interpretations. These regulations are about as respected on the Street as the Idaho law that prohibits fishing from the back of a giraffe, or the Indiana law that prohibits residents of Gary from going to the theater four hours after eating garlic.

When Salomon Smith Barney management suggested that Grubman wait at least six months after helping Global on its merger with another telecom company, Frontier Corp., before issuing new research reports on Global, that advice didn't sit well with Winnick. He hated losing his most enthusiastic huckster. So Winnick complained to Salomon, and, presto-chango, Salomon took another look at the rules and decided that Grubman now only needed to lie low for two months. You can almost imagine Winnick sliding $100 across the table and saying, "My friend Ben Franklin here wonders if you wouldn't mind checking that little rule book just one more time."

The relationship between Jack Grubman and Global Crossing has been described in press reports as "unusually cozy." In fact, "typically cozy" is more like it, given his chummy relationships with WorldCom, Qwest, Metromedia, and McLeod.

It also seems that his relationship with Winstar Communications, a former Wall Street pinup that filed for bankruptcy in 2001, was also a little on the "cozy" side. In September 2002 the National Association of Securities Dealers filed charges against Grubman, alleging that he violated securities rules and misled investors by pushing the company's shares despite signs that Winstar was in serious financial trouble.

In 1998, Grubman began advising clients to start buying into Winstar—which just happened to be a Salomon investment banking client. The company was trading at $20 and Grubman's initial price target was $71. At its height in March 2000 Winstar reached just over $64. A year later, it was trading at under $10 and Grubman was still screaming "buy." As late as March 2001, with Winstar trading at just over $7, Grubman wrote in his "State of the Union" report: "We think the business metrics at Winstar continue to exceed expectations and are quite robust." The next month the company sought bankruptcy protection and its shares were delisted from the NASDAQ. It was only at this point that Grubman stopped covering the company.

PUSHING CRAP

	Company	Stock Price at peak	Stock Price Now (As of 10-07-02)
Henry Blodget	Aether Systems	$315	$2.60
	Excite@home	$189	Out of business
	Infospace	$130	$4.58
Jack Grubman	Winstar	$64	Less than 1 cent
	WorldCom	$64.50	9 cents
	Global Crossing	$61	2 cents
Mary Meeker	Yahoo	$475	$9.06
	Priceline	$162	$1.28
	CNET	$208	92 cents

In September 2002, the National Association of Securities Dealers fined Citigroup, Salomon's parent company, $5 million for Grubman's misleading research report. Hardly a fine that will register with Citigroup, which had revenues of $80 billion in 2001.

The Bulls Hit the Fan

The disgusting degree of duplicity that analysts are capable of became breathtakingly clear in early 2002 as crusading New York Attorney General Eliot Spitzer revealed a series of e-mails from the upper echelons of Merrill Lynch's research department. After examining more than 30,000 documents—which included thousands of e-mails—from the company, Spitzer went public with the fact that researchers were hawking as a "buy" stocks that they were privately ridiculing as "such a piece of crap." InfoSpace, an Internet infrastructure designer, was on Merrill's star analyst Henry Blodget's "Favored 15" list for more than four months. Spitzer revealed that, during those same four months, Blodget and his team of analysts privately called InfoSpace a "powder keg" and a "piece of junk" run by a "sleazebag." And those were just the compliments.

In public, of course, Blodget's recommendations about the company were rosy. Why? Seems he was keeping InfoSpace happy just long enough for Merrill to get its cut for brokering a deal between InfoSpace and another Internet flash-in-the-pan, Go2Net. Blodget knew full well that that company was also a dud. When asked in an e-mail what was interesting about Go2Net, he responded "Nothin'." The Internet Capital Group, another company recommended by Blodget, saw the value of its stock plummet 94% between December 1999 and October

2000, ending up at $12.38. At the time, Blodget e-mailed a colleague predicting that it would fall as low as $5. But Merrill's public rating? "Accumulate."

Who did this hurt? Moms and dads, schoolteachers, firemen, farmers, mechanics, retirees, and secretaries for starters— people who took the investing advice because they saw the analysts on TV, where they sounded like they were in the know. Hey, from the analyst's point of view, it's just a damn shame that the guy sitting in the La-Z-Boy in Des Moines, Iowa, watching the stock picks is already way behind the curve.

In an inspiring indication that at least some analysts are capable of being as appalled by all of this as the rest of the public, one courageous party pooper in Blodget's department, Kristin Campbell, expressed what she called "extreme reservations" about the continued pumping of Go2Net and told Blodget in no uncertain terms that she didn't "want to be a whore for fucking management." She summed up the sorry state of investment research standards: "The whole idea that we are independent from banking is a big lie."

With the tenacious Spitzer breathing down his neck, Henry Blodget finally stepped down from the stage in November 2001. Announcing that he was leaving Merrill (with a reported $2 million golden handshake), Blodget said that he planned to write a book, the title of which may or may not be *Eliot Spitzer Is a Big Bald Idiot*. Friends say that he still believes in the stocks he promoted, even though many of the companies he praised have disappeared altogether and many of the others are on life support.

Spitzer's revelations shamed Merrill CEO David Komansky into offering a mea culpa. Although, typically, it was more of a mealy culpa. "Anything that happens on my watch," said Komansky, "I'm responsible for. Those e-mails were embarrassing to me . . . and I truly regret that they ever happened."

Notice that he doesn't regret the out-and-out fraud the e-mails reveal; what he regrets is that the e-mails "happened." How much do you bet that the newest Merrill Lynch employee training session is something along the lines of "Making the Delete Key Your New Best Friend"?

Komansky's carefully calibrated contrition was the very model of the latest in PR-approved damage control: apologize quickly, accept responsibility, and put the past behind you. Only you don't really apologize, and you don't really accept responsibility.

So Merrill Lynch has gone from gold standard to "crap" pusher. And, to help it regain its lost luster, it hired high-profile power players, including Rudy Giuliani who, before he was "America's Mayor," had zealously prosecuted the junk-bond fraudsters of the eighties as a U.S. Attorney.

Meanwhile, Spitzer, whose investigation forced the sheep-in-wolves-clothing SEC to launch its own inquiry into the matter, was being told to back off. Spitzer was, in effect, reprimanded for not leaving the matter to the big boys in Washington. While being careful not to cross jurisdictional swords, SEC chairman Harvey Pitt gently reminded Spitzer that "only the federal government can set nationwide standards." And Representative Richard Baker, whose Capital Markets subcommittee held hearings on conflicts of interest on Wall Street, cautioned Spitzer: "It is essential that the SEC now lead the concluding phase of this inquiry."

So now Spitzer is having to take on both the bad guys and the guys who are supposed to protect the public from the bad guys. If Congress and the SEC had done their jobs, there would be no need for Spitzer.

The good news is that he is a man on a mission and won't be easily deterred. "Nobody can force me to pull back," he told me, "and I have no intention of doing so." As for the urgings of Messrs. Pitt and Baker, Spitzer didn't pull any punches: "The hearings conducted by Mr. Baker were pointless. They didn't ask the right questions and they didn't produce the kind of evidence necessary to bring about real reform. As for the SEC, it clearly didn't step up and prevent these abuses from occurring."

When By-Lines Become Buy-Lines

The Fourth Estate had a track record almost as bad as the analysts. The editors of *Fortune* voted Enron the "most innovative" of the magazine's "most admired" companies six years in a row. Shamed Tyco CEO Dennis Kozlowski was lauded as America's "Most Aggressive CEO" in a 2001 *Business Week* cover story. Unbelievably, the magazine even went so far as to hail him as a "tax master," a maestro of strategies that allowed his company to report billions of dollars in earnings every year, while building up $24 billion in debt. In 1999 *Fortune* named WorldCom (or MCI WorldCom, as it then was), then under the guidance of CEO Bernie Ebbers, as one of ten stocks to "grow with," a company with "the size, stability, and earnings power to see you through the market's ups and downs."

The media–Wall Street nexus was the subject of a study co-authored by doctors Jeffrey Busse and Clifton Green from Emory University's business school. Their study found that trading in shares that CNBC's stock market analyst Maria Bartiromo was about to cover increased ten minutes before she revealed her picks on air, reaching a "hectic pace" in the last five minutes.

Wall Street denizen and co-founder of TheStreet.com James Cramer talked regularly with Bartiromo and other reporters. If he picked up clues or suggestions as to what stock was going to be recommended, he admitted to the paper, he would have no problem trading before the news broke. "Yeah, I did that game," he said. "It's found money."

The relationship worked both ways. A disgruntled former employee of Cramer's, Nicholas Maier, handed over to the government a tape-recorded conversation between himself and another trader at Cramer's hedge fund which showed that Cramer would sometimes buy shares in a company before calling his friends at CNBC to spill some news into their willing ears. Once the news was made public, Cramer would clean up.

Like Jack Grubman's overly friendly relationship with Gary Winnick, this is not illegal. Cramer explains it away by claiming that he and his colleagues were "merchants of the buzz," shop stewards in the vast rumor mill of Wall Street. When knowledge is money, and insider knowledge is even more money, the "buzz" is clearly a lucrative commodity to trade.

Meet the New Economy

What happened to elevate people like Meeker, Blodget, Cohen, and Grubman to the Wall Street pantheon? Why were the analysts treated as such soothsaying geniuses? How hard was it really to predict growth in an economy that was booming beyond belief? How brilliant do you have to be to ride a wave and give no warning when it's about to break? In part the analysts were products of their environment. If they hadn't existed, we would have had to invent them. As Blodget liked to say, "I plucked the chords of the Zeitgeist."

They were in good company. All the financial gurus who believed that the economy had undergone an amazing transformation—including former President Clinton, one of the giddiest cheerleaders of the "new" economy—were not only fooling themselves, they were duping the American public out of billions of dollars. The one stock picker who didn't buy into the craze was Warren Buffett. The legendary investor shunned the tech sector, refusing to invest his money—and the money of his investors—in something he didn't understand.

But millions of others *did* buy into the madness, betting their retirement funds and even running up debts on credit cards to cover stock buys, not knowing that, caught in the raging conflict of interest that investment banking is built on, they were always going to be the losers. And as Martha Stewart might have said, "That's not a good thing."

But, perhaps a painful lesson is being learned. In May 2002, Jeffrey Evans, president of the New York Society of Security Analysts, noted that "the era of the celebrity analyst is over." Pay for top Wall Street analysts has dropped. In 2001 the average pay packet was $800,000, down more than 50% from the previous year's average of $2 million. The new rules preventing analysts from making money on investment banking deals could drive that even lower. Those poor souls! Now when they eat out, they'll only be able to afford lobster, not caviar.

Furthermore, the media also claim to be using analysts less and less. CNBC, which given its current volume of public contrition may have to turn itself into the Self-Flagellation Channel, is, according to CNBC senior news editor Ellen Egeth, "much less likely to peg a story on an analyst upgrade or downgrade now." Indeed, CNBC's morning show *Squawk Box* ridicules analysts as penguins mindlessly following each other over the edge, into the icy water.

TOP 10 STUPIDEST THINGS SAID ABOUT THE NEW ECONOMY

1. "We've got corporate profits that are continuing to grow. We're benefiting from the tax cuts of the early eighties, the restructuring of American corporations of the 1980s. The world is perfect." (David Williams, Managing Director, Alliance Capital, 8-14-97)

2. "Even if the market tanks, the vast majority of us will stay in the game. We have to. Because for more and more Americans, our money is no longer in the hands of schlumpy stockbrokers or fancy-Dan fund managers. Our money is with ourselves. We have become the land of the self-invested." (Andy Serwer, *Fortune* magazine, 10-11-99)

3. "In short, investors' enthusiasm is well founded. The risks of stock investing—never so great as imagined—really have declined. In 1952, a New York Stock Exchange survey found that only 4% of Americans owned equities; today, the figure is nearing 50%. It is this broad ownership of stocks that is the most profound evidence that investors have become more rational and that Dow 10,000 is only the beginning." (Economists James Glassman and Kevin Hassett, authors of *Dow 36,000, The Wall Street Journal*, 3-18-99)

4. "The dominant event of the late 20th century is the bull-market prosperity of the 1980s and 1990s. This was caused largely by a shift back to free-market economics, a reduction in the role of the state and an expansion of personal liberty. At the turn of a new century, taking the right road will extend the long cycle of wealth

creation and technological advance for decades to come. By 2020 the Dow index will reach 50,000, and the 10,000 benchmark will be reduced to a small blip on a large screen." (Economist and current host of *Kudlow & Cramer*, Lawrence Kudlow, *The Wall Street Journal*, 3-18-99)

5. "Amazon—the company everyone wants to be like—could lose nearly $350 million this year . . . but Amazon's losses are also a sign of the New Economics of Internet commerce." (*Time* magazine's Joshua Ramo, in announcing Amazon founder Jeff Bezos as the magazine's Person of the Year, 1999)

6. "As increasing numbers of Americans joined the middle and upper-middle classes . . . a great democratization of the investment business began." (Andy Serwer, *Fortune* magazine, 10-11-99)

7. "I'm really optimistic about the future of this great country. I believe that the next century will be a time of incredible prosperity . . . a prosperity that must be sustained by low taxes, unleashed by lighter regulation, energized by new technologies and expanded by free trade; a prosperity beyond our expectations, but within our grasp." (Governor George W. Bush, 9-02-99)

8. "This is really the best of times. I don't think anyone at this table has seen better times." (Citigroup Chairman and CEO Sanford Weill at a meeting of the Business Council, 1999)

9. "The stock market itself is a much better measure of economic progress than a barrelful of government statistics. Market prices reflect the collective judgment of millions of profit-seeking individuals who buy and sell each day

10. "The traditional industrial economy was a Newtonian system of opposing forces, checks and balances, in which disequilibria of demand and supply arose, only to be equilibrated by adjusting prices. While in contrast, the right metaphors for the new economy are more Darwinian, with the fittest surviving, and, as modern Darwinians have come to understand, accidents of history casting long and consequential shadows." (Then-Treasury Secretary Lawrence Summers in a speech to the Kennedy School of Government, 9-27-00)

Schizophrenics in Suits, Part Two: The Accountants

Every scandal, it seems, produces at least one classic and defining euphemism—a judiciously chosen word or phrase diligently employed to sugarcoat the sour reality at hand.

During Watergate, press secretary Ron Ziegler ingeniously dismissed all his previous egregious dissembling as "inoperative." In Vietnam, the military referred to the appalling number of killings of American soldiers by American soldiers as "friendly fire."

Now we have corporate America's glittering contribution: "restatement of earnings." It sounds so innocuous and benign. Earnings are good after all, and "restating" is just the boardroom equivalent of asking for a do-over on the playground. The term connotes a mere slip of the tongue, a wrongly chosen word, or a silly, but perfectly understandable, failure to carry the *1* when doing your math homework. In plain language, restatements are revisions (almost always downward) of the revenues claimed in the supposedly meticulous annual reports prepared by a company's auditors. In the out-of-control world of corporate America, however, they've become one of the methods of choice for perpetrating out-and-out fraud.

In June 2002, three former executives of drugstore giant Rite Aid were indicted for an overstatement of earnings, which led not only to a $1.6 billion restatement, but, prosecutors alleged, to an artificially inflated stock price, which in turn artificially inflated the executives' pay packages. At the time, Rite Aid's restatement was the largest in history. Now it looks like small change.

Three days later, restating earnings moved out of the smoky backrooms of corporate America and onto the front pages. Telecom giant WorldCom revealed to a disbelieving public what could be one of the largest accounting frauds in history. WorldCom had improperly recorded $3.8 billion in expenses as capital expenditures, grossly inflating cash flow and profits over the past five quarters. Without this "aggressive accounting" maneuver, WorldCom would have reported a net loss for 2001, as well as for the first quarter of 2002. Instead, it listed more than $1.5 billion as profit for those periods. On news of the restatement, WorldCom stock promptly fell 93% to close at six cents. Of course later we found out we knew only half of the truth: WorldCom had really overstated its earnings by $7 billion.

Three days after WorldCom, Xerox announced that it would have to restate five years of results to "reclassify" more than $6 billion in revenues. Shares in the company immediately lost 18% of their value. Xerox spokeswoman Christa Carone, apparently seeking to reassure investors, blithely dismissed the gravity of the announcement with this deft exhibition of doublespeak: "There's no revenue that is going away. . . . It's just going from one place to another." Be forewarned: that level of weasely wordplay is for professionals only. Just try saying something like that to the IRS if they catch you shifting some income over to the "deductions" side of your tax return.

Restatement of earnings has become the Ebola virus of corporate America, with over 1,000 U.S. corporations restating their earnings since 1997. (Which means, I suppose, that Xerox could argue that it was merely copying others.)

The bug has spread to the federal government. In the summer of 2002, the Commerce Department "restated" first-quarter growth down 1.1% from its original 6.1%. It also revised its numbers for 2001's economic growth, revealing that there had been three quarters of negative GDP, rather than just one. Although President Bush tried to put a positive spin on things by emphasizing the fact that the first two quarters still showed positive growth, the *New York Times* editorialized that he "could not have reassured anybody when he said he remained committed to making his fiscally disastrous 10-year tax cuts permanent. It seemed especially surreal to mention this, as he did, after saying that he would ask Congress to show some fiscal restraint."

Restatements—corporate or governmental—are not just disembodied numbers. They inflict disastrous losses on, who else, the gullible shareholders who thought they could believe those super-glossy annual reports.

One of former SEC chief Arthur Levitt's deputies—chief accountant Lynn Turner—estimates that, in the six years prior to the Enron implosion, the steady erosion of accounting standards and the dishonesty it fostered cost investors $100 billion. WorldCom's crisis alone cost telecom investors $180 billion, while the investors in Enron lost $80 billion. By the fall of 2002, the scandals surrounding Enron, Adelphia, Global Crossing, Qwest, Kmart, Tyco, Citigroup, and WorldCom had led to a collective loss of almost $700 billion in shareholder value since the shares were at their peak.

As the number of restatements has shot up, so has bankruptcy. After all, these companies wouldn't be restating their earnings if their backs weren't up against the wall. They'd happily continue to defraud investors if they thought they could keep playing the shell game. In 2001, 257 public companies, with total assets of $258 billion, declared bankruptcy. That was a record—the previous one was set the year before, with 176 companies going under with $95 billion in assets. That only sounds like a lot because it is.

WHAT'S ANOTHER WORD FOR "DOUBLESPEAK"?

The Random House Dictionary defines "euphemism" as "the substitution of a mild, indirect or vague expression for one thought to be offensive, harsh or blunt." The wizards, goblins and devils of Wall Street have taken corporate doublespeak and raised it to levels previously unheard of. What follow are some of my favorite examples of scandal doublespeak and their translations.

1. When a CEO announces that his company has to "restate earnings" from a previous year, what he really means is:
   a. Crap! The Internal Revenue Service, Eliot Spitzer, or the SEC caught us cooking the books. Now we have to tell investors we really lost billions of dollars instead of making them.
   b. Guess what! We've been stealing from mom and pop investors just like you as far back as '96.
   c. For the love of God, don't start dumping our stock. This is a financial hiccup, not a cancer on the company.

d. I'm telling the truth about the company's finances now so I don't have to testify before Congress, go to jail, or lose my country club membership later.

e. All of the above.

2. When an analyst from a Wall Street brokerage firm tells investors watching CNBC that the market has "bottomed out" and urges them to "buy" a particular stock, what he really means is:

a. Buy this stock . . . my company is doing the IPO. And with the bonus money this thing generates, I can get new marble tile with gold inlay in my Hamptons toolshed.

b. Of all the companies doing what this company does, this one sucks the least.

c. An investment in this company could earn you as much as 2 or 3% over the next five years. Or you could lose your shirt. Which you wouldn't do if you hid your money in the cookie jar.

d. Sell!

e. How the hell should I know, I'm making this stuff up as I go.

f. All of the above.

3. When an analyst from a Wall Street brokerage firm urges investors watching CNBC to "accumulate" shares of a particular company, what he really means is:

a. This company will be bankrupt and the CEO will be in jail within six weeks.

b. My bosses told me to say this and I don't want to get fired.

c. The SEC has opened an investigation into financial malfeasance.

    d. This stock sucks. I know it and you know it. But my investment bank is hoping to land the company's mergers and acquisitions business. ·

    e. All of the above.

4. When an analyst from a Wall Street brokerage firm tells investors a particular stock is going to "under-perform," what he really means is:

    a. It's too late, Grandma. You've already lost your life savings. Good luck filling out the Medicare forms.

    b. This company went bankrupt last week, the workers are all looking for jobs, and the CEO has hired Johnnie Cochran.

    c. Call your cousin who works there—next week she's going to need help paying the mortgage.

    d. All of the above.

5. When a company CEO talks about "synergy," what he really means is:

    a. The company's vastly disparate parts are elegantly working in harmony . . . to steal billions from investors, employees, and customers alike.

    b. Despite our raised expectations, the buyout of our media company by the world's largest funeral home conglomerate has been a failure on a par with AOL/Time Warner.

    c. Both of the above.

6. When a company's financial statement lists "other related charges," that's a euphemism for:

    a. Expenditures so outrageous even our shady accountants can't figure a way to hide, mitigate, or inexplicably call them "revenue."

    b. Money spent on booze, drugs, and hookers.

c. Don't bother investigating this. Either we've lost the receipts or we're just going to lie about them anyway.

d. All of the above.

7. In his June 28, 2002, tongue lashing of Wall Street, President Bush promised to "punish companies and executives . . . who fudged the numbers." What he really meant was:

a. I will do nothing.

b. I might do something, but it's mostly for show.

c. Don't worry. Nothing will change. My friends in big business will be allowed to continue getting rich, ripping off customers, and stealing from investors.

d. I have to hurry up and get home. Nick at Night is showing a *Rawhide* marathon.

e. Did I just say "fudge?" I love fudge. Mommy, can I have some fudge?

f. All of the above.

8. When a company CEO announces that previous financial statements "misreported earnings," what he really means is:

a. That old lie about our earnings is no longer accurate; this new lie about earnings is the one you should trust.

b. Our old accounting firm did a crappy job of cooking the books, so we're hiring someone much more devious.

c. We thought we stole enough that year, but as it turns out, we need to steal a little more.

d. Please don't send me to jail. I'm afraid to shower in front of other men.

e. All of the above.

9. When a CEO announces that his company's earnings "failed to meet projections," what he really means is:
   a. After the board, the vice presidents, and I got our bonuses, there were no more profits. My bad.
   b. Instead of making money this quarter, the company lost billions of dollars.
   c. The lie we told you three months ago about how prosperous the company is was way too big.
   d. The board lent my family and me $3 billion which we lost when our Internet start-up, gasoline-and-fertilizer.com, inexplicably went belly-up.
   e. All of the above.

10. When a company spokesman says that the preferential access to hot new IPOs given to major clients "conformed to industry norms," what he really means is:
    a. The entire industry is crooked, not just us.
    b. Thanks to generous donations to powerful Washington lobbyists, we convinced Congress that down is up, bad is good, and two plus two equals seven.
    c. Thanks to a large collection of photos of Washington's elite naked, we convinced Congress that down is up, bad is good, and two plus two equals seven.
    d. I know what we're doing is illegal and you know what we're doing is illegal, but the SEC doesn't give a rat's ass—and that's what counts.
    e. In three months our company will be bankrupt, our CEO will be on trial, and I'll be cutting a deal with the Feds and ratting out my friends to avoid prison.
    f. All of the above.

11. When the vice president's spokeswoman says that her boss was "given no special consideration whatsoever," yet still managed to walk away with a $45,000 profit from extremely juicy IPOs conveniently given to him by his broker, what she really means is:

    a. My boss was given a lot of special consideration.

    b. What, ordinary people don't get this kind of preferential treatment?

    c. Mr. Cheney was treated the way all his powerful friends are treated. They got privileged access to lucrative share deals, they made money, and now I'm lying about it for them.

    d. Please believe me and don't investigate this. My boss won't survive prison: His heart's not in great shape.

    e. All of the above.

A Restatement of Yearnings

In a classic Monty Python sketch, Michael Palin plays an accountant who visits a career counselor, played by John Cleese. Palin tells Cleese that he's sick of accounting and what he really wants to be is a lion tamer. Cleese, however, talks him out of any career change by explaining that, according to his tests, Palin is ideally suited to accounting because he is "an appallingly dull fellow, unimaginative, timid, lacking in initiative, spineless, easily dominated, no sense of humor, and irrepressibly drab and awful." "In most professions," Cleese continues, "these would be considered drawbacks. In accountancy, they are a positive boon."

During the 1990s, accountants from the Big Five accounting firms began to get in touch with their long-repressed lion-tamer side. No longer content to just be the bag men, they became the enablers in the rape and pillage of America's 401(k) plans and stock portfolios.

Along the way, the accountants squandered their reputation for incorruptible probity that had long been the bedrock of the capital markets. Since 1934, public companies have been required to publish annual reports audited by certified public accountants, who are supposed to be serving the interests of the public, even though they are being paid by their corporate clients.

Despite hopping desperately from one accounting firm to another as scandal after scandal broke, companies have found themselves without really much of a choice at all. Take, for example, Qwest, which specializes in communications networks. Qwest has been so brilliantly managed that its stock fell 98% between March 2000 and August 2002, going from $96 to just under $2. Which, of course, didn't stop the company from paying Qwest CEO Joseph Nacchio a compensation package worth $87 million. After an SEC investigation was launched into Qwest's accounting practices in February 2002, the company quickly fired its accounting firm, Arthur Andersen, which had served Enron so loyally, and picked new accountants out of the remaining Big Four—Deloitte & Touche, Ernst & Young, PricewaterhouseCoopers, and KPMG. KPMG, Qwest's choice, may not be much help, though, since it is currently being investigated for the accounting irregularities at Xerox.

Xerox, in turn, has now dumped KPMG and hired PricewaterhouseCoopers, as has the desperate Adelphia Communications, after firing its auditor, Deloitte & Touche, in June 2002. But PricewaterhouseCoopers had just paid $55 million to settle a class action suit over its bookkeeping and book-cooking for MicroStrategy, whose shareholders have lost $11 billion. And in 2001, discount retailer Dollar General fired Deloitte & Touche and went shopping for another auditor, settling on Ernst & Young, which is currently being investigated by the SEC for apparent accounting irregularities at Computer Associates.

There's no one left untainted among the Big Four.

Diogenes, the Greek philosopher who searched with his lantern for just one honest man, would have had to give up his search for an honest accounting firm. What would seem a fairly straightforward process of adding up assets and liabilities has gone from being part of the solution to being part of the problem. That was the result of a practice called, in yet another oh-so-clever euphemism, "creative accounting."

"If men were angels," James Madison might have said, "no accounting precautions would be necessary." But we're no angels. And even the accounting firms acknowledged that some boundaries were in order, especially when the company being audited is also one of your biggest customers.

A web of both written and unwritten rules had evolved over the years. For one thing, accountants didn't bid out their services to clients, and didn't try to poach the business of companies that weren't looking for new auditors. Nor did they advertise. For years, these constraints prevented unscrupulous CFOs from shopping around for a more compliant accountant and stiffened the accountants' backs when they had to give big-ticket customers bad news.

But then it all changed. In one fell swoop, the time-honored Code of the Green Eyeshade—the canon of behavior that had made accountants "proper English gentlemen," in the words of a former chief accountant for the SEC (although not, perhaps, the kind of English gentlemen who get invited to the better parties)—was swept away.

Nineteen-seventy-eight was the year that the Federal Trade Commission allowed the accounting firms to start selling their booty on Main Street like every other vendor of corporate services, from the copier salesmen to the coffee concession-aires. They caught on fast.

In a flash, bookkeeping, that boring old mainstay of the profession, became a loss leader, the poor man's ghetto of the trade, as firm after firm built up lucrative consulting practices. Accounting hucksters began hawking a fabulous repertoire of expensive services. "We'll cut costs. We'll streamline production. What do we have to do to put you in a new car today?" You can just imagine the flashy new mottos: "PricewaterhouseCoopers, now with a sparkling drop of Retsyn," or "Your profits will 'Snap, Crackle & Pop' with Arthur Andersen."

And, of course, right along with competition came the accounting profession's own special brand of conflict-of-inter-est. Just like the banks, the firms built Chinese walls between the consulting and auditing sides. And those walls came tum-bling down just as readily as they had at the banks. The newly flush firms began to pay hefty bonuses to employees directly linked to the amount of consulting work they landed, along with dangling less quantifiable incentives like the doling out of precious partnerships. It was only a matter of time before the accountants crawled into the lap of Mammon.

Congress also did its part to undermine the profession's ethics by passing laws limiting the firms' liability if caught in fraud.

After that, the deluge.

Unfettered by those stuffy, bureaucratic restrictions, the accountants were now able to run with the bulls like everyone else in Pamplona-on-the-Hudson. The notion that the job of auditors was actually to serve investors had become as anachro-nistic as the notion that stock analysts were objective. The client was the company that paid the bills, and accountants competed just the way everyone else does in a market: they offered a more attractive service than their competitors.

What's a Little Fudge
Between Friends?

The greatest lure accountants offer these days is a guarantee of favorable results. "Earnings management," if you will. To produce results that please, the accountants stretch every loophole they can find in order to boost their clients' earnings. "Stretch" is actually way too soft a word. Really what accountants have done is driven a truck bomb through every loophole and looked the other way when management was driving the truck. As when Enron set up its labyrinth of off-balance-sheet partnerships. Just in case Arthur Andersen was tempted not to glance away, Enron offered 27 million reasons to play dumb.

So Andersen was working as a highly paid consultant pocketing a cool $27 million from Enron for its services, while also playing the objective inspector of the company books. Now there's a double-dipping recipe for "earnings management." It's just a tad harder to blow the whistle when you're making a mint, as Andersen partner and audit expert Carl Bass discovered when he was removed from auditing the Enron account after the company's chief accounting officer Richard Causey criticized him for the "caustic" and "cynical" view he took toward certain Enron transactions.

By 1999, consulting services—including design and implementation of financial information, consulting on financial issues, tax problems and partnership questions—made up 50% of total revenue, and by 2000 brought in up to three times as much revenue as auditing services. In 1981, consulting had generated just 13%.

In a world where the "generally accepted accounting principles" are so generally and deliberately Byzantine—and over 100,000 pages long—consulting fees were a good investment for companies seeking to add a little to their balance sheets. But don't, for a second, think any of it is illegal. Far from it.

Responding to the bombshell revelation that senior bankers at Citigroup actively helped Enron hide billions in debt, Enron Lawyer of Last Resort Robert Bennett deftly summed up the real reason for the current economic crisis: "Most of the problems—not all of them—are things that have been legal and acceptable."

And Bennett is actually telling the truth. How can any right-thinking person consider legal, for example, a stock that counts as debt on the company's tax return but as equity on its balance sheet? And yet that's exactly what the white-coated geniuses at the Goldman Sachs loophole lab created when they invented Monthly Income Preferred Shares—given the cute and cuddly nickname "Mips." This shape-shifting security was hailed as "a breakthrough" by Goldman and "a coup" by the starry-eyed cheerleaders in the business press.

It is emblematic of the kind of corporate culture we live in that a practice that the man on the street would consider blatantly illegal is not only legal but touted as a breakthrough and a coup. And it is a breakthrough, of a sort. After all, it's not easy to take something so unequivocally wrong and make it legal.

Indeed, back in 1997, when the Treasury Department was trying to curtail the use of Mips, Jon Corzine—now a member of the Senate Banking Committee, then Goldman Sach's CEO—signed an overheated letter to Congress that decried government efforts to "impose completely arbitrary" distinctions between assets and liabilities.

Which is tantamount to saying that people should stop making "completely arbitrary" distinctions between right and left or black and white. Or, perhaps more to the point, right and wrong. Yet it is precisely this inconvenient distinction between what is debt and what is not that Citigroup helped

Enron eradicate. It's as if I went out to dinner and, when the check came, offered my phone bill as payment.

It is very hard to deny the effect the consulting fees had on the outcome of the audits. In fact, it's hard to see much difference between this sort of consulting and outright bribes. Accountants solicited the consulting work in what former SEC Chairman Arthur Levitt called "a game of nods and winks" by offering to present a company's earnings in a more positive light if the company would pay it something extra. The more creative the accounting firms would be in the quest to hide losses and deliver phantom profits, the higher their consulting fee would be.

So records filed with the SEC in early 2001 showed that Tyco, for example, paid PricewaterhouseCoopers $13.2 million in auditing fees, but nearly $38 million for its consulting prowess. Motorola paid KPMG $3.9 million for auditing and a whopping $62.3 million for other services. Sprint paid Ernst & Young $2.5 million to check its books, but $63.8 million in other fees. And AT&T paid PricewaterhouseCoopers $7.9 million for auditing services, while shelling out $48.4 million for other services.

Conveniently, the accounting industry began making this outrageous amount of money from consulting at the same time the SEC's bite was becoming more like a sloppy kiss. Budget cuts meant corresponding cuts in the number of cases the agency could pursue. In 1980, the SEC routinely examined all company filings. By 2000 it was able to check only 8% of them. Whereas it used to go after entire firms, by the time the dot-com boom rolled around it was investigating only individual partners.

Given that reduced oversight was the wood and wind for the firestorm of scandals that would engulf investors' portfolios in 2002, any responsible member of the accounting profession should have seen the flames a mile off.

YOU GOTTA BE KIDDING ME!

Here is a list of seemingly questionable business practices. See if you can discern the activities that are illegal from the ones that are legal. Give yourself one point for each correct answer.

1. Under new SEC guidelines, U.S. companies are now permitted to forcibly transfer the children of American workers to third-world nations to live in squalor and work in factories for pennies a day.
   (*Illegal.* U.S. companies operating in third-world nations are only permitted to do that to indigenous populations.)

2. Under the Generally Accepted Accounting Principles, a company can move an entity off its books if it pays another company to put that subsidiary on its books, even if the risks and rewards stay with the first company.
   (*Legal.* According to a new proposal by the Financial Accounting Standards Board.)

3. Phone companies can switch you to their long-distance service without your consent.
   (*Illegal.* It's called "slamming" and if you've been "slammed," you can report the allegations to the FCC, or you can lodge a complaint with former WorldCom CEO Bernie Ebbers—whose company was the number one generator of FCC slamming complaints and paid $8.5 million in 2002 to settle a lawsuit charging deceptive marketing in California. Good luck.)

4. Under the Generally Accepted Accounting Principles, a company can hide billions in trading profits from long-term contracts in undisclosed cash reserves, while at the same time hiding corporate borrowings and losses in off-the-book partnerships.

(Illegal but commonplace. Enron did this as energy prices leaped in California in late 2000 and early 2001. For more information on Enron's shady business practices, visit any unemployment office in the Houston area.)

5. Goldman Sachs invented a security it called "Monthly Income Preferred Shares" (Mips) which counted as debt on the company's tax return, but as equity on its public books. *(Legal. To learn why, write to crusading Senator Jon Corzine (D-NJ) who was at Goldman Sachs when Mips were invented.)*

6. Thanks to a loophole in recent business regulations, companies can advertise one price for a product and then capriciously charge you a grossly inflated price once you buy it.
(Illegal. Unless you're a home construction contractor or a carpet cleaning company, where this practice is de rigueur.)

7. Because of the market downturn, many existing stock options will cost more to exercise than they are worth. As an enticement, some companies are allowing employees to exchange these worthless options for new ones. One common method is the six-and-one swap, which accounting law conveniently treats as a regular options grant. Employees turn in their existing options, and six months and a day later are granted new, lower priced ones.
(Legal. And terrible for investors who rightly expected "bonuses" to be paid when the company showed growth and profit, rather than the opposite.)

8. Banks that routinely charge customers additional fees for bouncing checks, for using other banks' ATMs, and for falling below minimum specified balances may now charge an undisclosed additional fee on top of the previous fee as a "processing processing charge."

(*Illegal*. This is what's known as "stealing." But it won't be for long—if the banking lobby can just convince a majority of the House and Senate and President Bush.)

9. Thanks to regulatory loopholes, companies can transfer profits earned in America to a paper company in Barbados or Luxembourg, which, through accounting sleight of hand, allows them to transform taxable profits into expenses they can deduct on their American tax return. The paper company then sends the money to the U.S. company's headquarters in Bermuda, which has no income tax. In short, taxable profits have been turned into virtually untaxed dollars for use anywhere in the world. Using this scheme, companies can reduce taxes on American profits to as little as 11%.
    (*Legal*. And despicable.)

10. In an effort to minimize customer confusion as it pertains to product prices, company CEOs regularly confer with one another and agree to sell similar items at the same "set price."
    (*Illegal*. It's known as "price fixing." It's the crime Al Taubman, the head of Sotheby's auction house, was convicted of, and for which he's serving a one-year-and-a-day sentence in jail.)

11. During the 1980s, General Motors protested a move on the part of the Financial Accounting Standards Board to change pension accounting. A compromise was reached whereby companies could guess what profits their pension plans might return, and then report profits as if they had actually done so.
    (*Legal*. And totally confusing. Give yourself one point for just reading it and another point even if you only half understood it.)

Willful Disregard

Although the analysts and the members of the financial press rushed around the corporate barnyard like chickens with their heads newly lopped off when the scandals broke, they'd had all the information they needed to cry foul for many years.

Back in 1999, Ernst & Young paid $335 million to settle allegations that its audit of CUC International failed to reveal $500 million in inflated earnings. By then, WorldCom's accounting fraud was in full swing. But no one was paying attention and drawing parallels with what had happened even further back with Sunbeam. When the company needed to hit some earnings forecasts in 1997/1998, Al Dunlap, its ever-ingenious CEO, came up with this bright idea: even though it's still winter, I'll get several giant retail chains to go ahead and buy their summer items now—things like barbecue grills, lawn chairs, etc.—and let them store the merchandise in Sunbeam warehouses until they needed it shipped. This worked great for the winter numbers, but then summer rolled around and there were no new sales, because everything had been charged to the winter quarter. Sunbeam ended up in bankruptcy, and its accounting accomplice in the lame-brained scheme, none other than Arthur Andersen, paid $110 million to Sunbeam stockholders.

Later that same year Arthur Andersen, long considered the dullest firm in a hyper-square profession, again had flown its freak flag high and wide at the huge garbage disposal conglomerate Waste Management. Over several years it had overstated pretax profits by $1.4 billion. Andersen was accused by the SEC of fraud for okaying false financial statements for four years beginning in 1992, and eventually agreed to pay part of a $220 million Waste Management settlement.

But it was allowed to set a dangerous precedent: paying a fine with no admission of wrongdoing. No Andersen executives even lost their jobs and, in fact, several of the very same executives were involved in the Enron fraud just three years later. One of them, Richard Kutsenda, putting his Waste Management experience to good use, was actually given the task of determining what the shredding policy should be for sensitive documents. That policy would, of course, come in awfully handy when Enron hit the headlines.

And the early warnings didn't come from only Andersen. In what should have been a truly stunning revelation, an internal investigation at PricewaterhouseCoopers in 1998, undertaken at the SEC's behest, exposed over 8,000 cases of PwC executives making investments in companies they audited.

Perhaps the only consolation is that in the dog-eat-dog world of corporate collusion, despite the starring role the accountants played in this burlesque of sleaze and greed, they were betrayed at curtain call. Playing Prince Hal to the accountants' fat Falstaff, the corporate chiefs, who had paid so handsomely for special services, claimed to "know them not." On the witness stand before Congress, Enron's president Jeffrey Skilling was the first to utter the fateful words, "I am not an accountant," no less than seven times. It turns out the glamorous executive boys never really accepted the geeks.

Returning the favor when WorldCom announced its restatement, Arthur Andersen immediately laid all the blame on

WHAT A FINE MESS:
ARTHUR ANDERSEN'S LONG ROAD TO RUIN

1982 In the wake of the Delorean collapse, Andersen pays $60 million to settle investor claims.

1988 When Home State Savings Bank collapses amid charges of bogus accounting, Andersen pays the state of Ohio $5.5 million to cover taxpayer losses.

1993 Andersen pays $82 million to settle a suit brought by the Resolution Trust Corporation contending that Andersen had been negligent in its auditing of Charles H. Keating's Lincoln Savings and Loan Association.

1998 Amidst allegations it helped Waste Management defraud investors, Andersen pays out $95 million to settle lawsuits.

1999 Andersen is accused of signing off on an overly optimistic economic forecast for Colonial Realty, a Connecticut real estate company whose collapse cost investors $300 million. To settle allegations of fraud, Andersen pays out $90 million.

2001, May To settle allegations made by investors of faulty accounting on behalf of the appliance company, Sunbeam, Andersen pays out $110 million.

2001, June After the SEC charges the firm with misstating earnings at Waste Management, Andersen agrees to pay a $7 million fine.

2001, November To settle Waste Management shareholder lawsuits accusing the firm of misstating earnings, Andersen pays out $20 million.

2002, June A Federal District Court jury in Houston finds Andersen guilty of obstruction of justice for destroying thousands of Enron's financial documents.

2002, August On August 31, 2002, the Arthur Andersen accounting firm officially closes its doors.

WorldCom's CFO Scott Sullivan, lamenting "that important information about line costs was withheld from Andersen auditors." But isn't a major accounting firm supposed to be at least as good at accounting as the companies it keeps?

Ultimately, Arthur Andersen took the fall and turned itself in to the government for its "waste management" of crucial documents relating to Enron's baroque corporate structure. Even before the government pounced and the jury pronounced its death sentence, the ratty clients had begun deserting Andersen's sinking ship. So eager were they to display their newfound disdain that commentator Mike Kinsley wrote of the new corporate prudishness, "it's not true that some companies attempted to hire auditors from Arthur Andersen just for the thrill of firing them with a sanctimonious flourish."

With Andersen gone, the remaining four major accounting firms have been busy divesting themselves of their consulting businesses. The jury, however, is still out on how much real reform will make its way into their accounting practices.

The Really Deep Troughs: The Boards

While the accountants conspired with them, and the analysts and business press lauded and glamorized them, CEOs have had no better teammates in the gaming of the system than their collaborators on the corporate boards.

Adelphia Communications imploded in May 2002, the victim of a Shakespearean family drama. If anyone was going to slow down the cash withdrawals from the company, it was not going to be Adelphia's board of directors. That's because the Rigas family and the Adelphia board were pretty much the same thing, with five out of nine directors coming from the Rigas clan. They were a sort of media mafia, a Gambino family for the new media age.

John Rigas, the chairman and CEO, was joined on the board by his three capos—I mean, sons—all of whom also served as executives with Adelphia. Rigas' son-in-law, also a board member, pitched in as a managing partner of an Adelphia-funded vanity project called Praxis Capital Ventures.

Adelphia is a textbook case of what can happen when the dining room becomes the boardroom. After John Rigas resigned in May 2002, Erland Kailbourne was appointed interim-CEO, which showed that, even if the board could no longer keep it all in the immediate family, it could at least keep it in the corporate family: Kailbourne had been head of the company's audit committee since 2001 and must be either extremely stupid or extremely corrupt or both not to have noticed the mind-numbing financial sleaze going on around him.

The family-friendly Adelphia board approved the egregious multi-billion-dollar loans given to the Rigases, while many other Rigas family enrichment projects were undertaken without even getting the board's rubber stamp. The unwittingly generous Adelphia shareholders bought John Rigas his own golf course, his own hockey team, and his far-flung apartments. Adelphia also paid a company owned by John Rigas $2 million dollars for the maintenance of those new properties, including snowplowing and lawn mowing (grass doesn't mow itself, you know). In one especially creative deal, Adelphia was nice enough to finance Rigas' purchase of 3,656 acres of land in Potter County, Pennsylvania, for a paltry $465,000—a good price, which was the least the seller could do after Adelphia also picked up the tab for the timber rights to the same land for $26.5 million. The deal also came with this little rider: the timber rights would automatically revert to Rigas if the family lost control of Adelphia.

Which, of course, is what happened. You'd think at least one person on the board might have asked why a cable company needed timber rights.

And while he might be corrupt, Rigas is no misogynist. Every day was "Take Your Daughter to Work Day" at Adelphia. Ellen Rigas Venetis helped break the glass ceiling by helping herself to loans from Adelphia of more than $3.8 million to finance companies of her own, ErgoArts and SongCatcher Films. Some of the money was spent on the film *Songcatcher*, the story of a woman who collects folk songs in rural Appalachia. According to a plot summary on the Internet Movie Database, when the heroine falls in love with Tom, "a handsome hardened war veteran," he forces her to confront a difficult question: is she "no better than the men who exploit the people and extort their land?" Perhaps it was some sort of $3 million cry for help.

But the nepotism didn't stop there. While daughter Ellen was producing ironically themed movies, her husband, Peter Venetis, was pressing his nose to the pillow-soft grindstone at Praxis Capital, an investment fund to be financed with $65 million in start-up money from Adelphia. While paying Peter Venetis $1.3 million per year for his money management expertise, Praxis made exactly one investment for $1 million.

Bruce Greenwald, a professor at Columbia University Business School, explains the dangers of such family-dominated public companies thus: "In some cases the families that control companies come to treat investors as bondholders. The family thinks its job is to give them a good return. Anything over that return belongs to the family. They don't see equity investors as co-owners." Sounds straight from the Rigas coat of arms.

By the time the Adelphia board came to its senses and finally ended the family feast, the tab for the feeding frenzy was a 99% decline in the company's stock, which wiped out some $6 billion in shareholder equity.

But family-run firms are, of course, not the only businesses that pack their boards with directors who will reliably look the other way. In fact, almost all corporate boards operate with something like the rigor of, say, your average security screener at the Islamabad International Airport. All too often, the corporate directors that make up boards are overpaid, underworked, and excessively beholden to the CEOs they are supposedly paid to oversee, and who have very likely appointed them.

The boards themselves are free to operate with virtually no oversight. The lack of regular and rigorous assessment of the performance of corporate boards is astounding. A National Association of Corporate Directors commission revealed that 63% of CEOs say they've never been part of a board evaluation as a director on an outside board. Furthermore, 40% admitted that their own firms don't have any regular board-performance assessments.

It's clear that the recent spree of corporate crimes and cover-ups couldn't have been pulled off quite so profitably without these largely unnamed co-conspirators.

Take Global Crossing. At least 10 of the 30 directors who sat on its board during its short, disastrous life had close business ties to the company. Four of the directors were Global Crossing executives, and former director Norman Brownstein was actually a company attorney. A fifth board member—and member of Global Crossing's audit committee—Maria Elena Lagomasino, was chairwoman of the wealth management division of the J. P. Morgan Private Bank, one of the company's leading creditors and willing victims.

When the directors realized Global Crossing was beginning to flounder, they got out while the getting was good, which is to say, golden. After making, one supposes, their first accurate assessment of the company's real prospects, most of the directors gave up their board seats, promptly sold their shares, and left the little-guy investors to fend for themselves. James McDonald and Douglas McCorkindale, CEOs of Scientific-

Atlanta and Gannett, were two of the first to leave the Global Crossing board. Though they refused to comment on the reasons for their departure, I imagine it's because they wanted to spend more time with their families.

Global Crossing's boardroom had always been little more than a corporate pit stop. Almost 60% of Global Crossing's directors served less than three years, a very poor record considering that 60% of all corporate directors in the U.S. serve for six years or more. As the company's stock price started to drop, directors began jumping ship at an ever-increasing rate. In 2001, 10 out of the company's 11 directors quit.

In fact, Global Crossing's board had such a high turnover rate that just introducing the members to one another must have taken up the first hour of every meeting. While Adelphia board meetings looked like the Rigas family Thanksgiving dinner, Global Crossing's were like chance encounters in an airport lounge. The only thing the directors knew for sure is that the next time they met, if they met again, they'd be surrounded by new faces.

This absurd system ensured that none of the directors had the expertise necessary to assess the risky strategies being promoted by the large-living chairman Gary Winnick. Not that they would have interfered with Winnick anyway. Many boards are incentivized (Wall Street-ese for "bribed") to forget everything they ever knew, if anything, about proper corporate governance.

The breakdown of corporate oversight at Global Crossing resulted in the fourth largest bankruptcy in U.S. history, wiped out $57 billion of shareholder equity, and destroyed 9,000 jobs.

The insidious process of corrupting outside directors by bribing them with fees or payments of one sort or another is all there in the fine print of a company's annual report—if you can find it. Frequent laundering terms for these expenses are the meaningless headings "certain other" or "related charges."

But I Want to Direct!

Given all of the conflicts of interest and the clubby coziness of the boardroom social set, is it any wonder that boards cast such a lazy eye on their companies' true performance? A board generally has both an audit committee, which is supposed to keep a close and informed watch on the company's finances, and a compensation committee, which determines executive pay. In most cases—90% by one recent measure—the compensation and audit committees of the board are composed of outside directors. That's the good news. But don't pop the champagne quite yet.

These "outsiders" are often insiders in all but name, if you factor in all the consulting deals, legal retainers, and cross-investments. And, in the rare instance in which a board member really is an outsider, there's the common fetish for committing and/or overlooking any acts of fraud that bolster the bottom line. Most directors are senior executives themselves and they have a general and mutual interest in keeping executive pay high and safely immune from unpleasant things like poor company performance.

Ken Lay sat on the board of Eli Lilly, Dennis Kozlowski sat on the board of Raytheon, and former Johnson & Johnson CEO Ralph Larsen sits on the boards of Xerox, AT&T, and GE. This is how a cozy industry standard is established that will trickle across, up, but seldom down, in the fullness of time. Or at least until the fullness of Chapter 11.

Social ties also incline directors to side with the well-heeled managers against the grubby individual shareholders. After all, corporate directors are members of the most exclusive club in the world: the secretive "National Association for the Advancement of Incredibly Rich Guys." If they're not

CEOs themselves, then they're probably longtime friends of CEOs—like Martha Stewart, who sat daintily on Sam Waksal's board at ImClone—or fellow members of any number of other boards or fashionable charities.

Although the ties that bind corporate directors and CEOs are informal, subtle, and difficult to quantify, they're powerful enough to foster a collegial spirit in the boardroom that frowns upon criticism or any genuine attempt to exercise real oversight.

This is not to say, of course, that these boards can't be corrupted much more directly, too. At EMC, a large producer of computer storage media based in Hopkinton, Massachusetts, Chairman of the Board and CEO Richard Egan (his wife, son, and brother-in-law also happen to sit on the board) actually appointed himself to the compensation committee, where I'm sure he can be counted on to be rigorously impartial in determining his own salary.

And if compensation committees are only too happy to pad corporate executives' pay, audit committees seem all too willing to be bamboozled. The purpose of audit committees is to validate a company's financial reporting. Therefore, the committees' members are supposedly held to a higher standard than run-of-the-mill board members. Companies listed on the New York Stock Exchange must have audit committees made up entirely of independent directors, but only one member is actually required to have accounting or "related financial management expertise."

The only bar that audit members of NASDAQ companies are required to clear is that they "be able to read and understand financial statements." I'm sure investors are reassured knowing that the same set of skills one needs to understand a *Dilbert* cartoon is all it takes to qualify you to become an audit committee member. But, sadly, even this standard is apparently so high that companies feel the need to qualify it. The annual report of blue chip financial giant Goldman Sachs includes the wonderfully comforting disclaimer that "the members of the Audit Committee are not professionally engaged in the practice of auditing or accounting and are not experts in the fields of accounting or auditing." Then what are they doing on an audit committee? And for an investment bank, no less. It sounds like perhaps they'd be better suited on the "committee" that, say, cleans the offices at night. But, of course, I'm sure Goldman requires actual experience for that job.

Similar statements, essentially attesting to the incompetence of a company's hand-picked audit committee, appear in virtually every proxy report. The Washington Post Company, for instance, helpfully explains that its audit committee "relied . . . without independent verification, on management's representation that the financial statements have been prepared with integrity and objectivity." Board members also probably believe it when the proctologist says "you won't even feel this."

You Scratch My Back, and I'll Scratch Yours, and Yours, and Yours, and Yours

Former elected officials are sought after as board members because they can always be counted on to call in some Beltway favors from their former government colleagues who will no doubt at some point join them on a board or two. In fact, this luxurious little rest stop on the way to retirement is so popular in Washington that some former pols sit on a stunning number of boards.

Here are some of the most in demand powerbrokers:

William H. Gray III (D-Pa.) is a former member of the U.S. House of Representatives. He currently sits on nine boards: Dell Computer, EDS, J.P. Morgan Chase, the Municipal Bond Investors Assurance Corp., Pfizer, Prudential Insurance, Rockwell International, Visteon, and Viacom. Clearly worried that all this corporate exposure might make him too much of a fat cat to pass through the eye of a needle, he is also a senior minister at Bright Hope Baptist Church in Philadelphia.

Former Senate Majority Leader George J. Mitchell sits on so many corporate boards it's a wonder his behind isn't shaped like the seat of a high-backed, padded leather executive chair. Mitchell holds board directorships at Casella Waste Systems, FedEx, Staples, Starwood Hotels & Resorts Worldwide, Unilever NV, UnumProvident, Disney, and Xerox. And that's all on the side. By day he toils away as a partner at the law firm of Verner, Liipfert, Bernhard, McPherson, and Hand. Mitchell is also president of the Economic Club of Washington, Chancellor of Queen's University in Belfast, a senior fellow at Columbia University's School of International and Public Affairs, and one of the principal architects of the Northern Ireland peace plan. He slices, he dices, he does it all.

Former Senator Sam Nunn (D-Ga.) is a director on seven boards: Coca-Cola, Dell Computer (with Gray), General Electric, Internet Security Systems, Scientific-Atlanta, ChevronTexaco, and Total System Services. Nunn is also a partner at the Atlanta law firm King & Spalding.

As you would imagine, in addition to lots of cash, one byproduct of all this cozy camaraderie is a huge pile of conflicts of interest. Nunn's firm, for instance, does considerable legal work for GE, a company he's ostensibly "supervising," while Disney paid Mitchell's law firm nearly $1.3 million for legal and regulatory work. In addition, Disney paid Mitchell $50,000 for consulting services in 2001.

The big kahuna in the world of corporate directors is longtime Washington insider Vernon Jordan. Jordan sits on a full dozen boards, including American Express, DaimlerChrysler, Dow Jones, Revlon, Sara Lee, and Xerox. He's also a partner at the Washington law firm Akin, Gump, Strauss, Hauer & Feld. On top of all of this he's a board member at Howard University and the LBJ Foundation, a trustee at the Brookings Institution and a senior managing director at Lazard Freres & Co. Just trying to manage Vernon Jordan's schedule could crash a PalmPilot.

Experts in corporate governance say a director should spend a minimum of four hours per week executing his duties for the board. In the case of many directors, unless they are bionic, cloned, or have days that are 36 hours long, lots of board meetings are going to have a few leftover doughnuts.

Then there's an entirely new category, with an entirely new kind of inexperience: the celebrity directors. These are people with admirable accomplishments but in entirely unrelated fields, like the distinguished cancer researcher and Enron director Dr. John Mendelsohn, who was presumably researching cancer and saving lives while Ken Lay, Jeff Skilling, and crew worked their accounting magic. Mendelsohn is also a director of ImClone, a company much more in Mendelsohn's wheelhouse but now embroiled in the Waksal indictment.

Of course, among Mendelsohn's fellow ImClone directors was the ultimate celebrity director, that doyenne of domesticity, Martha Stewart. While Martha's skill at weaving a holiday wreath out of bittersweet canes is undisputed, it does not appear to have translated into aptitude for evaluating cures for cancer. She did prove her flair for finance, however, when she frantically unloaded nearly $250,000 worth of stock hours ahead of the release of an eviscerating FDA assessment of ImClone's experimental drug, Erbitux. Don't try that one at home. But then you probably wouldn't, since you're not likely to find yourself getting phone calls from people who know about such reports before the public does.

Corporate Boards Know Where
Their Bread Is Buttered

Given how clubby corporate boardrooms are, it's no wonder they so readily look the other way while CEOs loot their companies. Sometimes, however, the boards go even further than just blind acquiescence. Often, a board will actually circle the wagons around a CEO under the gun. That's just what the board of Starwood Hotels (part of former Senator Mitchell's vast directorship collection) did in 2001 when it awarded a generous raise to Starwood's CEO, Barry S. Sternlicht, despite tumbling profits and a bloodbath at the top that cost most of Sternlicht's deputies their jobs. (After all, somebody had to be the scapegoat, and I wouldn't be surprised if Sternlicht likes to be known as a good delegator.) The individual, small-fry investors, however, knew exactly who was to blame. Responding to the turmoil, an almost-unheard-of three-quarters of Starwood's shareholders passed a resolution demanding changes in the board. But in a telling demonstration of their lack of accountability, the board and Sternlicht simply noted the voting results, chuckled to themselves, and carried on.

Or, take the case of the ex-high-flying E*Trade Group, one of the biggest duds of the Internet boom. CEO Christos M. Cotsakos has such a talent for wasting money that he would even waste money to brag about wasting money: he once bought ad time during the Super Bowl to show a wind-up toy monkey playing the cymbals with the tag line, "Well, we just wasted two million bucks." But he was being modest.

For he wasted much, much more than that—and mostly on himself. In 2001, the board awarded Cotsakos an astonishing $80 million pay package, an increase of over $75 million from his pay for the prior year of $4.6 million. Yes, the share price for E*Trade rose a couple of bucks that year, but then it just as quickly dropped again and is now trading at just over $4.50. For that Cotsakos deserved a 94% pay increase? And $15 million to cover a forgiven loan and another $15 million to cover the taxes on that loan? E*Trade's board justified the package by citing Cotsakos' "vision." He must have had something more impressive than vision, say a very large gun. Or at the very least something sharp in his hand, a pair of scissors, perhaps, or a threatening-looking pair of tweezers. That would at least give the board of directors some defense as to why it emptied the vault so quickly.

Under fire from shareholders after the package was announced, Cotsakos resolutely refused to replace his board's compensation committee. The chairman of the over-compensation committee was David Hayden, who is also the chairman of the board of Critical Path, a struggling supplier of corporate e-mail systems. While Hayden was scratching Cotsakos' back with gigantic paychecks, Cotsakos was scratching right back by serving as a dutifully cooperative member of the Critical Path board. And why shouldn't he? After all, E*Trade was both an investor in Critical Path and a customer, purchasing e-mail services from the company. Imagine Cotsakos' surprise when, in July 2000, Hayden dumped millions of dollars worth of Critical Path's stock just before the SEC announced it had uncovered accounting violations at the company.

A similarly arrogant, "screw the public" indifference to shareholder opinion appears to have informed the boardroom decision-making at Tyson Foods. This is the Arkansas chicken-processing behemoth that distinguished itself by paying $6 million in 1997 to settle accusations that the company made illegal gifts to Clinton's agriculture secretary, Mike Espy, while regulations that would have affected Tyson were being considered by Espy's department. Don Tyson, the company's chairman at the time, and his son John Tyson, then vice chairman, were named unindicted co-conspirators and accused of arranging for the gifts, which included a college loan the Tyson Foundation arranged for Mr. Espy's girlfriend.

Tyson's board includes four corporate consultants, three of whom are former employees who, collectively, have millions of dollars worth of contracts with either retired Tyson chairman and current director Don Tyson or current CEO John Tyson. Despite a 50% decline in Tyson's shares since 1997, the board thought that Don Tyson needed an $825,000 bonus and an $8 million, 10-year consulting contract. Another director on the Tyson board has a 10-year, $4 million consulting contract, and Tyson junior got a $2.1 million bonus.

Perhaps the longest running battle between a CEO shielded by a toadying board and exasperated shareholders came to an end in 1999, when William Farley, a leveraged buyout specialist, was finally ejected from the top spot at Fruit of the Loom, which itself went into Chapter 11 a few months later. Farley, who acquired the underwear maker in 1985, spent a merry 10 years pillaging the company, until shareholders wearied of what the *National Journal* called "plundering assets, bungling business deals, hiding financial problems, and profiting from insider trading," and began to clamor for Farley's ouster. Astonishingly, Fruit of the Loom's board—hand-picked by Farley— defended him for almost five more years, okaying $103 million in sweetheart loans to the CEO and agreeing to a relocation of the company's nominal headquarters to the Cayman Islands to limit its liabilities.

Tips for Aspiring Pigs

Another crafty way to limit corporate liability, and, thus, accountability, can be found in the Chancery Court of Delaware. Sixty percent of all Fortune 500 corporations are incorporated in Delaware for a very simple reason: the state has a tradition—dating back to 1792—of backing managers and directors in legal disputes with shareholders. These notoriously friendly laws offer boardroom miscreants even more cover when skirting their corporate responsibility.

The only price a director pays for helping to steer a company down the tubes is a short-lived—and getting shorter—stink by association. Not only do these indestructible executives fail all the way to the top, many of them are able to survive corporate failures with their good name and other directorships amazingly intact. Why? Largely, because of a sort of mutually assured destruction pact among the corporate business class. I won't penalize you for looting your company while running it into the ground, if you won't penalize me for looting my company while running it into the ground. It's a win-win strategy. At least, for them.

The poor service that we, the public, receive from corporate directors does not, alas, come cheap. The average salary for a director at the largest 200 companies in America is $137,000, although many directors make far more. AOL Time Warner's board members raked in about $843,200 in stock for their attendance at board meetings in 2001. If the board had four two-hour meetings a year—about par for the course—the lackadaisical directors would have made roughly $29 a second. That adds up to about $17,500 per 10-minute trip to the bathroom. And that's just for *bad* advice. You can only imagine what they'd charge for advice that would actually *help* the company. As it was, the policies upon which the AOL board advised and consented have yielded a precipitous 86% drop in AOL's share price since December 1999. The company would have fared better if it had just given all the directors a million dollars apiece not to show up at all.

But, as with executive compensation, juicy paychecks are only the beginning. Corporate directors also harvest filthy lucre more indirectly: as the recipients of a plethora of sweetheart deals with the companies they oversee. According to Executive Compensation Advisory Services, about 10% of the Fortune 1,000 companies pay outside directors additional consulting fees. Per director, those fees average $224,300 a year.

And shareholders can't even find out about such payments because they're so often deliberately hidden beneath the same euphemistic language that shrouds the misdeeds of the rest of corporate America. In 2001, Tyco paid outgoing director Frank Walsh $10 million but "disclosed" it to the SEC as a "certain other" expense. If you called it what it really was—"a bribe," "free money," "a huge ass kiss," or a "$10 million accounting trick"—that might be more likely to raise a flag with the IRS. And with the shareholders. But who needs that?

Just as CEOs were given huge amounts of stock options, supposedly to further align their interests with those of the shareholders, starting in the 1980s, directors too were given tantalizing option packages. But to directors who hold options, an exorbitant spree of acquisitions financed by a massive debt load may seem like a brilliant idea, just as long as it gooses the stock price long enough for them to make a killing by unloading their shares. Of course, many corporate directors aren't motivated by money alone. Perks are just as good. General Motors, for instance, gives its directors a new car (repair bills included) every three months as part of the company's "product evaluation program." Calling it the "Free Car for Keeping Your Yap Shut" program was soundly vetoed by management. And does the fact that board members need a new car every three months really speak very well about the quality of the company's products?

Directors on the board of UAL, the parent company of United Airlines, get unlimited free first-class trips, as do their families. Plus seconds on the warm fresh cookies baked prior to landing. And AT&T directors get free long-distance phone service and phone and computer equipment, all installed gratis.

Then there's the alluring bonus Callaway Golf gives its board members. All new products are immediately dispatched to the board members' homes, including new golf balls, irons, and, of course, the treasured Big Bertha drivers.

With goodies like these, you almost have to feel bad for Tyson's board of directors. What are they going to do with a lifetime supply of lousy frozen chicken?

THE BINGE AND
THE RECKONING

The Chickens Come Home to Roost

"The greatest price of refusing to participate in politics is being governed by your inferiors."

—PLATO
The Republic

THE PRESIDENT HAS TRIED to explain away the avalanche of corporate corruption—the billion-dollar restatements, fun-with-numbers accounting, the sweetheart deals for corporate insiders—as nothing more than the predictable result of a little too much economic hooch, the inevitable hangover from a decade-long corporate binge.

As always, Bush likes to keep things simple and down home. America got a little sloshed at the big Wall Street office party, and now all it has to do is down the congressional equivalent of Alka-Seltzer—a hearty swig of some stomach-soothing reforms—put an ice bag on its head and sleep it off.

The hangover theme is an interesting metaphor given the president's well-publicized background as a reformed party animal. After all, he's famously recounted how, on the morning after his fortieth birthday party, following a night of boisterous, boozy celebration, he awoke with a killer hangover and suddenly knew what had to be done. He had to quit drinking. And he did. And if it worked for him, it'll work for America.

But apparently America's corporate hangover isn't quite killer enough for the president because, despite his public pronouncements to the contrary, he has steadfastly refused to swear off the corporate hard stuff. He's still giving his boardroom buddies ample wiggle room to keep bellying up to the corruption bar. Or maybe he's just a believer in the "hair of the dog that bit you" school, where the best cure for drinking too much is a few more drinks.

If Bush were serious about sobering up corporate America, he would have pushed for much more substantive reforms, and not just after WorldCom hit the front pages, but right after the Enron scandal broke.

After all, our reformaphobic elected officials must know that what corporate America needs is a full-scale intervention—shipping CEOs off to greed detox. But they just can't bring themselves to do it because they are under the influence of their own powerful addiction: their dependence on massive doses of campaign cash.

The World Before and
After WorldCom

The collapse of WorldCom in June 2002 marked the dividing line between two distinct phases of the post-Enron corporate reform movement. Up until then the Enron scandal was about to be added to the list of recent Next Big Things that fell far short of expectations—an ignominious inventory that includes the Y2K bug, killer bees, New Coke, and the Segway scooter.

Lawrence Lindsey, the president's top economic advisor, and a former advisor to Enron, went so far as to claim that the

Enron disaster was "a tribute to American capitalism." And 9/11 was a tribute to Islamic ingenuity.

One salivating banking industry lobbyist even crowed "Enron is over." And, as is so often the case in Washington, the official spinmeisters started circling the carcass, offering all the lame rationalizations they could muster why nothing ever came of all the promises to change the sleazy status quo. The simple truth is that if they could have gotten away with it, our politicians would have done nothing at all.

Here's a Beltway sampler of the most popular excuses for doing nothing that made the rounds pre-WorldCom.

The "Chicken Little" Excuse. This is a favorite of business lobbyists who love to run around Washington yelling, "The Dow is falling, the Dow is falling!" Their stock warning is that any legislation limiting the unfettered practices of corporate America could send an already sputtering economy into an irreversible death spiral. This is like suggesting that a dying cancer patient not have surgery to remove a malignant tumor because the procedure might leave a scar.

The "We Shall Pass No Law Before Its Time" Excuse. In this moldy oldie lawmakers claim they're for reform—it's just that they want to "be careful" and "do it right." So they hem and haw and appear ever so grave and thoughtful. And then just wait out the public's attention span while the reform in question dies a slow, quiet death. A textbook example was offered by Mike Siegel, spokesman for the Senate Finance Committee: "We are more interested in getting it done right than getting it done fast." Sounds sensible until you realize that, before WorldCom imploded, reform legislation languished for months in the Senate and had been written off as almost certain not to pass.

The "Buck Stops There" Excuse. In this venerable dodge, any hard-nosed inquiry is sabotaged by suggesting that someone—anyone—other than the entity doing the investigating is better suited to the task. For instance, if Congress is holding hearings on Wall Street malfeasance, you quickly suggest that this is a matter better suited to the regulators at the Securities and Exchange Commission. If the SEC is leading the probe, you suggest it could be better handled by the Justice Department. And as soon as those Justice Department subpoenas start flying, you immediately close the circle and say that this, really, is a job for Congress. It's just a question of filling in the blanks and shuffling the players. Think of it as three-card monty for the K Street crowd. It's quick. It's easy. And the winners have been determined long before the cards are dealt.

An especially deft post-Enron twist on the "right idea, wrong venue" excuse saw Republicans—those diehard champions of states' rights—deriding the rights of states like New York and California to curtail abuses. Suddenly, those laminated cards of the 10th Amendment that so many GOP candidates carry in their breast pockets were replaced by crib notes on the virtues of federal power.

The "Reformers are Just a Bunch of Grandstanding Politicians Looking to Grab the Spotlight" Excuse. Well, even a stopped watch is right twice a day.

And finally, the "Not Enough Oxygen in the Room" Excuse holds that, because the president's Homeland Security proposal—referred to by "Not Enough Oxygen" devotees as "the most massive reorganization of the federal government since the New Deal"—was so, well, massive there would be no room on the legislative calendar for anything else in the foreseeable future. In the classic trade-off between guns and butter, our legislators selectively emphasize the former over the latter whenever it suits their larger purpose of corporate-inspired inertia.

Corporate Big Guns,
Loaded with Money

The real reason no reforms were passed in the many months after the Enron revelations was the one we didn't hear: there was no Enron-inspired reform because the big donors were determined there would be no Enron-inspired reform. And they were willing to pay through the nose to guarantee it.

Case in point: in March 2002, the House Energy and Commerce Committee, fresh off its public flogging of Enron execs, sent letters out to the big securities firms seeking information about their involvement with Enron's shadier practices. Several of those firms responded not with humble compliance but by threatening to turn off the campaign contribution spigot unless the reformers cooled their jets. National Republican Congressional Committee chairman Tom Davis confirmed the donor uprising: "They were very free with their complaints." (They were also very free with their money—the securities and investment industry has given a monumental $273 million in campaign contributions since 1990.)

Then came WorldCom, and our Washington lapdogs suddenly remembered they were on the public leash. Even the most seasoned money grubbers know that the only thing that trumps big money is big public outrage. One of the last to catch on was Senator Trent Lott. The Trent Lott Leadership Institute at the University of Mississippi had, after all, been the recipient of $1 million in WorldCom donations.

I'm sure, completely coincidentally, Lott had appointed a senior WorldCom executive to a commission on Internet commerce, a major interest for the telecom industry, and had taken WorldCom's side in the battle over Internet broadband legislation. And when WorldCom had to come clean on its multi-billion-dollar accounting fraud, Lott very decently declined to join in the bashing. "Well, obviously we are very disappointed," he said. "I don't know the truth yet of what happened. I don't know yet, is this an Arthur Andersen problem or is this some sort of something that our corporate officials did wrong. I don't know. But it is a concern and we have to address it." Attention, big business! This kind of mealy-mouthed defense is what your millions of dollars in donations buys.

But it was too late. With WorldCom the scandals had finally reached critical mass. Our political leaders realized that something must be done, and now the issue became just how little they could get away with.

Watching the president unleashing his newfound outrage after months of virtual silence and ho-hum shrugs conjured up the image of Louis, Claude Raines' police chief in *Casablanca,* announcing that he is "shocked, shocked!" to find that gambling has been going on at Rick's Café just seconds before picking up his winnings from the previous night. After all, phony-baloney accounting tricks helped Bush collect his own winnings of $848,560 in 1990 on an insider transaction at Harken Energy, which his father's SEC investigated but ultimately declined to prosecute. All he needed was Raines' pencil-thin mustache and Brit-doing-a-Frenchman accent. And given the fact that the SEC is currently investigating shady bookkeeping at Halliburton under former CEO Dick Cheney, one can easily picture Rick and Louis—I mean, Dick and Georgie—ambling off down the tarmac at Andrews Air Force Base after dispatching their underlings to "round up the usual suspects" and embarking on what promises to be the continuation of a beautiful—i.e. highly profitable—friendship.

Back in those days you could already tell the president's heart wasn't really in his new tough rhetoric. He called, for example, on corporate executives not to "fudge the numbers." Given the daily revelations of corporate criminality and its devastating impact—on jobs, savings, and faith in our economy—admonishing crooked CEOs not to "fudge the numbers" is as lame as suggesting that suicide bombers not "spoil the day" of their intended victims. The desultory nature of Bush's commitment to cleaning up the corporate sewer was made all the more evident in a rare instance of unscripted presidential musing: "I believe people have taken a step back and asked, 'What's important in life?' You know, the bottom line and this corporate America stuff—is that important? Or is serving your neighbor, loving your neighbor like you'd like to be loved yourself?" Yes, I bet Ken Lay is out loving his neighbor as he'd like to be loved himself right now.

Meanwhile, Harvey Pitt tried to recast himself as a combination of Dirty Harry and Howard Beale. This was the same Harvey Pitt who once authored a white paper arguing against government efforts to eliminate conflicts of interests among corporate accountants. And the same Harvey Pitt who continued to meet privately with former clients under SEC investigation even after taking office. Suddenly he wanted to be seen as the "very tough cop on the beat." Like a wannabe Clint Eastwood, he reacted to the WorldCom revelations with his best tough-guy snarl: "Criminal charges may be too good for the people who brought about this mess." What does he have in mind instead—public execution? Thanks for your enthusiasm, Harvey, but the public would actually be very happy with criminal charges. Lots of them.

Pitt went so far as to actually quote Beale's famous "I'm mad as hell, and I'm not going to take it anymore" rant from *Network*, during a speech at the Economic Club of New York. Hearing Pitt go ballistic over corporate malfeasance was about as believable as hearing Al Gore fume "to hell with the polls" and promise to really "let it rip" next time he runs.

In his essay "Politics and the English Language" George Orwell wrote: "The great enemy of clear language is insincerity.

. . . Political language . . . is designed to make lies sound truthful and murder respectable." And to allow corporate coddlers like Pitt and Bush to repackage themselves as born-again crusaders for reform while they continue to tolerate a corporate culture in which CEOs can call fraud a "restatement," and don't have to admit wrongdoing even when caught picking their shareholders' pockets, I'm sorry, fellas, but the nation doesn't buy your "restatement of yearnings."

Wacko in Waco: The Brunch Bushians Drink the Kool-Aid

The same mood of unreality laced the air during a much-touted gathering in the middle of August 2002.

At the behest of their charismatic leader, the cult members gathered in Waco, a hot, dusty town on the flat, featureless central Texas plain. They had been summoned to hear an endless series of droning sermons from the leader himself and his fellow fanatics.

Thunderously denouncing all doubters as heretics, the speakers put forward a bizarre religious vision, one that no sane person could accept. The only thing missing was Janet Reno and her flamethrower.

The revival meeting in question, otherwise known as "The President's Economic Forum," gained added significance from the fact that the president took precious time—a whole half-day, in fact—away from his month-long vacation to attend, though it's not like he had to travel very far. No, this time the mountain of true believers came to Mohammed.

The forum ended with the steady whoosh of departing corporate jets instead of a fiery apocalypse. This time the conflagration wasn't in Waco but on Wall Street, where one airline declared bankruptcy, another threatened to if it didn't get what it wanted, and a third announced a massive restructuring with 7,000 lost jobs. In Washington, meanwhile, Alan Greenspan declined to embarrass his boss by lowering interest rates— although the Fed had assessed the current economic outlook in unusually gloomy terms.

While the President may have acknowledged that our economy was "challenged," an understatement akin to saying that David Koresh was "a tad kooky," the hallelujah chorus that was determined to drown out facts with blind faith had clearly won the day. No one mentioned, for example, the expanding budget deficit or the exploding trade deficit, and no one dared bring up the heresy of reconsidering the president's disastrous tax cut.

Like the Branch Davidians, the Brunch Bushians found comfort by withdrawing from a world that was confusing, complicated, and just a little too unfriendly of late. But while Bush preached to the choir at Baylor University, an ominous rumbling was coming from outside. This time, it was not ATF sharpshooters and tanks, it was those ordinary citizens the Brunch Bushians had pretended to include in Waco. They kept losing jobs and losing their savings while their president kept telling them that, despite the increasingly grim realities of their daily lives, they still gotta believe in the Bushians' Holy Trinity: more tax cuts, less regulation, and more domestic energy exploration.

Amen, and pass the marshmallows, pardner. I feel a political firestorm coming on.

Reform Sleds a Slippery Slope

Substantive, tough reform was never on the agenda, but after the collapse of WorldCom, the "genius of capitalism" crowd knew it had to adopt a new strategy: publicly embrace reform while working diligently behind the scenes to undermine it. Hug it closely, get it under control, and then quietly stab it in the back.

The fools on the Hill practiced a time-honored Washington game plan: start with brash resistance, move on to insincere support, take control by going on a full-steam offensive, and then, hidden by swirling layers of demagoguery, engage in back-channel efforts to kneecap whatever meager reforms manage to survive the legislative process. Call it How to Succeed in Killing Reform While Looking Like a Reformer.

For a textbook example of how this game works, one need look no further than the efforts of the Business Roundtable, a powerful lobbying group made up of the CEOs of 150 of the largest corporations in America. The Roundtable's griddle must be overheating from all the waffling they've been doing lately.

Even as late as mid-May 2002, some seven months after the Enron story broke, the Knights of the Roundtable were still in Stage One: full-throated resistance to change (known to students of the campaign finance reform wars as the Mitch McConnell Method). Standing shoulder-to-shoulder with such anti-corporate reform stalwarts as Senator Phil Gramm, Representative Michael Oxley, and, yes, President Bush, these knights in manure-splattered armor helped lead the charge against reform in general, and Senator Paul Sarbanes' accounting bill in particular.

In a letter sent to the members of Sarbanes' Banking Committee—part of yet another massive lobbying effort organized by the astonishingly militant accounting industry—the Business Roundtable expressed concern that the bill would "inhibit the ability of U.S. public corporations to compete, create jobs and generate economic growth." Note to the 18,550 employees who are the collateral damage of the accounting-triggered explosion at WorldCom: be sure to send your résumés to the Business Roundtable. No doubt they'll help you find a new position with the same zeal and alacrity with which they cost you your old one.

Instead of strict new laws, the Roundtable came out in favor of—who'd have guessed?—industry self-regulation. It's the classic beginning of Stage Two. Acknowledge *some* change is needed, but not any new laws. No, what we need is to "enforce the current laws more vigorously." In this case, the point was made emphatically by a public call for corporate executives to, apparently out of the goodness of their hearts, simply obey the best practices of doing business.

The Roundtable also offered a stale set of "Principles of Corporate Governance." These "guiding principles" included such stern pronouncements as "The corporation has a responsibility to deal with its employees in a fair and equitable manner," and "It is the responsibility of the independent accounting firm to ensure that it is in fact independent." Slow down, fellas! Rome wasn't built in a day. Reassuringly, the Roundtable also called on all firms to carry out their work "in accordance with Generally Accepted Auditing Standards." Generally accepted by whom, Arthur Andersen? Or by the pharmaceutical giant Merck, which claimed in July 2002 that a $12 billion sales pad was in line with generally accepted accounting practices? And the terrifying thing is, they're probably right. The problem is, the accounting industry is obviously able to generally accept conduct that our country can't generally afford.

Which brings us to WorldCom—and Adelphia, and Xerox, and Tyco, and Merrill Lynch, and Martha. As the avalanche built up speed, the Business Roundtable quickly shifted to the full-blown mature period of Stage Two, also known as the old "hug and mug," according to which you reverse your rhetoric, while your goal remains exactly the same—in this case gutting any prospect for meaningful reform. In this phase, you hit the political talk-show circuit, as Roundtable chairman John Dillon did in the summer of 2002, and tout your support of the very bill you were, only weeks before, working so hard to kill. Or, better yet, you introduce your own Trojan horse reform bill. Ideally, this will drain away the critical number of votes from the real reform bill, while also allowing your fellow anti-reformers to go back to their districts claiming to have voted for reform.

These gambits are particularly effective when your interviewers courteously neglect to probe you on your "Come to Jesus" transformation. A Get-Out-of-Jail-Free attitude that may account for how brazenly these guys switch sides—as if all they have to do is change jerseys and suddenly they're on our team. Watching John Castellani, president of the Roundtable, Senator Jon Corzine and all the rest of the ersatz corporate reformers, I wondered: Where were they in the nineties when, you know, all this corporate mischief was going on? After all, a lot of the clues were there—even filed with the SEC—available to anyone who had chosen to look for them. Why weren't they—and why, for that matter, wasn't the financial press—crying foul about these things ten, five or even one year ago? Were they unable to find the SEC in the phone book? Or were they too caught up in the irrational exuberance to notice?

No one held President Bush's feet to the fire over his own miraculous foxhole conversion, either. After all, Bush is as adept at the abrupt face-saving about-face as anyone. In his schoolmarmish post-WorldCom lecture to Wall Street, he called for arming the SEC with 100 new enforcement officers—just months after proposing cutting back the SEC's fraud investigators. And in October 2002, just months after authorizing a $776 million annual budget for the SEC, he proposed cutting it by $200 million.

One of the main goals in this second stage of reform resistance is to blur the distinctions between real and phony reformers and between real, concrete reform and the vague principle of reform in general. Lots of smoke. Many mirrors. Toward this obfuscatory end, the Roundtable took out a full-page ad in the *New York Times*, proclaiming, "Enough is enough" and trumpeting its so-broad-it's-meaningless support for "the proposals for reform put forward by The President, Members of Congress, and the leading stock exchanges." Exactly which members of Congress might those be, guys? And which proposals? The ones offered by Senator Sarbanes or the feeble fixes put forth by Representative Oxley? Or doesn't it really matter, just so long as you dress up as "reformers"?

You Call That Reform?

The smoke-and-mirrors approach was evident when, goaded by a rash of bad press, a very public lashing at the congressional whipping post, and a 38% drop in the company's stock, mighty Citigroup announced in the middle of August 2002 a major change in the way the banking giant does business. CEO Sandy Weill characterized the move as part of Citigroup's campaign "to be a leader in defining and adopting higher standards."

Notice he didn't say "high," but, rather, "higher." Relative to what the standards have been, yeah, I guess "higher" shouldn't be too much of a problem. And what exactly were these higher standards, deemed worthy of such public self-congratulation? The headline-grabber was that Citigroup will no longer provide financing to companies that conceal debt from shareholders. In other words: it's no longer going to aid and abet the fraudulent acts of corporate crooks. How noble. What's next, a splashy press release touting the fact that Citigroup will be lowering Osama bin Laden's overdraft limit?

At the same time Citigroup was pledging to mend its ways, it continued to defend its role in helping Enron hide billions in debt by claiming that it never knew that Enron was using shady transactions to defraud shareholders. It's a bit like the driver of the getaway car proclaiming his innocence because the guys running out of the bank with masks and bags of money never told him they were robbers. Maybe they were just really shy and didn't like carrying wallets.

Saint Sandy also vowed that Citigroup will start expensing stock options in 2003, and gave himself another proud pat on the back for complying with the SEC's demand to certify the accuracy of his company's financial reports. It's an indication of how low corporate America has sunk that Weill's pale concessions earned major coverage around the country. I guess we're living at a time when "Big Corporation Announces It Will Do The Right Thing" really is news.

Sadly, we can't rely on selfless, conscientious business leaders to police themselves. Thank goodness we have Eliot Spitzer launching multiple investigations, including a probe of Weill's role in Jack Grubman's pumping of AT&T stock in order to win the company's business. The new "financial crimes SWAT team," which has been flooded with allegations of corruption since its creation in the summer of 2002, is supposed to take on the career corporate criminals, the pension plan hostage takers, and the stock option shysters.

How will that work, you ask? Will the team have the stomach for the fight? Can we expect to see undercover "narc-accountants" infiltrating what's left of the Big Four accounting firms? Middle-of-the-night no-knock raids on companies that restate their earnings by billions of dollars? Confiscation of an executive's entire assets simply on the suspicion of fraud? Will corporate cops get to emulate their drug-fighting counterparts and be allowed to keep a percentage of the money they confiscate? I bet that would do wonders to change the reluctance to target corporate corruption.

But, as Frank Rich wrote in the *New York Times*, in reality the president's SWAT team "exists mainly on paper, as a cutely named entity with no real assets. It calls for no new employees or funds and won't even gain new F.B.I. agents to replace those whom the bureau reassigned from white-collar crime to counterterrorism after Sept. 11."

The Incredible Shrinking Reform Bill

With so much public fury swelling, the politicians realized they had to produce some version of reform before they could move on to Stage Three: Accept and Reload.

Lame as the reform bill is, we can still expect the members of the Roundtable and other mock-reformers to work cleverly behind the scenes to undermine the new measures in any ways they can, and those ways are considerable. In this "reload" phase of Stage Three, you quietly propose new rules allowing exceptions for almost everything covered by the original bill. Or you strangle the funding of the oversight agency so it has no power to enforce the new law. Or, another Washington favorite, you pack the regulatory agency with people dedicated to undermining the law they're sworn to uphold. Like putting Gale Norton—a woman who once suggested a "right to pollute" for property owners—in charge of the Department of the Interior.

The gradual undermining of the hard-won campaign finance reform bill serves as a telling example of what to expect with the campaign to reform finance. After years of bloody congressional battles, supporters were finally able to pass a bill banning soft-money donations. The president reluctantly signed the bill into law and it looked like a done deal. But never underestimate the resourcefulness of those looking to maintain the status quo. The administration's friends at the Federal Election Commission took a carving knife to the new regulations, slicing open loopholes through which millions in soft money can continue to pour into party coffers.

Under the Commission's generous interpretation, not only can state parties still raise large amounts of soft money for themselves, but federal candidates can also go on raising soft money for the state parties as long as they don't actually ask for the money outright, but just use a wink and a nod. As FEC Commissioner Scott Thomas put it, the four anti-campaign finance reform commissioners fighting to neuter the legislation have "so tortured this law, it's beyond silly."

As they say on K Street: "It ain't over till the fat cats sing."

Before the Ink Was Dry

The cover offered by the fusillade of public pronouncements by the new reform converts was used to good effect by the anti-reform lobby. In the unusually hot summer of 2002 these frantic efforts came to a boil. With the public and public-spirited legislators (sure, there are a few) crying for Congress to close the offshore incorporation loophole and end the Bermuda tax holiday for American companies, business fought back, Hollywood fashion, by pulling grizzled veterans out of retirement to return to their old stomping ground for one last stand.

Accenture, the consulting arm of the Evil Empire of Arthur Andersen, which had been spun off as a Bermuda-based separate entity in 2001, sent Dennis DeConcini, a former Democratic senator from Arizona, on an urgent assignment to slap some sense into the backs of his friends in high places. And to cover the Republican flank, Accenture hired two agents of influence on the other side of the aisle: Kenneth Duberstein, a blast-from-the-past onetime chief of staff for Ronald Reagan, and Steven Symms, once a Republican senator from Idaho.

On the principle that you can never be too rich or too thin or have too many lobbyists in your corner, Accenture also signed up former Representative—now lobbyist—Robert Livingston who was all set to become Speaker of the House in 1998 until revelations that he had been less than faithful in his marriage drove him out of the House and into the less ethically stringent (imagine such a thing!) field of lobbying.

Accenture's Hail Mary play to hang on to the Bermuda dodge is only one of many such anti-reform lobbying campaigns that worked. Even disgraced companies continue to take advantage of the status quo. Tyco, for example, initially refused to certify its financial reports on the grounds of its Bermuda incorporation. It must have helped that among its lobbyists was that Viagra-powered Washington godfather Bob Dole. In the spring of 2002, when Tyco's troubles were already a-bubble, the erstwhile presidential candidate registered as a lobbyist for the company on corporate tax matters.

The Financial Certification Frenzy

After the SEC issued its order that the 942 largest companies in America submit signed statements attesting to the accuracy of their financial reports, two big-deal corporate lawyers— Dixie Lynn Johnson and Stanley Keller—sent the SEC what is known as "a strongly worded letter" on June 12, 2002, protesting the action. We can assume that Harvey Pitt at least read the missive since Johnson was a former law partner of his. On what grounds, you wonder, could anyone object to such a common-sensical request that you stand by your numbers?

But it took only days before the corporate clean-up specialists were hanging out a shingle pointing out possible technical flaws in the SEC rule and waving it in the face of CEOs who knew or suspected that their reports, current and past, were a few cheeseburgers shy of kosher. Invent a better mousetrap and the world will beat a path to your door. Invent a way to escape from a better mousetrap and watch the world skip the path altogether and climb through your windows and down your chimney. Who wants to bet me that the lawyers' bottom fishing pays off with a whole new client pool and a new sort of damage-control practice (with a whole new fee scale, natch)? Any takers?

Welcome to the Big House: How Many CEOs Will Learn the Real Meaning of "Hostile Takeover" in Prison?

In the summer of scandal, the new consensus along that other Axis of Evil, the one connecting Washington and Wall Street, was that the very public hauling of a few corporate crooks to jail would be a very good thing for the market, for the economy—and for our political leaders' reelection prospects.

As soon as corporate crime finally started to register on pollsters' seismographs, all of official Washington was suddenly drunk on the idea of tossing CEO scofflaws in the slammer. A day after President Bush took Wall Street to the woodshed and proposed doubling the maximum prison term for mail fraud and wire fraud, the Senate did him one better, voting 97-0 to adopt stiff new criminal penalties for securities fraud, document shredding, and the filing of false financial reports. "Somebody needs to go to jail," Senator Tom Daschle intoned ominously. "We're going to shackle them and take them to jail," growled Representative Tom DeLay, sounding like he couldn't wait to slap on the handcuffs himself.

You can count me in with the law-and-order crowd. But the question is, How many of corporate America's new breed of robber barons will ever actually see the inside of a jail cell? Truth be told, despite the well-deserved roasting they're currently getting over the media spit, many of the most notorious boardroom bad guys are continuing to live the high life to which they became accustomed while plundering their companies' coffers.

In July 2002, while visiting friends in Aspen, I had a close encounter of the disgraced CEO kind: I spotted Kenny Lay, garbed in a spiffy jogging suit, getting in a little morning cardio not far from one of the two multi-million-dollar vacation homes he keeps there. I realize that life isn't fair. But wouldn't it be nice if it were a little more just? If Lay, instead of jogging around the streets of Aspen in sweats, were jogging around a jail-yard track in stripes?

But if the past is indeed prologue, very, very few of America's new robber barons will end up in jail. In the last 10 years, the Securities and Exchange Commission—which, despite being the government's top corporate watchdog, doesn't have the authority to toss even the worst Wall Street cheaters in prison—turned 609 of its most offensive offenders over to the Justice Department for potential criminal prosecution. Of those, only 187 ended up facing criminal charges. And of those, only 87 went to jail. Eighty-seven. In 10 years. And far too many white-collar criminals land in one of those ritzy country-club prisons, where inmates perfect their backhand and make collect calls to their brokers.

To make the current climate even more temperate for corporate crime, most prosecutors are reluctant to take on these kinds of cases, passing up more than half of the ones the SEC sends their way. For one thing, proving fraudulent intent is a tricky business—and in criminal cases, it has to be proven beyond a reasonable doubt. For another, with rare exceptions, most prosecutors have neither the passion for making corporate criminals pay nor the zeal to pursue complex and challenging fraud cases. Too busy busting prostitutes in New Orleans, I guess.

Even Eliot Spitzer, one of the few who has shown the determination to take on Wall Street's elite, allowed Merrill Lynch to walk away with a fine but without having to admit guilt for brazenly misleading investors.

Another impediment to a vigorous legal campaign is that prosecutors like to win. When they go after a corporate player, they know they'll be locking horns with the best legal talent that billions can buy—not running roughshod over some overworked public defender. It's a high-stakes game that many aren't willing to play.

So despite the PR value of pumping up maximum sentences for corporate crimes, it's not going to make much of a dent in boardroom thievery because so few of the perpetrators will ever face criminal prosecution. For a corrupt corporate chieftain crunching the numbers, the odds will still justify the crime. Doubling the penalties for those convicted of breaking laws that are so rarely enforced is hardly serious reform.

Compare this tiptoeing on eggshells to the ardor with which our criminal justice system pursues even the lowest-level drug offenders. In 2000 alone, 646,042 people were arrested in America for simple possession of marijuana. And while the Drug Enforcement Administration has a budget of $1.8 billion, even with the extra funds Bush wants to toss its way, the SEC will have to make do with less than a third of that.

The sentencing side of the criminal justice ledger exhibits the same inequity: the average sentence for even the biggest white-collar crooks is less than 36 months; nonviolent, first-time federal drug offenders are sent away for over 64 months on average. So much for letting the punishment fit the crime.

The bitter truth is that, unlike the majority of nonviolent drug cases, corporate malfeasance is not a victimless crime. Not with tens of thousands of laid-off workers, $630 billion lost from corporate pension plans, and more than $9 trillion in shareholder assets wiped out in the scandal-fueled stock market swoon.

Here's the bottom line: despite their tough talk, our political leaders are not serious about declaring war on corporate crime. So are we merely going to enjoy the pleasure of seeing Sam Waksal, John Rigas, and Andrew Fastow in handcuffs, and move on?

Cleaning Up the Mess

"To destroy this invisible government," wrote Theodore Roosevelt nearly a century ago, "to befoul the unholy alliance between corrupt business and corrupt politics is the first task of the statesmanship of the day."

Any real change has to start at the top. That means, for starters, that President Bush should come clean about his own history of shady dealing, authorizing the SEC to release all documents connected to his Harken deal. He should also demand the resignation of Enron-tainted Secretary of the Army Thomas White.

Dick Cheney should also be held accountable for what went on during his time at the helm of Halliburton. Jon Corzine should be held accountable for the "breakthrough" business practices introduced when he was at Goldman Sachs. And Robert Rubin should be held accountable for what went on under his watch—both at the Treasury and at Citigroup— especially since, as part of his $40 million-a-year gig at Citigroup, he phoned both Bush's Treasury Department and a top credit-rating agency in an effort to delay the downgrading of Enron's credit rating, and thus allow the company to continue defrauding the public for a few last, desperate weeks.

WHO'S BEEN INDICTED?

RITE AID "Four executives were indicted last month in an alleged accounting fraud scheme, including former CEO Martin L. Grass and former CFO Franklyn M. Bergonzi. The smoking gun in the case is a tape made by a former employee who secretly recorded his colleagues." (*National Law Journal*, 7-08-02)

ADELPHIA "The federal grand jury indictment names John Rigas, 77, who is the company's founder and recently ousted chairman, two of his sons and two other former Adelphia executives. Based on the conspiracy, wire fraud and bank fraud counts, including 16 securities fraud charges not included in the original complaint, a judge could theoretically put each in jail for up to 250 years and fine each $19.5 million." (*Los Angeles Times*, 9-24-02)

TYCO "Dennis Kozlowski was indicted in June for evading sales taxes on six paintings he bought for $13.2 million." (*Bloomberg News*, 8-01-02)

"Charging Kozlowski and former Tyco CFO Mark Swartz with corruption, conspiracy and grand larceny, prosecutors say the men secretly tapped two corporate funds to splurge on luxury homes and yachts and take massive personal bonuses and loans. The two stole more than $170 million from the firm and fraudulently obtained $430 million by selling securities, prosecutors say." (*USA Today*, 9-13-02)

WORLDCOM "Federal prosecutors accused Scott D. Sullivan, the 40-year-old former chief financial officer of WorldCom, and Buford Yates Jr., the company's former director of general accounting, of directing a two-year scheme to conceal $3.9 billion in company expenses and boost profit." (*Los Angeles Times*, 8-29-02)

"WorldCom Inc. ex-controller David Myers pleaded guilty last month to federal securities fraud, conspiracy and filing a false document with the U.S. Securities and Exchange Commission. Myers said he plotted with WorldCom's 'senior management' to hide more than $7 billion in expenses." (*Bloomberg News*, 10-02-02)

IMCLONE "Samuel D. Waksal, the former chief executive of ImClone Systems, pleaded guilty yesterday to six charges, including securities fraud, perjury and obstruction of justice, stemming from his role in a flurry of stock sales that occurred late last year." (*New York Times*, 10-16-02)

SOTHEBY'S "Former Sotheby's Holdings Inc. Chairman A. Alfred Taubman, the controlling shareholder in the company, was convicted in December of plotting with his counterpart at Christie's International Plc, Sir Anthony Tennant, to fix fees paid by sellers of art, antiques and other valuables. He was sentenced to a year and a day in federal prison." (*Bloomberg News*, 8-01-02)

CENDANT "Cendant Corp. Chairman Walter A. Forbes and E. Kirk Shelton, the former vice chairman, were indicted in February 2001 for inflating earnings at CUC International Inc. for a decade to fund corporate acquisitions and boost share price." (*Bloomberg News*, 8-01-02)

TYSON FOODS "Six former Tyson Foods Inc. managers were indicted in December in an immigrant-smuggling case that stemmed from a U.S. Immigration and Naturalization Service investigation." (*Bloomberg News*, 8-01-02)

ANDERSEN "Justice Department officials obtained an indictment against Enron's auditor, Arthur Andersen, and a federal jury in Houston convicted Andersen of obstruction of justice in June." (*Los Angeles Times*, 8-02-02)

WASTE MANAGEMENT "Garbage giant Waste Management's founder and his top aides were charged yesterday with cooking the books to inflate profits by $1.7 billion. The Securities and Exchange Commission accused the former executive team of staging a 'massive fraud' for five straight years—with help from its auditor Arthur Andersen—in order to meet earnings targets and reap bonuses, among other benefits." (*New York Post*, 3-27-02)

HOMESTORE "Three former executives of Homestore.com, the USA's largest online real estate company, have agreed to plead guilty to falsely inflating the company's earnings." (*USA Today*, 9-26-02)

ENRON "Yesterday Michael Kopper, a former managing director of Enron's global finance unit, pleaded guilty to federal money-laundering and fraud charges . . . these are the first criminal charges brought against an Enron insider." (*New York Times*, 8-22-02)

"Andrew S. Fastow, the financial wizard dubbed "Fast Andy" for his alleged off-the-books finagling that led Enron Corp. into bankruptcy and disgrace, was charged Wednesday with fraud, money laundering and conspiracy. Fastow also is charged with personally enriching himself, sometimes at the expense of Enron." (*Atlanta Journal and Constitution*, 10-03-02)

What is stunning is that even after all the suffering caused by Enron's deception became apparent, when questioned about his ill-advised phone call to the Treasury, Rubin maintained: "I would do it again."

So, I suspect, would many, many others. And they'll continue to do it again and again until they're given a strong enough reason not to. So far, such disincentives do not exist. Which is why Tom Daschle did not think twice, a day after he killed John McCain's amendment to force companies to report stock options as an expense, about boarding a corporate jet for a weekend retreat in Nantucket, organized by three generous corporate contributors—Eli Lilly, BellSouth, and FedEx. He was joined on this little jaunt by 15 of his fellow senators, including Hillary Rodham Clinton and Ted Kennedy, and 250 of his party's most generous campaign donors.

This defiant arrogance is still the order of the day in Washington. Which is why Harvey Pitt was the fox guarding the henhouse at the SEC for so long.

When the Bush administration picked SEC nemesis Pitt to replace Arthur Levitt and lead the watchdog agency, it was a little like naming Osama bin Laden to run the Office of Homeland Security.

Now I'm not saying that Pitt was corrupt—just that he was the wrong man for the job. Soon after taking office, Pitt promised to turn the SEC into a "kinder, gentler" agency. But we don't need regulators who are kind and gentle—we need feral dogs who can't differentiate between the scent of accounting malfeasance and the blood of fresh kill.

Pitt's also the man who vigorously defended the Big Five's consulting practice, going so far as to venture the bizarre opinion that "A firm that does only audits may be incompetent."

In another example of our leaders' blurry oversight, many of those on the Hill now calling for the heads of corporate executives were noticeably silent when Pitt sailed through his confirmation process, unanimously approved by the Senate Banking Committee.

Back in December 2001, I called, in a column, for Harvey Pitt to resign. Eleven months later he finally did. In the meantime, he coddled his old pals in the accounting industry, allowing them to continue to double-dip as highly paid consultants, took halfhearted sloppy seconds on the New York attorney general's probe of Wall Street, and illustrated why our conflict-of-interest laws should be stronger by holding meetings with former clients currently under investigation by his own agency. And, in a truly clueless maneuver, he responded to almost unanimous criticism of his performance by requesting a raise in salary and elevation to cabinet status.

When I ran into Pitt at the White House Correspondents' Dinner in May 2002, I asked him what he thought of the latest wave of corporate misconduct. "There is no doubt," he told me with confidence, "that we need to find out if some companies went too far." Find out if some companies went too far? Gee, Harvey, are you sure you want to go out on a limb like that? And if only we had an agency whose job it was to find those sorts of things out.

It's crystal clear that Pitt just didn't get it. In fact, it wasn't even in Harvey Pitt's DNA to notice the stink wafting up from the corporate sewer, let alone get down into the muck and clean it up. Which is why Pitt-watchers were not surprised when he caved to pressure from his friends and former clients in the accounting industry and backtracked on his choice of John Biggs, CEO of TIAA-Cref, a large pension plan, to head the new board that will oversee the accounting industry. Nor were they surprised when he withheld from the SEC commissioners damaging information about William Webster before they voted on him for chairman of the oversight board.

Once more with feeling: Pitt was the wishy-washiest watchdog since Scooby-Doo.

Unfinished Business

Since, at its heart, the corporate scandal is a political scandal—corporate money corrupts politicians who by passing or neglecting to pass laws make corporate crime possible and profitable—it's hard to see how we will ever get rid of this corporate hangover until we cure our politicians' unslakable thirst for campaign cash and their corporate masters' "infectious greed," to use Alan Greenspan's oft-quoted phrase. Teddy Roosevelt was the driving force behind a tough ban on corporate donations that was enacted in 1907, but Roosevelt's reforms were eventually circumvented by the soft money loophole, now supposedly closed by the campaign finance reform bill. As we've seen, the Federal Election Commission has already been trying to undercut the reform. So it's essential that we purge the Commission of commissioners who don't believe in its mission, and that we fortify it with some real enforcement bite.

But even before the commissioners and the lobbyists and the lawyers started sniffing out the new loopholes like pigs snorting for truffles, the ban on soft money was hardly the end of the overwhelming influence of money on our campaigns. The fact is soft-money donations made up less than 20% of the nearly $3 billion spent in the 2000 elections, while hard-money donations totaled roughly $1.75 billion. But it's a start.

Politicians from both parties were immediately tripping over themselves in a desperate stampede to cash in before soft money went the way of DDT, Dalkon Shields, and the Ford Pinto. The fund-raisers started revving up their databases and putting out the call to fat-cat donors across the land: "Gentlemen, start your checkbooks!"

Leading the revels at the big-buck bacchanal were the president and the vice president, who were the main draw at, on average, two fund-raisers a week in the spring of 2002, playing more dates than Steve and Eydie.

But the juiciest morsel of bait in the Republican tackle box was Rudy Giuliani who, in a particularly distasteful example of cashing in on September 11, headlined a March 2002 fundraiser for House Republicans touted as a "Salute to America's Heroes." Here was Rudy trading in his September 11 halo for an enormous deposit in his personal favor bank, which he can cash out whenever he decides to make his next political move. To paraphrase Todd Beamer: Let's bankroll!

There can be no clearer indication of how undemocratic the way we finance campaigns is than the fact that only one-quarter of 1% donate $200 or more, and only one-tenth of 1% gives $1,000 or more. Of course, politicians from both parties insist that the contributors who coughed up half a billion dollars in soft money during the 2000 election cycle are getting nothing for their donations other than the warm glow of participating in the democratic process. In fact, that pricey quid comes with an even more generous quo, and the corporate leaders who are cutting the checks are very clear on what they are buying. Take the persuasive little memo Enron's political action committee sent to employees in June 2000, soliciting "voluntary" contributions of between $500 and $5,000. In it, company execs made no bones about why they needed the money, saying it would help the company overcome the numerous legal and regulatory challenges it was facing on a range of tax and environmental issues. The memo was deafeningly silent on the virtues of participating in the democratic process.

But it isn't just the likes of Ken Lay who understand the value of political donations. Vice President Dick Cheney practiced similar spending habits when he was running Halliburton.

The company was facing a potentially devastating firestorm of asbestos-related lawsuits. But instead of arguing its case, it decided it would be cheaper to simply change the law.

As a former member of Congress and longtime Washington fixture, Cheney knew the quickest way to a politician's heart was through his wallet. So he and Halliburton doled out $494,452 to congressional candidates from 1997 to 2000, with $157,000 going to 62 lawmakers who, whaddyaknow, co-sponsored bills limiting the liability of asbestos producers. Cheney, clearly a man committed to leading by example, personally contributed $12,500 to politicians helping to push his company's agenda.

Such donations are the equivalent of soft-money smart bombs: precisely targeted to where they'll have the most impact. It is clear that those giving the money know that it tilts the scales in their favor. It simply defies common sense to imagine that they would give for any other reason. Even at the height of the bull market, no IPO ever delivered a rate of return as high as an investment in a politician—and elected officials' willingness to sell off public policy is immune to market ups and downs.

But now, the lights have been turned on and the roaches are scattering. While continuing to insist that political contributions have absolutely no influence on them, the good folks in Washington can't seem to decide on the best way to prove it. So some have been rushing to refund contributions from disgraced companies like Enron, Adelphia, Tyco, and Global Crossing. If the money didn't buy influence, why the mad scramble to return it? And where was the refund money coming from—new donations? If so, what made these new donations any purer than Enron or Tyco's? And, come to think of it, wasn't that how Charles Ponzi's original scheme worked?

Our elected leaders cite the absurd cost of political ads—the single greatest expense of almost all modern campaigns—as the main reason they need to fund-raise so aggressively. But consider this. It was they who, in 1997, in an example of everything that's wrong with Washington, gave away the digital spectrum to broadcasters—a little gift now worth hundreds of billions of dollars. Demanding that the broadcasters, who are now making massive profits using the public airwaves, offer political candidates free TV time is a small price to pay in return.

But ultimately the only way to dramatically diminish the corrupting influence of special-interest money is by adopting the Clean Money, Clean Election model, which replaces the nonstop money-grab with full public financing of elections. No hard money, no soft money, no endless dialing for dollars, no quid pro dough deals. Just candidates and elected officials beholden to no one but the voters.

And this is no pie-in-the-sky fantasy. Clean Money laws in states like Maine and Arizona have proven remarkably effective: reducing campaign spending, shrinking the influence of outside money, and encouraging more—and better—people to run.

In the meantime, there is a whole raft of specific corporate reforms urgently needed:

Treat stock options as the expenses that they are.

This reform was dropped from the Sarbanes bill even before it hit the Senate floor. And then, in July 2002, Tom Daschle, fresh from getting an earful from venture capitalist and big-time Democratic Party donor John Doerr (Doerr and his wife have given $619,000 to Democrats since 1999), pummeled John McCain's attempt to force a vote on stock-option reform before jetting off to Nantucket. Next, Phil Gramm—a top recipient of big business donations—used a procedural cudgel to bash Carl Levin's backdoor attempt to reintroduce the issue.

Make bridging the Chinese wall between research analysts and investment bankers illegal.

The Sarbanes-Oxley bill has done nothing to make it harder for investment banks to deceive investors with overly optimistic research, using their research departments to land banking business. It is hard to believe that something so blatantly fraudulent is still legal.

Prohibit accounting firms from providing any consulting services while auditing a company's books.

Under Sarbanes-Oxley, the provision of consulting services by audit firms is not made illegal. It is restricted somewhat in that the accounting firm has to seek prior approval for consulting work from the company's audit committee and disclose the services in public reports.

Outlaw offshore tax havens, and, in the meantime, bar companies that move their headquarters overseas from competing for government contracts.

The Sarbanes-Oxley bill neither bans nor restricts the use of tax havens by American corporations. Nor does it ban or restrict government contracts going to such companies.

In 2001 alone such contracts topped $1 billion. Although there are half a dozen bills in Congress at the moment designed to prohibit the massive windfall corporate America gets from these tax havens, some provisions in these bills would actually make things worse, prolonging the high-level—and perfectly legal—gaming of the system.

House Republicans, cloaking themselves in the mantle of reform, have brazenly crafted a bill that temporarily closes the $6.3 billion Bermuda loophole while creating two much larger—and permanent—loopholes that will net American multinational tax fugitives a combined $60.8 billion. The new bill would also create incentives for companies to invest and create jobs overseas rather than here at home.

Congress is currently considering legislation that will bar the Pentagon and the new Homeland Security Department from doing business with companies that have set up offshore tax-cheat havens since January 2002. Which means that all the corporations that had the foresight to profit early from their disloyalty, depriving the government of $70 billion a year, are A-okay. If something is so wrong on January 1, what made it right on December 31?

***Regulate the special-purpose entities used for the
complex, off-balance sheet transactions that were
at the heart of the Enron debacle.***

No new rules governing special-purpose entities were included
in the Sarbanes-Oxley bill, so, for the moment, they can still be
hidden off the company's books. Senator Carl Levin is considering legislation to rein in these shady entities.

Any serious corporate reform bill would also have to outlaw the "rent-a-balance-sheet" practice, according to which a
corporation can fail to include an entity on its books if it pays
another company to put it on its books, even if the risks and
benefits remain with the original company.

***Strengthen whistle-blower protection and ensure
that it shields all workers equally.***

This vital reform was covered in the Sarbanes-Oxley bill, but
only with very ambiguous language that allowed the president,
hours after signing the bill into law, to issue a White House
interpretation limiting whistle-blower protection to those providing information during a congressional investigation.

Responding to bipartisan criticism of the order, the White
House then announced that it will "leave it up to Congress to
determine through their own rules and procedures who would
get whistle-blower protection."

Clearly the law needs to be made watertight to limit the
possibility of such bad-faith interpretations.

***Begin to address the question of restitution by
repealing the provision in the Private Securities
Litigation Reform Act of 1995 that makes it
extremely hard for investors to recover losses
sustained through corporate fraud.***

The Sarbanes-Oxley bill directs the SEC to create a new restitution fund from what it recovers from executives under inves-

tigation. But the amounts collected are normally minuscule—between 1995 and 2001 only 14% of the $3.1 billion in ill-gotten gains of convicted white-collar criminals was recouped.

It is also necessary to repeal a provision in the 1995 Litigation Reform Act that protects executives from liability for hyped projections, as long as they hide behind a disclaimer. Many disgraced executives—Ken Lay among them—are using this loophole to evade shareholder lawsuits. Also, under current law, corporations can, simply by filing a motion to dismiss, put a halt to discovery, without which plaintiffs have no access to corporate documents to verify their restitution claims.

Eliot Spitzer is once again leading the charge. He has filed suit against WorldCom's Bernie Ebbers, Qwest's Joe Nacchio and Phil Anschutz, Metromedia's Stephen Garofalo, and McLeod's Clark McLeod, demanding the return of $1.5 billion pocketed in stock trading schemes and $28 million in profits from selling IPO shares offered in exchange for multi-million-dollar fees.

Strengthen the independence of corporate boards.

Despite the consensus that corporate board independence needs to be backed by regulation, the Sarbanes-Oxley bill is silent on this thorny issue. At the moment, the NYSE and the NASDAQ are proposing that companies have a board with a simple majority of independent directors.

If approved by the SEC, the new rules will apply to the 2,300 U.S. companies listed on the Big Board, which will have two years to comply. Companies that fail to do so are facing the daunting prospect of a slap on the wrist—i.e. a letter of reprimand from the NYSE.

Drastically overhaul current accounting standards.

Warren Buffett, Alan Greenspan, and Henry Paulson, CEO of Goldman Sachs, among others, have argued that the current accounting standards are—in Paulson's words—"ripe for manipulation" and need to be overhauled. But there is no overhaul in Sarbanes-Oxley and none being proposed in Congress.

Indeed, Standard & Poor's, the private bond-rating agency, announced that it plans to apply its own earnings standards to companies in its benchmark S&P 500-stock index. And it will follow its own core earnings figures in assigning its debt ratings. It will correct company numbers by treating stock options as a business expense, excluding from earnings items such as pension plan investment gains, and including as a cost the "one-time" expenses that many companies exclude from their earnings reports. These new, more upfront calculations slashed profits for the S&P 500 companies by a bogusly inflated 25%.

Outlaw accounting gimmicks—like "Monthly Income Preferred Shares"—that make it impossible for the public to have an accurate picture of a company's financial health.

The Sarbanes-Oxley bill leaves such gimmicks untouched so, for the moment, they remain legal.

To this day, even as Senator (and former Goldman Sachs CEO) Jon Corzine stands amidst a business landscape strewn with the body parts of exploded companies and blown-up retirement plans, he continues to defend what he calls his former company's "aggressive tax policy" including the liberal use of Mips, the security which manages to show up as debt on a company's tax return but equity on its balance sheet. "Lawyers said it was right. Accountants said it was right. . . . And the courts said it was right." In other words, shut up and pass the New Economy Kool-Aid.

Institute real pension reform.

Even though the savage impact on ordinary Americans' pensions has been one of the harshest consequences of the corporate scandals, there is still no pension reform signed into law.

The crisis in retirement security is such that half of all Americans have no pension plan at all, and half of those who do will now have to put off retirement because of stock-market losses.

There is also a blatant injustice in the way companies provide pension plans to disproportionately benefit their top executives. So-called "Top Hat" plans are now offered by 86% of the Fortune 100, compared to 10% in the 1980s. "Top Hat" plans, unlike 401(k)s, are exempt from all rules regarding participation and fiduciary duties. Reserved primarily for upper-level management, these plans are similar to traditional pension plans calculated by multiplying final annual pay by number of years of employment. Because the pension is paid regardless of what state the company is in, they are significantly less risky than contribution plans like 401(k)s which are heavily dependent on the company's share price. Twenty-five years ago, 43% of workers were covered by guaranteed pension plans. Now, with the proliferation of defined contribution plans, that figure is down to 20%.

As if this were not enough, the pension reform bill passed by the House of Representatives in April 2002, if signed into law, would further exacerbate the inequalities by making it easier for companies to reduce the number of employees covered by pensions while increasing the pension benefits of the most highly compensated executives.

Institute some basic lobbying reform.

Begin by reinstating the mandatory five-year "cooling off" period between the time an official leaves a position in the administration and when he can begin lobbying for a related industry. This elementary rule was instituted by President Clinton on the first day of his administration and then rescinded during his last days in office.

Also make it illegal for family members of legislators to become lobbyists. Until this is done, demand full financial disclosure of lobbying and board-of-director fees earned by family members of elected officials.

Repeal the Financial Modernization Act.
The act, passed in 1999, ended the separation of banking functions instituted during the New Deal to protect the public from the kinds of fraud and deception that have been rampant in the last few years.

Stop the Bankruptcy Reform Act from becoming law.
The Bankruptcy Act would not only significantly add to the burden of consumers struggling to rebuild their lives amid tough economic times, it also contains a provision that loosens some crucial conflict-of-interest restrictions. Under the new law, it would be easier for lawyers, accountants and investment bankers who are involved with a company before it declared bankruptcy to be retained by the same company to help clear up its post–Chapter 11 mess and allocate its remaining resources.

As Elizabeth Warren, a Harvard Law School professor, put it: "In a bill that largely focuses on consumers, this provision that has received almost no attention would be very helpful to some of the biggest players in the current scandals."

The exploitation of the bankruptcy bill shows beyond any doubt that even in the middle of all the public clamoring to clean up the Augean stables of corporate America, there is a whole industry working overtime to shovel sackfuls of manure in even as we are taking a few teaspoons out.

End the ability of mutual funds to both own huge amounts of stock and administer 401(k) plans and other employee-benefit services for the companies in which they hold substantial positions.
Mutual funds are now among the largest owners of American corporations—controlling close to $3 trillion in stock. The 75

largest mutual fund companies control 44% of the voting power at U.S. companies. So there are enormous consequences for all of us when owners elect not to act like owners, but like timorous lackeys desperate to please management.

But that's exactly what's happening because of a gargantuan conflict of interest: the giant mutual funds are serving two masters. As owners of huge amounts of stock, it is their job to hold incompetent or self-interested management accountable. But there are massive fees coming their way when corporate executives award them 401(k) and pension fund assets to invest. And sticking a thorn in a CEO's side is unlikely to endear a fund manager to him.

For instance, the nation's largest mutual fund, Fidelity, which owns 5.3% of Tyco's stock, also earned $2 million in 1999 for its part in running Tyco's 401(k) plans. In 2001, over 50% of Fidelity's $9.8 billion in revenues was generated by administering 401(k) plans and other employee benefit services for some 11,000 companies, including Philip Morris, Shell, IBM, Monsanto, and Ford.

Mutual Funds:
Corporate Crime's Narcoleptic Giant

This last reform is not even debated because the two-faced status of mutual fund managers, though a combustible conflict of interest, has yet to hit the headlines. With the monster mutual funds too afraid of losing the profitable 401(k) and pension fund business to ever rock the boat—with ownership essentially AWOL—irresponsible corporate execs have been allowed to run wild. This is how this mother of all conflicts of interest begets her malevolent progeny.

It's definitely controversial to make a stink about excessive CEO pay packages, blank-check loans to senior executives, or abusive accounting strategies. That's why the whistles they should be blowing seems stuck in their throats.

So they hold their tongues, don't ask the tough questions, and time and again refuse to disclose how they vote on proxy ballots. And as California Treasurer Phil Angelides told me: "That silence speaks volumes." Angelides is at the forefront of demanding that mutual funds be more transparent, but, so far, to no avail.

With their financial clout, if mutual funds demanded change, they would not—indeed, could not—be ignored. In fact, they could have insisted on—and gotten—all the rules and standards the new corporate reform law imposes. And much, much more. But because of their competing interests, they didn't—to their lasting shame, the detriment of their investors, and, indeed, to the detriment of us all.

Imagine how different things would be if these funds, instead of abrogating their responsibility as owners, had embraced it. If you owned hundreds of millions of shares in a company, would you be sitting on your duff waiting for the SEC to rush to the rescue and protect your assets? Or would you be taking matters into your own hands? Mutual funds are not just sleeping giants. They are giants with a serious case of narcolepsy.

And it's not like there are no role models for responsible behavior. Take the example of Bill Gross, founder and managing director of Pacific Investment Management Co. (PIMCO), which manages over $250 billion in bond funds. This spring, after Gross took General Electric to the woodshed for misleading investors about the company's debt, he unloaded most of PIMCO's $1 billion in GE bonds.

"I picked on GE," Gross told me, "because I wanted to alert the investment universe that it wasn't just Enron, Tyco, or WorldCom pulling some fast ones, but GE—the biggest guy on the block—and probably everyone in between. GE definitely changed things in the last six months and I sort of think I nudged them along the way."

He didn't just nudge them along the way. He bloodied them enough to force them to clean up their balance sheet. Gross' speaking out was as remarkable for its effectiveness as it was for its rarity.

The debate has so far focused on accounting firms not mixing auditing with consulting, and investment banks keeping research independent of banking. It is now time to hold mutual funds accountable. Isn't their fiduciary obligation to their investors paramount? Or are they using the money of working Americans as a come-on to generate more servicing fees?

The biggest mutual funds like to adorn themselves with high-minded monikers like Fidelity, Puritan, Flagship, and Strong American. They now need to start living up to their true-blue names.

Looking for Reformers in All the Wrong Places

The revelations of infectious greed that have come in wave after wave for so many months have the potential to ignite an explosion of populist outrage—one with the power to remake our democracy. The question is: who will light the fuse?

The unfortunate reality is that truly substantive changes are clearly not going to come from our leaders in Washington. Our elected representatives are so compromised, such an integral part of the scandal, that if they set off a populist petard, they'd only be hoisted by it themselves. Those currently in power have proven themselves chronically unable to bite the corporate hand that feeds and feeds and feeds them.

Just as they've worked, and are still working, against campaign finance reform, the enemies of financial reforms will be spending millions of dollars—and every waking hour—making sure there are enough loopholes in the fine print to keep the pigs fat and happy. So, instead of real reform, we get watered-down initiatives, slap-on-the-wrist fines, and showy arrests. The only thing that will make it possible for the handful of real reformers to keep the corporate swine at bay is public outrage. So it's up to us to keep demanding that the stirrings of reform are not stillborn.

As our collective anger collides head-on with our political system's intransigence, we're stuck with a classic case of an irresistible force meeting an immovable object. Something has got to give. In the past, it's been us. But it doesn't have to be.

We can't count on a white knight riding to the rescue. Look around at the political landscape—100 senators, 435 members of the House, 50 governors. Is there anyone—anyone—who strikes you as capable of breaking the logjam, of tapping into the American people's longing for fairness and justice and equity?

I hear silence. The spark will have to come from outside the current political gene pool.

Will it be, say, a younger, charismatic Ralph Nader? A Ross Perot without the corporate baggage or bats in the belfry? A real-life version of Jimmy Stewart's Jefferson Smith, who arrives on the scene funded by $1 donations from paperboys and soda jerks, or, these days, video store clerks and cubicle drones?

My guess is none of the above. Instead, it will be a critical mass of individuals and groups mobilized by the injustice given flesh and blood by the current scandals. This time we have a story to organize around, a story that has it all: narrative power, colorful crooks, sympathetic victims, juicy details (who can forget Kozlowski's $6,000 shower curtain?), political intrigue, global fallout. A story so compelling that even our part-of-the-problem media giants can't ignore it.

Looking Beyond the Knights in Shining Armor

Beneath the media radar, people are organizing across the country—from established organizations engaging in grassroots work like Public Citizen, Common Cause, Global Exchange, the Center for Public Integrity, the Pension Rights Center, Workingassetsradio.com, and United for a Fair Economy to newer groups like Citizen Works and Junction-City.com to Jim Hightower's traveling road show, "The Rolling Thunder Down-Home Democracy Tour."

And there is a lot happening at the local state level. In July 2002, for example, California State Treasurer Phil Angelides released a list of 23 companies—including Tyco and Ingersoll-Rand—that the state has blacklisted because of their use of offshore tax havens. California will divest from these companies and refuse to sign further contracts with them. Angelides also urged two powerful pension funds in the state—the nation's first and third largest—to pull out their money from such companies. The California Public Employees Retirement Systems (Calpers), which manages $137 billion, has, in the meantime, announced that it will not do business with any bank that breaches the Chinese wall between research and banking, and is considering Angelides' proposal that it divest from any company that has moved offshore to avoid paying taxes.

"What we've tried to do," Angelides told me, "is ask the question: how can we use our power to send a clear message to the market about the importance of corporate responsibility and conduct?"

While an overreliance on market-based solutions may have gotten us into this mess, here's hoping that the growing de-

WILL ANYONE EVER ADMIT WRONGDOING?

Jack Grubman "While I regret that I, like many others, failed to predict the collapse of the telecommunications sector and I understand the disappointment and anger felt by investors as a result of that collapse, I am nevertheless proud of the work I, and the analysts who worked with me, did."

- *(Letter of resignation, August 15, 2002. Grubman, a $20 million-a-year analyst for Salomon Smith Barney, failed to predict the meltdown of the telecommunications industry in general and WorldCom in particular, waiting until the day before it announced one of history's largest accounting frauds to cut his rating on the company to "underperform." Yet another decision Grubman could be "proud of.")*

Merrill Lynch "At the end of the day, we believe that the integrity of our research was maintained." (Stan O'Neal, President & COO)

"The actions we are taking will ensure that analysts are compensated only for activities intended to benefit investors." (David Komansky, CEO)

- *(On May 21, 2002, Merrill Lynch agreed to pay $100 million in fines to settle charges that its analysts had given tainted advice to investors, describing one stock as a "piece of crap" privately, while maintaining a "buy" rating on it publicly. The integrity of Merrill's research may, in fact, have been maintained. The integrity of Merrill's financial advice, well, that's a "piece of crap." Merrill Lynch never admitted wrongdoing.)*

Xerox "Xerox is best served by putting these issues with the SEC behind us." (Anne Mulcahy, CEO)

"This is an issue that deals with changes in time and allocation of revenue, not fictitious actions, accounting or phony revenue. It is revenue moving from one period to the next." (Xerox Spokeswoman Christa Carone)

- *(On April Fools Day 2002, Xerox restated its financial reports for the previous five years and agreed to pay a*

$10 million fine, the largest ever in an SEC enforcement case. The company did not admit wrongdoing. Plus, my copier's still broken.)

Al Dunlap "This agreement with the SEC, in which Mr. Dunlap neither admits nor denies the allegations of the SEC's complaint, will allow him to pursue his retirement and, therefore, is a welcome outcome." (Dunlap's lawyer, Frank Razzano)

- *(On September 4, 2002, Al Dunlap, one of the most infamous corporate hatchet men in history, agreed to pay an SEC-levied $500,000 civil penalty for his crooked bookkeeping at Sunbeam. In addition to the fine, Dunlap was barred from ever serving as a director or officer at a public company again.)*

First Boston "This case raised enormously complicated and novel legal questions . . . Messrs. Ehinger and Coleman have decided that it is in the best interests of all concerned to resolve the case without admitting or denying the NASD's failure-to-supervise charge."

- *(On August 15, 2002, the National Association of Securities Dealers (NASD) fined Anthony Ehinger and George Coleman, two senior executives of Credit Suisse First Boston, $200,000 apiece and imposed a 60-day suspension on both men for overseeing their firm's collection of millions of dollars in inflated commissions from the huge IPOs of the Internet boom. The fine is expected to teach the men a valuable lesson: that for just $200,000, you can get a 60-day vacation from First Boston.)*

AOL "AOL's accounting was always fully disclosed and AOL did not admit any wrongdoing in its settlement agreement." (company spokeswoman Ann Brackbill)

- *(On May 15, 2000, AOL agreed to pay $3.5 million to settle the SEC's charges that the company was guilty of $385 million worth of improper accounting. There's no truth to the rumor that Warner Bros. is developing a film on the financial fiasco called: "Dude, Where's My $385 Million?")*

Ashford.com On June 10, 2002, the SEC fined then-Ashford CEO Kenneth Kurtzman and then-CFO Brian Bergeron $85,000 for improperly deferring $1.5 million in expenses. In the settlement, neither Kurtzman, Bergeron, or Ashford.com, an online jewelry store, admitted wrongdoing.

mand for fairer, saner, and more democratic answers for America's problems may increase their supply.

"We have the chance," Scott Harshbarger, former president of Common Cause, says, "of combining the traditionally disenfranchised with a new investor class that now sees pensions and college funds disappearing. This is a unique opportunity to organize and politicize them."

Just this kind of spirit of true reform is demonstrated in a truly important movement among American companies that has huge potential for lasting reform, and has hardly received any attention.

More than a hundred companies in America are seeking to redefine the bottom line—moving away from conventional corporate accounting, where the only consideration is profit, to one that also includes the social and environmental impact the company is having. It's called the Triple Bottom Line.

Yes, stock price is important, say triple bottom liners, but so is how you treat your workers, the effect you're having on the environment, and whether the McNuggets you sell are made from chickens raised in deplorable conditions.

The key idea is that corporations need to pay attention to both their stockholders and their stakeholders—those who may not have invested money in the company but clearly have a de facto investment in the air they breathe, the food they eat, and the communities they live in.

Among the leading crusaders for this shift in corporate priorities is Ray Anderson, the founder and chairman of the board of Interface, Inc., the world's largest commercial carpet company, and the co-chair of the President's Council on Sustainable Development during the Clinton administration. A corporate polluter and single bottom liner for two decades, Anderson became a devoted convert to the triple bottom line after reading *The Ecology of Commerce,* Paul Hawken's visionary book about socially responsible businesses.

Deciding that he wanted to "pioneer the company of the next industrial revolution," Anderson set out to remake Interface into what *FastCompany* magazine hailed as "the most highly evolved big company in the country"—a $1.2 billion model for "social responsibility and economic growth."

He now travels the country giving speeches about this new kind of corporate responsibility. "There is a real hunger," he told me, "for companies that stand for something other than the conventional bottom line. Beyond profits, there must be purpose. Beyond success, there must be significance. And by doing good, you'll end up boosting your bottom line, as well." Anderson estimates that his company has saved $185 million on waste-reduction efforts alone.

But Ray Anderson remains the exception—not just among CEOs but even among triple bottom line CEOs. Most of them have made the shift not because of a personal conversion but because of public pressure and protest.

Nike, for instance, has moved to the cutting edge of environmentally conscious production techniques—phasing out the use of the controversial carcinogenic chemical PVC in its products—but only after facing boycotts and reams of bad PR over its unfair treatment of overseas workers. And Starbucks began aggressively marketing Fair-Trade Certified coffee—a line that pays its coffee farmers far more than the going rate—after it became the target of human rights activists.

However these yuppie stalwarts came to change their ways, they are now at the forefront of a growing movement. And with corporate America under siege, there has never been a more opportune moment to adopt better business practices. But for this change to occur, pressure will have to come from three sources: the government, the media, and, above all, the public.

The government needs to reward socially conscious companies with tax credits, incentives, and subsidies while levying higher taxes on polluting and wasteful companies. The business press needs to stop running adulatory cover stories on America's most cutthroat CEOs, and replace them with glowing profiles of the most forward-thinking ones (good-bye, Dennis Kozlowski; hello, Ray Anderson).

And, most important, the public has to keep the heat on. We can't settle for companies like Citigroup promising to no longer help corporate crooks intent on fleecing us.

Demanding that companies stop being bad is not enough. We have to demand that they start being good. That has to be our bottom line on corporate reform. But before we get too comfortable, pointing our Monday morning fingers at these white-collar crooks without a conscience, we need to admit that their anti-social behavior couldn't have flourished in a vacuum. We allowed it. Even celebrated it.

Like the klepto-CEOs, our culture also suffered a severe empathy shortage during the irrationally exuberant nineties. The last decade saw a marked decline in media coverage of the homeless. And how many cared that, even as the market boomed, we still had over 14 million children living in poverty? But who had time to notice, especially when another hot new IPO was about to turn some 20-something computer geek into a dot-com billionaire?

During the nineties, it was as if denial had replaced baseball as the national pastime. We buried our heads in the sand— unwilling to question the integrity of the bulls rushing down Wall Street for fear it might jeopardize the 30% rate of return we had come to see as our birthright. And the buoyant pronouncements of our political leaders only served to hammer home the communal delusion that the party would go on forever.

"Never has the promise of prosperity been so vivid," said candidate George W. Bush in the days leading up to the 2000 election, while his opponent, Al Gore, blithely hailed "the greatest prosperity ever" and promised voters: "You ain't seen nothing yet." For his part, Bill Clinton, in his final economic report to

Congress, assured the nation that "the expansion will continue"—even though economic growth had already slowed by 60%.

This shared denial provided convenient camouflage for corrupt CEOs. In America, we keep score with money and the trappings of wealth—so the psychopaths fit right in. They were nothing more than the winners of a game we all wanted to play—a game that we knew rewarded certain aberrant tendencies.

As well as prosecuting all the crimes these Wall Street wolf boys committed, and instituting all the major reforms needed, we should take the opportunity as a culture to lie down on the couch and see what it was in our collective unconscious that created these nightmares.

But only for a little while. Because we have work to do. We were told again and again during the nineties that our unprecedented prosperity was fueled by consumer spending. Well, the time has come for the shoppers to leave the malls and take to the streets—to go from invigorating our economy to reinvigorating our democracy.

PUTTING THE "ACT" BACK INTO ACTIVISM

"Few will have the greatness to bend history itself, but each of us can work to change a small portion of events and in the total of all those acts will be written the history of this generation."
—Robert F. Kennedy

Here is a list of groups working to bring about political and corporate reform. Some inform, some help empower, and some organize. They are groups that I have either been personally involved with or whose work I drew from in completing this book. Go to their websites, or call, to find out more about how to get involved.

1. Campaign for America's Future
An organization that works for working people, monitors corporate accountability, and has led the struggle to save Social Security. Find out more at *www.ourfuture.org*.

> 1025 Connecticut Avenue, NW
> Washington, D.C. 20036
> Tel: (202) 955-5665
> E-mail: *info@ourfuture.org*

2. Center for Public Integrity
The Center, which scrutinizes all aspects of politics and government, has written over 100 investigative reports on accountability and ethics-related issues. For its latest expose, visit *www.publicintegrity.org*.

> 910 17th St. NW, Seventh Floor
> Washington, D.C. 20006
> Tel: (202) 466-1300
> E-mail: *contact@publicintegrity.org*

3. Center for Responsive Politics
A Washington, D.C.–based research group that tracks political money and studies its effect on policies and public elections. The organization seeks to promote a more informed voter as well as a more responsive government. To find out more, visit *www.opensecrets.org*.

1101 14th St., NW, Suite 1030
Washington, D.C. 20005-5635
Tel: (202) 857-0044
E-mail: *info@crp.org*

4. Citizen Works

Citizen Works promotes strengthening citizen participation in creating a sustainable and just society. To get involved, visit *www.citizenworks.org*.

PO Box 18478
Washington, D.C. 20036
Tel: (202) 265-6164
E-mail: *info@citizenworks.org*

5. Common Cause

Founded by John Gardner in 1970, this citizen's lobbying group promotes grassroots-level activism for an open and accountable government. To become involved in shaping our nation's public policies, visit *www.commoncause.org*.

1250 Connecticut Ave., NW #600
Washington, D.C. 20036
Tel: (202) 833-1200
E-mail: online form

6. Corporate Accountability Project

An organization of activists dedicated to—you guessed it—holding corporations accountable for their actions. Learn "how to overthrow corporate rule in five not-so-easy steps" at *www. corporations.org*.

1434 Elbridge St.
Philadelphia, PA 19149
Tel: (215) 743-4884
E-mail: *catalyst@envirolink.org*

7. CorpWatch

The San Francisco–based group counters corporate-led globalization through education and activism. Grassroots mobilization is underway at *www.corpwatch.org*.

PO Box 29344
San Francisco, CA 94129
Tel: (415) 561-6568
E-mail: *corpwatch@corpwatch.org*

8. Democracy Rising

Founded by Ralph Nader in 2001, Democracy Rising is a non-profit grassroots group advocating corporate reform. Empower yourself at *www.democracyrising.com*.

> 320 SW Stark Street, Suite 202
> Portland, OR 97204
> Tel: (202) 465-2764
> E-mail: *jkafoury@democracyrising.org*

9. Friends of the Earth (FOE)

An environmental organization, with affiliates in 63 countries, dedicated to preserving the health and diversity of the planet for future generations. Learn how to influence decisions affecting the quality of your environment at *www.foe.org*.

> 1025 Vermont Ave., NW
> Washington, D.C. 20005
> Tel: (202) 783-7400
> E-mail: *foe@foe.org*

10. Global Exchange

Global Exchange has launched numerous campaigns, fighting for corporate accountability, democracy, civil rights, and environmental protection. To learn more about becoming a Global Citizen, please visit *www.globalexchange.org*.

> 2017 Mission Street #303
> San Francisco, CA 94110
> Tel: (415) 558-9486
> E-mail: *info@globalexchange.org*

11. Jim Hightower's "Rolling Thunder Down-Home Democracy Tour"

Jim Hightower, along with several progressive organizations and constituencies, mixes music and education in a democracy-organizing tour that seeks to empower people. To assist in revitalizing American democracy, please visit *www.rollingthundertour.org*.

12. Natural Resources Defense Council (NRDC)

This national advocacy group uses law, science, and the support of more than 500,000 members across the country to ensure a safe and healthy environment for all living things. Speak out at *www.nrdc.org*.

40 West 20th Street
New York, NY 10011
Tel: (212) 727-2700
E-mail: *nrdcinfo@nrdc.org*

13. Natural Step
A consulting group that assists businesses in redefining their bottom lines to include social and environmental considerations. Please visit *www.naturalstep.org/*

116 New Montgomery Street, Suite #800
San Francisco, CA 94105
Tel: (415) 318-8170
E-mail: *services@naturalstep.org*

14. Pension Rights Center
The Pension Rights Center is dedicated to protecting and promoting retirement security for all Americans. For more information, please visit *www.pensionrights.org*.

1140 Nineteenth Street, Suite 602
Washington, D.C. 20036
Tel: (202) 296-3776
E-mail: *PNSNRIGHTS@aol.com*

15. Program on Corporations, Law and Democracy (POCLAD)
Thirteen activists are researching and rethinking corporate America's influence on democracy. Join the debate at *www.poclad.org*.

P.O. Box 246
S. Yarmouth, MA 02664-0246
Tel: (508) 398-1145
E-mail: *people@poclad.org*

16. Public Campaign
Public Campaign seeks to create a network with other organizations and citizen groups to increase campaign reforms in order to drastically reduce special interest and big money influences in American politics. Get involved in cleaning up politics at *www.publicampaign.org*.

1320 19th Street, NW, Suite M-1
Washington, D.C. 20036
Tel: (202) 293-0222
E-mail: *info@publicampaign.org*

17. Public Citizen

Founded by Ralph Nader in 1971, Public Citizen fights for consumer justice and government and corporate accountability. The umbrella organization sponsors six watchdog groups, including Congress Watch and Trade Watch. Take action at *www.citizen.org*.

> 1600 20th St., NW
> Washington, D.C. 20009
> Tel: (202) 588-1000
> E-mail: *member@citizen.org*

18. Shareholder Action Network

> (A project of the Social Investment Forum)

The organization seeks to create a central network of shareholder advocates, providing information and uniting investors to demand corporate responsibility. Take action at *www.shareholderaction.org*.

> 1612 K Street NW, Suite 650
> Washington, D.C. 20006
> Tel: (202) 872-5313
> E-mail: *san@socialinvest.org*

19. Sierra Club

Founded in 1892, the Sierra Club's environmental grassroots network is over 700,000 members strong. Join the fight at www.sierraclub.org.

> 85 Second St., Second Floor
> San Francisco, CA 94105-3441
> Tel: (415) 977-5500
> E-mail: *information@sierraclub.org*

20. Social Investment Forum

A shareholder advocacy organization that promotes socially responsible investing. Learn how investors have the opportunity and responsibility to challenge corporate misconduct at *www.social-invest.org*.

> 1612 K Street, NW, Suite 650
> Washington, D.C. 20006
> Tel: (202) 872-5319

21. Stakeholder Alliance

A grassroots effort that seeks to change the corporate system through comprehensive public disclosure. Join its call to action at *www.stakeholderalliance.org*.

733 15th St. NW, Suite 1020
Washington, D.C. 20005
Tel: (202) 234-9382
E-mail: *stakeholder@stakeholderalliance.org*

22. United for a Fair Economy (UFE)
A Boston-based advocacy group that focuses public awareness on wealth inequality. Join its activist network at *www.ufenet.org*.

37 Temple Place, 2nd Floor
Boston, MA 02111
Tel: (617) 423-2148
E-mail: *info@faireconomy.org*

23. United Students Against Sweatshops (USAS)
This international student movement was created after 11 college students spent the summer of 1997 as interns at UNITE, a textile workers' union. Learn about their fight for sweatshop-free labor conditions at *www.usasnet.org*.

888 16th St., NW, Suite 303
Washington, D.C. 20006
Tel: (202) 347-7417
E-mail: *emailusas@yahoo.com*

24. Working Assets
Founded in 1985, Working Assets is a phone, credit card and on-line services company that has donated over $25 million to groups like Greenpeace, Oxfam, and the Children's Defense Fund. In 2000 alone, Working Assets' members generated more than 900,000 letters and calls to Congress, the White House and business leaders. You too can speak out at *www.workingassets.com*.

101 Market Street, Suite 700
San Francisco, CA 94105
Tel: (877) 255-9253
E-mail: *info@workingforchange.com*

EPILOGUE

PR POLITICS. It's become a hallmark of the Bush administration. Have a big photo op, declare victory, move on, and hope the public will consider the problem solved.

We saw it with education. We haven't heard much about that since the president signed his prized Leave No Child Behind Act—which has turned out to be more of a Leave Millions of Children Behind, but Hopefully Not Your Own Act.

We saw it with Iraq. The president donned his formfitting flight suit, made a memorable tailhook landing of a Navy S-3B Viking on the deck of the USS *Abraham Lincoln,* and proudly declared: "Mission Accomplished." I guess that focus-grouped better than "Quagmire Accomplished." But the body count and the post-occupation price tag continue to soar.

And we saw it with the tidal wave of corporate scandals documented and dissected in this book. The president smiled for the cameras, signed the corporate responsibility bill into law, vowed "No more easy money for corporate criminals, just hard time," and acted as if the Enrons, WorldComs, and Global Crossings were now a thing of the past. Corporate reform was another "mission accomplished."

But a quick survey of the news since then reveals that it's actually been monkey business as usual on Wall Street. Even *Fortune* magazine, the corporate playbook, adorned its April 28 cover with a CEO with a pig's head and the title "Oink! CEO Pay Is Still Out of Control." Clearly, when it comes to learning from its mistakes, corporate America has fallen off the rehab wagon more times than Rush Limbaugh.

Last spring, high-ranking executives at HealthSouth, the nation's largest provider of rehabilitative health care services, pleaded guilty to routinely cooking the company's books. And this wasn't just happening back in the bad old days when everyone was doing it—no, these guys were fraudulently inflating earnings well into 2002, even as Enron, WorldCom, Adelphia, and Tyco were front-page news. How's that for clueless?

Next up on the "They Just Don't Get It Tour" are the good folks at Electronic Data Systems (EDS), with proof of just how little has changed when it comes to corporations rewarding failed execs with massive severance packages. After pushing CEO Dick Brown out the cockpit door for overseeing a 50 percent drop in share price over the last seven months of his tenure—as well as for steering the firm into an SEC investigation—EDS handed him a golden parachute worth $37 million. So Brown managed to Dick shareholders even past the bitter end.

Then there was New York Stock Exchange chairman Richard Grasso's jaw-dropping decision—mercifully stymied by Eliot Spitzer—to appoint scandal-tainted Citigroup chairman Sandy Weill to its board to, I kid you not, represent the public. It's a move that made about as much sense as naming Khalid Abdul Muhammad to the 9/11 Commission.

Of course, both Grasso and Weill were soon looking for new business cards: Weill stepped down as Citigroup CEO in the wake of the company's $400 million payment in the landmark Wall Street conflict-of-interest settlement, and Grasso was forced to resign after it was revealed that as head of the world's largest stock exchange he had received a $140 million salary and benefits payout from the people he was charged with regulating.

You'd think this country's CEOs would have gotten the message. They have, after all, in the course of the last few years gone from American Idols to America's Most Wanted—the most stunning transformation since Ozzy Osbourne morphed from a drug-addled, bat-chomping satanic rocker into America's cuddliest dad. But no matter how battered their reputations may be, they still appear determined to rescue themselves instead of their sinking ships. For today's captains of industry, the maxim in a crisis seems to be: "To hell with the women and children—save the lifeboats for us!"

Take American Airlines. While preparing to make a rough landing in bankruptcy court last year, executives at the dead-broke carrier extracted from workers $1.62 billion in wage and benefit concessions the bosses claimed were needed to keep American Airlines aloft. At the same time, the execs secretly gave themselves massive cash bonuses and a $41 million trust fund to guarantee their pensions should the airline crash and burn.

Even after the secret escape plan was revealed and all hell broke loose, the company held fast to its priorities. It canceled the cash bonuses. It tossed CEO Don Carty onto the tarmac. But it refused to relinquish the fund protecting its execs' nest eggs. In the end, the executives kept their cushy trust fund while the workers were forced to go along with a deal that led to thousands of layoffs and pay cuts of between 15 and 23 percent. I guess in today's business world, that's what amounts to a compromise.

Besides making one reach for the nearest airsickness bag, the American Airlines debacle highlights the growing disparity between the ways corporate America is preparing for the golden years of its executives and its rank-and-file employees.

In the clubby confines of America's boardrooms, the sky is the limit. Compensation committees are working overtime coming up with ever more creative—and devious—ways to boost the earnings of top executives. And super-charged pension plans are the hot new trend.

Among the gimmicks being used to goose the value of these plans is an accounting scheme that can dramatically increase a

CEO's retirement windfall by adding phantom years—even phantom decades—of service to the exec's pension. In theory, it works the same way as those jailhouse rules that reward a model prisoner with time off for good behavior—only these guys get rewarded no matter how many employees or shareholders they've knifed in the back with a shiv.

Thanks to this latest innovation in corporate accounting, Leo Mullin, Delta Airlines' CEO, has had an additional twenty-two years of service tacked on to the less than six he's actually worked for the company, while US Air's former CEO Stephen Wolf was given credit for twenty-four years he didn't put in. And this scam isn't reserved for the highfliers of the airline industry. When John Snow left CSX Railroad to become Treasury Secretary, he was given credit for having put in forty-four years at the firm, even though he'd actually punched a time clock there for twenty-five—a little fun with numbers that helped him walk away with a cool $33 million in pension booty.

Corporate directors, who have come under increasing fire from shareholders for approving excessive pay packages for high-level executives, appreciate the fact that these pension plan adjustments allow them to fly under the radar while continuing to funnel millions to CEOs. Unlike salaries and bonuses, which are regularly reported in the business press, the details of executive pension plans are usually hidden away in the extra-fine print of a company's SEC filings.

The picture is far bleaker for those down on the factory floor or crammed inside an office cubicle, where ordinary workers are seeing their pension plans slashed or eliminated altogether. Less than half of those currently employed in the private sector have any kind of pension coverage. And 40 percent of those companies that do offer pension plans are exploring the possibility of reducing benefits. Companies are also cutting back on matching contributions to their employees' 401(k) accounts. Some, like Ford, Goodyear Tire, and Charles Schwab, have decided to completely do away with matching contributions. They probably need the extra cash for their executives.

Even those workers who are able to hang on to their matching contributions can't rest easy: It turns out that the vast majority of corporate pension funds are critically underfunded. In fact, of the 343 S&P 500 companies that offer traditional pension plans, almost 90 percent of them are running a deficit. And we're not talking about being a few dollars short. General Motors' pension plan is $25.4 billion in the red, while Ford's has a shortfall of $15.6 billion. All told, the S&P companies are $206 billion in the hole; that's a shift of $457 billion since 1999, when the same pension funds had a collective surplus of $251 billion. In just a few short years, the nest eggs of the American worker have gone from sunny-side up to seriously scrambled.

And shareholders and employees are not the only ones being victimized by the ongoing culture of greed. Consider: All across corporate America, high-priced accountants are hard at work helping companies avoid billions in taxes by hiding profits in a host of tax-sheltering schemes. And they're doing a bang-up job: Corporations are currently turning over 30 percent less of their profits to the tax man than they did twenty years ago. Meanwhile, all across the country, state governments, facing the biggest budget crisis since the Great Depression, are being forced to slash programs and cut services. Gee, do you think there might be a connection? You can bet your vanishing after-school care, prenatal health program, and local law enforcement service there is.

According to a 2003 study by the Multistate Tax Commission, a nonpartisan coalition of state taxing authorities, corporate tax shelters robbed states of $12.4 billion in desperately needed revenues in 2001—a figure that represents more than a third of the money corporations rightfully owed. Companies sheltering their assets overseas are draining another $70 billion a year from the federal Treasury—funds that often make their way back to states through programs such as Head Start and AmeriCorps. But as damning as those statistics are, they're still just abstract figures. In order to really understand the devastating impact these lost revenues are having, we need to put flesh and bone to the numbers.

In Florida, for instance, which according to the Multistate Tax Commission lost $554 million to tax shelters in 2001, just $7.7 million would have saved a program that provided glasses and hearing aids for low-income people.

Oregon is dealing with $80 million in lost corporate taxes, and $14.5 million would have prevented the 19,000-student Hillsboro school district from shutting its doors seventeen days early last year.

In South Carolina, which also was denied $80 million because of tax shelters, a mere $1.4 million would have stopped the round of budget cuts that cost Traci Young Cooper, the state's 2001 Teacher of the Year, her job. The honor earned her a trip to the White House to meet President Bush; maybe if she knew what was coming she could have lobbied him to make all tax shelters illegal.

In Kentucky, which lost $150 million to tax shelters, $2.6 million would have allowed Governor Paul Patton to leave behind bars the 883 prison inmates he released early in a desperate effort to balance the state's budget. I have a sneaking suspicion that the twenty-five-year-old woman who was raped by one of these freed inmates just three days after his release would consider that $2.6 million money very well spent.

And the list goes on and on. Vital programs and services cut or eliminated that could have been saved had corporate America just done the right thing and paid what it owed.

But even with all this damning evidence, the most galling indicator that the corporate culture hasn't really changed is the aforementioned—and much-ballyhooed—$1.4 billion research settlement agreement between New York's crusading attorney general, Spitzer, and Wall Street's investment banks. The settlement didn't include the criminal indictment of a single person or institution. That's right: Not one of the flimflam men behind the high-level financial swindles will have to do any time behind bars. And, perhaps most infuriating of all, it didn't require any of those involved even to admit to any wrongdoing.

This kid-glove treatment of Wall Street crooks provides a profound example of how we continue to operate a two-tiered justice system in this country—one for a select group of elites and one for the rest of America. When common criminals are allowed to cop a plea, they plead guilty first as part of the bargain. Crooks in pinstripe suits, on the other hand, even those caught red-handed, don't have to come clean. It's the ultimate privilege—and the ultimate insult to our intelligence. What good is finding a smoking gun if the guys who fired it are allowed to pay a small fine, step over the bloody body, and reload?

Professor Paul Lapides, director of the Corporate Governance Center at Kennesaw State University, describes the sleazegeist thus: "I used to tell my students that if you commit a white-collar crime, the time will come when you will serve your time. Now I tell my students, if you commit a crime, commit a big one." Lapides adds, "If you commit a big enough crime, you'll probably have to return only some of the money, and you won't have to do any jail time. Is America a great country or what?"

A magnetic compass should always point north; a moral compass should always point out that lying, cheating, fraud, and conflicts of interest are dead wrong. This is not a question of right or left. It is a question of right or wrong. But our country's self-appointed morality czars have been deafeningly silent on this kind of economic indecency. I guess Bill Bennett—or as he's known in Vegas, "The $8 Million Man"—was too busy doubling down to notice.

How screwed up are the priorities of our business leaders? Well, Adelphia's John Rigas considered himself so moral that he refused to carry the Playboy Channel on his cable systems—but thought nothing of "borrowing" $3.1 billion from his company's coffers. Frankly, I think we all would have been better off if he'd have kept his hands off the money and shown a little skin.

Or look at Wal-Mart: pulling three men's magazines off the shelf at the same time that it treats women like second-class citizens, fires workers who try to unionize, is facing the largest sex-discrimination case in history, and is being sued in thirty states for refusing to pay workers overtime. Now that's something worth getting hot and bothered about.

To me, scantily clad girls are not immoral—cheating your workers is.

It's time for our business and political leaders to help redefine morality beyond sex, drugs, and rock and roll to include lying, hypocrisy, and callous indifference to those in need. That is the kind of leadership we must have if we're ever going to eradicate the culture of greed, corruption, and unethical behavior that has come to dominate both Wall Street and Washington.

Index